EVALUATION AND EDUCATIONAL PROGRAMMING OF DEAF-BLIND/ SEVERELY MULTIHANDICAPPED STUDENTS SENSORIMOTOR STAGE

EVALUATION AND EDUCATIONAL PROGRAMMING OF DEAF–BLIND/ SEVERELY MULTIHANDICAPPED STUDENTS SENSORIMOTOR STAGE

By

CARROLL J. JONES, Ph.D.

Associate Professor of Education
Methodist College
Fayetteville, North Carolina

CHARLES C THOMAS • PUBLISHER
Springfield • Illinois • U.S.A.

Published and Distributed Throughout the World by

CHARLES C THOMAS • PUBLISHER
2600 South First Street
Springfield, Illinois 62794-9265

© *1988 by* CHARLES C THOMAS • PUBLISHER

ISBN 0-398-05515-7

Library of Congress Catalog Card Number: 88-17694

With THOMAS BOOKS *careful attention is given to all details of manufacturing
and design. It is the Publisher's desire to present books that are satisfactory as to their
physical qualities and artistic possibilities and appropriate for their particular use.*
THOMAS BOOKS *will be true to those laws of quality that assure a good name
and good will.*

Printed in the United States of America
SC-R-3

Library of Congress Cataloging-in-Publication Data

Jones, Carroll J.
    Evaluation and educational programming of deaf-blind/severely
multihandicapped students : sensorimotor stage / by Carroll J.
Jones.
        p.   cm.
    Bibliography: p.
    Includes index.
    ISBN 0-398-05515-7
    1. Blind-deaf — Education — United States.   2. Handicapped —
Education — United States.   3. Teachers of the blind-deaf — Training
of — United States.   4. Teachers of handicapped children — Training
of — United States.   I. Title.
HV1597.2.J65 1988
371.91 — dc19   88-17694
                                                                      CIP

CONSULTANTS

JANET SORTH, M.A.
Assistant Principal
Litzsinger School
Special School District of St. Louis County
12110 Clayton Road
Town & Country, Missouri 63131

SUSAN MARSHALL, M.A., CCC-A
Audiologist
Litzsinger School
Special School District of St. Louis County
12110 Clayton Road
Town & Country, Missouri 63131

NANCY KENNEDY, O.D.
Private Practitioner/Consultant Optometrist
621 S. New Ballas
Tower A, Suite 228
St. Louis, Missouri 63141

MARION HOWELLS, M.Ed.
Speech/Language Pathologist and
Deaf-Blind Classroom Teacher
United Services for the Handicapped, Inc.
2027 Campus Drive
St. Charles, Missouri 63301

MARY GARAVAGLIA, B.S., P.T.
Physical Therapist
Litzsinger School
12110 Clayton Road
Town & Country, Missouri 63131

RICHARD SERANO, M.D.
Neurologist
V.A. Medical Center
2300 Ramsey Street
Fayetteville, North Carolina 28301

SUSAN POPE, M.Ed.
Teacher, Orthopedically Impaired
William Owen Elementary School
4533 Raeford Road
Fayetteville, North Carolina 28301

v

To Dr. Robert L. Ohlsen, Jr.

FOREWORD

"Find a need and meet it." The adage has long been the by-line for the business community. In the field of education, teachers search and long for that special resource which will fill the gap in their educational planning and remediation of students with special needs. In this book for severely/profoundly multiply handicapped and deaf-blind children, I believe Dr. Carroll Jones has truly "met the need."

One of the most desperate cries I have heard as a Special Education teacher trainer throughout my career is "What curriculum can I use that will be basic enough for the most handicapped learner?" I am happy to be able to point to this text as an excellent answer to that question. Dr. Jones has presented a very complete package of information for the educator of severely/multiply handicapped child. The package includes detailed diagnostic information so that the teacher will understand the physical, mental, social, and educational status of the student. She has presented excellent programming materials to allow the teacher to plan for skill development based on the specific deficits of the child in relation to the skills needed. Finally, Dr. Jones has provided an overall approach to monitoring and ongoing revision of the program plan to insure that each educational decision is worthwhile and affords the maximum benefit to the child. The text comes very close to that "Compleat Educator's Handbook" we all seek which will help make the path a little lighter as we teach a population of children in desperate educational need.

Dr. Carroll Jones is an excellent Special Educator and a meticulous educational curriculum planner and developer. Her experience with severely/profoundly multiply handicapped and deaf-blind students led to the birth of this text. It was her first-hand look at the needs of this population and the paucity of resources suitable to meet those needs which caused her to provide this noteworthy text. I believe that this book will greatly enhance the literature available related to this blessedly small, but vastly important aspect of society.

VIRGINIA DICKENS, PH.D.

Associate Professor of Special Education
Fayetteville State University

ix

PREFACE

The area of deaf-blind severely multihandicapped special education is a highly specialized area involving a close working relationship among medical and educational professionals. This book evolved as a result of that relationship and the assignment in January 1985 to provide multidisciplinary re-evaluations to all children enrolled in the Regional Deaf-Blind Program provided by Special School District of St. Louis County, Missiouri. In October 1985, the primary numbers of the diagnostic team presented, "From Evaluation to Programming of Young Deaf-Blind Severely Multihandicapped Children" at the 1st Annual National Early Childhood Conference on Children with Special Needs in Denver, Colorado. In December 1985, Janet Sorth, teacher of deaf-blind children, and I, chairperson of the diagnostic team/ educational diagnostician, presented "From Evaluation to Programming of Deaf-Blind Severely Multihandicapped Children" at the conference for The Association of Persons with Severe Handicaps (TASH) in Boston. Information from these presentations served as core ideas for beginning the current project and thus, these team members have been indicated as consultants on the project.

My first intention in writing this book was to provide a teacher-training text and resource volume for teachers and other professionals working not only with deaf-blind/severely multihandicapped children, but also with children of any handicapping exceptionality functioning within the sensorimotor stage of development. Secondly, I wanted, under one cover, both theoretical background information and diagnostic information; and specific information for classroom teachers to use in program planning, writing IEPs, collecting data to monitor IEPs, and hands-on materials teachers could use in their classrooms.

Thirdly, it is my intention to honor the superior professionals who served as the primary members of my 1985 Deaf-Blind Diagnostic Team from Special School District of St. Louis County, Missouri: Janet Sorth, Lead Classroom/Homebound Teacher; Susan Marshall, Audiologist; Nancy Kennedy, Consultant Optometrist; Marion Howells, Classroom Teacher/Speech Pathologist; Mary Garavaglia, Physical Therapist.

Each chapter of *Evaluation and Educational Programming of Deaf-Blind/*

Severely Multihandicapped Students: Sensorimotor Stage begins with a mini-outline, discusses background medical information and/or theory; discusses evaluation, diagnosis, programming, and IEP monitoring; and ends with a summary. The text is organized into eight chapters concerning the primary educational areas for deaf-blind severely multihandicapped children functioning within the sensorimotor stage of development. The book discusses historical background of deaf-blind assessment, suggests evaluation/re-evaluation procedures, general characteristics, and case studies (Chapter 1); delineates methods and materials used in evaluation, programming, and IEP monitoring for vision impairments (Chapter 2), hearing impairments (Chapter 3), secondary sensory impairments (Chapter 4), motor deficits and delays (Chapter 5), cognitive impairments (Chapter 6), communication delay/impairment (Chapter 7), and social and emotional deficits (Chapter 8). Each chapter includes sensorimotor stage developmental age norms, scope and sequence lists of programming skills, discussions of meeting deaf-blind guidelines, case studies of hypothetical children—Sally and Bud—including evaluation suggestions and reports, IEPs, and programming strategies.

Special acknowledgements to my colleague and friend at Fayetteville State University, Dr. Virginia Dickens, Coordinator of Special Education, who provided continuous encouragement and read rough drafts. Thanks to Richard Serano, Neurologist at the VA Hospital in Fayetteville, N.C., who provided suggestions on the vision chapter; and to Susan Pope, Teacher of orthopedically handicapped children in Cumberland County School District, N.C., who provided programming suggestions. Thanks always to my family, Merrell, Andrea, and Camille, for unfaltering faith in all of my projects.

Much of my original background knowledge and interest in severely handicapped populations was stimulated by my mentor and major professor at Kansas State University, Dr. Robert Ohlsen, Jr. He introduced me to numerous handicapped persons and helped me to "see" them first, as persons, and secondly, as persons with special needs. He shared knowledge gleaned from his previous work as a speech clinician, as Director of Special Education at the Institute of Logopedics, and as Superintendent of the Kansas School for the Visually Impaired. This volume is dedicated to Dr. Ohlsen, the first Director of Special Education in Kansas, to recognize his contribution to education during his 35+ year career as he retires from public service.

CONTENTS

EVALUATION AND EDUCATIONAL PROGRAMMING OF DEAF-BLIND/ SEVERELY MULTIHANDICAPPED STUDENTS SENSORIMOTOR STAGE

Chapter One

INTRODUCTION

The deaf-blind child is not a deaf child who cannot see or a blind child who cannot hear (McInnes and Treffry, 1982, 2).

- Historical Background for Identification
- Re-Evaluation to Re-Certify Students
- New Referral Evaluation Procedures
- Evaluation/Re-Evaluation Test Battery
- General Characteristics of Deaf-Blind Students
- Case Study Summaries: Pam and Sally
- Summary

In 1975 with the passage of Public Law 94-142, the Education for all Handicapped Children's Act, the evaluation and programming of deaf-blind and severely multihandicapped children and youth became areas of major concern to educators who had never before served these populations in the public schools. In many instances, it was nearly impossible to discriminate among young deaf-blind severely multihandi-capped children and young severely multihandicapped children whose profound mental retardation precluded using their vision and hearing appropriately.

HISTORICAL BACKGROUND FOR IDENTIFICATION

1975 Identification Guidelines

Early identification guidelines offered by the Bureau of Education for the Handicapped avoided definitive medical or intellectual criteria maintaining that to be eligible for services as deaf-blind, children must have

...auditory and visual handicaps, the combination of which causes

3

problems that they cannot properly be accommodated in special education programs solely for the hearing handicapped child or for the visually handicapped child (**Federal Register**, 1975).

These federal guidelines provided no real assistance in the identification/discrimination process because they required a determination that auditory and visual handicaps caused "severe communication and other developmental and educational problems." In an educational setting without medical information, it was nearly impossible to determine if the cause of the severe developmental delay was due to visual and auditory organic dysfunction, or if the students were organically intact but unable to use the vision and hearing functioning they possessed due to severe mental retardation, or to specific medical concerns such as hydrocephalus, seizure disorders, encephalopathy, and/or other neurological impairments. Educators not only lacked the expertise, but also the equipment to determine specific auditory and visual functioning levels.

In the absence of definitive characteristics, evaluation procedures and materials, and educational methods and materials, public school personnel attempted to comply with the law and serve these low-incidence populations by giving them the same diagnostic label and placing them in the same educational programs. Educators justified classifying and educating nonsensorily impaired severely handicapped children and deaf-blind severely multihandicapped children together because their instructional needs were often similar. Most state and regional centers accepted the justification.

Current Guidelines

In the past ten years, educators and researchers working with medical practitioners have expanded their knowledge about identification, developmental functioning, and educational programming for deaf-blind severely multihandicapped and severely multihandicapped children. By 1983, the Bureau of Education for the Handicapped had established 16 centers which established more than 300 programs in public and private educational institutions providing services in all 50 states and territories to the 5,998 deaf-blind children identified (Dantona, 1986).

State and Regional Center guidelines for determining eligibility for deaf-blind services have changed several times to become more specific in meeting the federal mandates to re-certify or de-certify all students in deaf-blind programs in order to discriminate among deaf-blind severely multihandicapped students and severely multihandicapped students with no sensory impairments. The current eligibility criteria among the states within the Mountain Plains Regional Center for Services to Deaf-Blind Children requires a combination of conditions including visual deficits, hearing deficits, and educational needs that cannot be served appropriately in programs for a single sensory deficit (Table 1). These guidelines add specificity to the **Federal Register** definition of deaf-blind and facilitate the diagnostic process.

RE-EVALUATION TO RE-CERTIFY OR DE-CERTIFY STUDENTS

The application of the federal mandate for recertification as deaf-blind involved all students currently served in deaf-blind programs. As per Federal/Regional Center regulations, the re-certification/de- certification process required a team including a vision specialist, a hearing specialist, and a teacher of deaf-blind children. Additional concerns of school districts included preparation of appropriate Individual Educational Programs (IEPs) and programming for those students de-certified as deaf-blind, and appropriately addressing the other deficit areas of deaf-blind severely multihandicapped students.

A multidisciplinary re-evaluation approach to the re-certification/de-certification process is recommended. Re-evaluation is a process based on a considerable amount of information due to years of data collected on students' classroom functioning in the areas of vision, hearing, communication, motor, self-help, socialization, and cognitive skills; medical reports; annual vision and hearing testing by the staff optometrists and audiologists; IEPs; and End-of-Year Progress Reports.

Since students currently enrolled in deaf-blind programs attend school on a daily basis, re-evaluation assessments can be spaced over a period of time and administered at optimum performance times. Evaluation instruments can be readministered, if necessary. Systematic Observation should be utilized by all diagnosticians and teachers in quantifying functioning levels. Systematic Observation (Mercer, 1987) is a specialized type of observation requiring data collection on duration and frequency of specific behaviors—not just anecdotal records. Systematic Observation requires a significant investment in time because the observation must be conducted over a period of time in numerous settings with various behaviors quantified.

TABLE 1
GUIDELINES FOR CERTIFYING A STUDENT
AS ELIGIBLE FOR DEAF-BLIND SERVICES

Regional Center regulations indicate that the determination that a child is a deaf-blind child shall be made on the basis of diagnostic evaluation conducted by a multi-disciplinary team of specialists, including at least but not limited to, specialists in the fields of hearing, vision, and education of the handicapped.

Criteria

A student may be determined as eligible when a combination of the following conditions from all three areas exists.

Vision:

1. Measured or estimated corrected visual acuity of 20/100 or less in the better eye, and/or a previous chronic visual condition has existed which has interfered with the visual learning mode.
2. In the presence of a normal peripheral vision apparatus as determined by an ophthalmologist, cortical blindness is determined; this blindness must be verified by reports indicating an absent optickinetic nystagmus as appropriate to age by an ophthalmologist, a pediatrician or a pediatric neurologist.
3. Field of vision of 20° or less in the better eye.
4. Visual acuity *cannot* be definitively measured and the student is suspected of being blind, thus "Functionally Blind." "Functionally Blind" means that the student does not visually track, localize or use his/her vision appropriate to the overall developmental level(s) as determined by appropriate assessment of development.

If: the measured or estimated visual acuity is better than 20/40 in one eye; there is no severe field limitation; the visual functioning appears to be appropriate to the child's developmental level as determined by appropriate developmental assessment;

Then the student shall be determined as *not* eligible.

Hearing:

1. Thirty (30) dB bilateral sensory neural hearing loss as a minimum across the speech frequency in the better ear with amplification, and/or a previous chronic condition of the auditory mechanism has existed which interfered with the auditory learning mode.
2. Sensitivity and middle ear functioning cannot be definitively measured and the student is suspected of being deaf, thus "Functionally Deaf." "Functionally Deaf" means that the student does not auditorally attend to, respond to or localize sounds, or use his hearing appropriate to his/her developmental level as determined by appropriate assessment of development.

If: measured or estimated hearing acuity, with amplification, is better than 30 dB bilateral sensory-neural hearing loss across the speech frequency; auditory functioning is appropriate to the child's developmental level as determined by appropriate developmental assessment;

Then, the student shall be determined as *not* eligible.

Education:

If it is determined that a student's educational needs based on the combination of his visual and hearing deficits cannot be served appropriately by the programs provided for (1) the visually handicapped, (2) the auditorily handicapped without extraordinary assistance necessary to accommodate the secondary impairment, then the student shall be deemed appropriate for deaf-blind program eligibility.

SOURCE: Mountain Plains Regional Center, 1985.

General Re-Evaluation Procedure

Adhering to general re-evaluation procedures assists in systematizing and objectifying the re-certification/de-certification process. Previously, many children had been enrolled in deaf-blind programs for as long as 5–7 years, although they clearly were not deaf-blind as per classroom functioning and annual audiology testing, but due to their severely multi-handicapped status remained in deaf-blind programs. The de-certification of these children was an emotional issue with parents. Thus, a systematic process serves to illustrate objective evaluations. A suggested re-evaluation process included preparation of a background summary report from permanent records, a multidisciplinary/multifaceted evaluation, conference scheduling that allows most of the diagnostic team and parents to attend, and completing the re-evaluation documents with a conference summary report (Table 2).

TABLE 2
RE-EVALUATION PROCEDURES

1. Background Summary Report from Permanent Records
   a. Medical history
   b. Vision history
   c. Auditory history
   d. Developmental history
   e. Previous labeling and services
2. Conduct Multidisciplinary Evaluations
   a. Vision
   b. Hearing
   c. Other developmental (e.g., self-help, social)
   d. Psychological – cognitive
   e. Motor – fine and gross
   f. Communication – receptive and expressive
   g. School and home adaptive behavior
3. Schedule Conferences/Conduct Conferences/Prepare Conference Summary Report

Background Summary Report

The Background Summary Report from permanent records serves several valuable functions. First, it provides information on the impact of educational programming, the rate and amount of growth made while the child was in the deaf-blind program. Secondly, background information coupled with current developmental functioning levels in cognition, motor, self-help, and communication skills can be used to help answer the question, "Are the child's vision and hearing functioning levels commensurate with overall developmental functioning?" Medical history provides information regarding neurological and relevant medical diagnoses and hospitalization reports. The student's current medical status will include information about medications taken including dosages and times, and other information relevant to classroom functioning and educational programming. Vision and auditory history provide ophthalmological and audiological diagnoses, including results of visual and auditory evoked response tests. Tracing visual and hearing functioning through the years provides data on functioning levels, the amount of improvement/no improvement/deterioration which is especially valuable in re-certifying or de-certifying questionable status students, and in determining functional blindness and/or functional deafness.

Multidisciplinary Re-Evaluation Team

Multidisciplinary evaluations should be performed by highly trained diagnosticians from diverse educational and medical backgrounds. Responsibilities need to be carefully delineated on an efficient team (Table 3). For deaf-blind evaluations, team members must include a vision specialist (e.g., optometrist), hearing specialist (e.g., audiologist), and a teacher of deaf-blind children. The team should also include a psychologist or psychological examiner, an educational examiner, physical and/or occupational therapists, a speech/language pathologist, a social worker, and a school nurse.

NEW REFERRAL EVALUATION PROCEDURES

The evaluation process for preschool children referred for deaf-blind program consideration must be substantially different from re-evaluation procedures to re-certify or de-certify students because the new preschool referrals are not attending school on a daily basis. For new referrals, there are no former IEPs or annual reports, and classroom teachers do not have data graphed on their current classroom functioning abilities. The majority of preschool referrals come from social agencies and social workers desperately trying to find program services for severely multihandicapped youngsters who may or may not have sensory impairments.

TABLE 3
MULTIDISCIPLINARY RE-EVALUATION TEAM
(Team Member)

Area	Responsible Person	Responsibilities
Team Coordinator	Chairperson	Prepares background information, collects release forms from parents, schedules conf., coordinates evaluation process, chairs conferences, prepares case study report, serves in public relations role.
Psychological Evaluation	Psychological Examiner or School Psychologist	Administers appropriate standardized and non-standardized instruments to determine intellectual and/or developmental functioning; Prepares psychological report.
Educational Evaluation	Educational Examiner	Administers assessment devices to evaluate information processing, academic achievement, behavior, and developmental functioning; Identifies functioning level, strengths and weaknesses, and determines educational needs; Prepares educational report.
Classroom Evaluation	Classroom Teacher	Prepares report of current classroom functioning; Assists with educational evaluation.
Vision Evaluation	Optometrist	Screens previous vision and neurological information. Uses formal and informal assessments to evaluate visual functioning; Determines if child meets vision portion of Deaf-Blind criteria. Prepares report.
Hearing Evaluation	Audiologist	Screens previous audiological and neurological information. Assesses current hearing functioning. Determines if child meets deaf criteria. Prepares report.
Physical Evaluation	Physical/Occupational Therapists	Secures Rx from child's physician to do physical therapy evaluation. Assesses ROM, fine and gross motor skills, oral motor-feeding, self-help skills. Prepares report.
Communication Evaluation	Speech/Language Pathologist	Screens previous speech/language and oral-motor functioning in receptive and expressive language. Assesses current functioning in receptive and expressive language. Prepares report.
Medical	School Nurse	Contacts parents to secure the most up-to-date information on medication and health conditions, immunizations, school health concerns. Prepares report.
Home/Family	Social Worker	Provides relevant information regarding family and child. Coordinates social agencies. Assists family with school transfers, and securing needed equipment such as wheelchairs. Prepares report.

A suggested evaluation procedure for new referrals begins with the social worker receiving the referrals from other social and medical agencies, followed by a scheduled home visit to meet parents, to explain the evaluation procedures, and to secure written permission to request all relevant data from social and/or medical agencies (Table 4). Once all of the requested information is collected, the chairperson schedules a records screening meeting.

TABLE 4
NEW REFERRAL EVALUATION PROCEDURES

1. Background Information
   a. School Social Worker receives *referral* from social agencies and makes a home visit to secure *permission* to request all relevant information (medical and social services).
   b. School Secretary or social worker collects all requested information (checklist) and notifies the chairperson when a file is completed.
2. Screening Team considers all information provided to determine:
   a. child appears appropriate for multidisciplinary evaluation;
   b. child appears inappropriate for multidisciplinary evaluation;
   c. insufficient information.
3. Clinic Evaluation at School
   a. Vision (optometrist)
   b. Hearing (audiologist)
   c. Communication (speech/language pathologist)
   d. Psychological (psychologist or psychological examiner)
   e. Fine and Gross Motor Skills Screening (pediatric nurse practitioner)
   f. Fine and Gross Motor Skills Evaluation (occupational and physical therapists)
   g. Classroom Functioning (classroom teacher)
   h. Parent Interview (all team members).
4. Diagnostic Conference (held after clinic evaluation)
   a. Diagnosis: "appears to meet deaf-blind criteria"
   b. Child Assessment Program Homebound teacher and therapist make bi-weekly visits to the home for 6 weeks to further evaluate and observe the child.
5. Diagnostic Conference to make Diagnosis.

SOURCE: Procedures utilized by Special School District of St. Louis County, MO, during Spring 1985.

Referral Records Screening

A records screening committee composed of at least a vision specialist (e.g., optometrist), an audiologist, and a teacher for the deaf-blind is required to analyze the vision, hearing, and educational information. Additional members of the school-based referral screening committee may include, as needed, the school principal, the diagnostic committee chairperson, and the pediatric nurse practitioner. The child's referral records should be analyzed to determine if the child appears appropriate for a multidisciplinary deaf-blind evaluation. Neurological information, ophthalmological evaluation reports, visual-evoked response testing results, and other vision functioning information should be analyzed to determine if the child appears to have an estimated visual acuity of 20/100 or less in the better eye, a chronic visual condition, cortical blindness, a field of vision of 20° or less in the better eye, or functional blindness (Mountain Plains Regional Center, 1985).

Medical records should be screened to determine if neurological reports, audiological evaluations, evoked response audiometry testing results, or other hearing functioning information suggests a 30 dB bilateral sensory neural hearing loss as a minimum across the speech frequencies in the better ear with amplification, a previous chronic condition of the auditory mechanism, and/or functional deafness (Mountain Plains Regional Center, 1985).

The developmental skills of cognition, fine and gross motor skills, self-help skills, and communication should be screened to discover the student's most recent functioning levels (usually assessed 6 months to 1 year previous to referral). In the absence of definitive vision and hearing deficit information or diagnosis, the developmental skills can be compared to vision and hearing functioning levels. If the records screening indicates the child's auditory and vision functioning levels appear commensurate with cognitive and other developmental skill levels, the child does not appear to be deaf-blind and thus does not meet the criteria for a deaf-blind multi-disciplinary evaluation. In cases where there is insufficient information to make a decision regarding vision and hearing functioning abilities, additional information should be requested.

If medical information reveals that the child shows conditions of both vision and hearing deficits, then the child appears appropriate for a multi-disciplinary evaluation. The school nurse or pediatric nurse practitioner should prepare a medical history summary of the child's current and past conditions to be included in the multi-disciplinary evaluation report.

Clinic Evaluation

In a clinic-type evaluation, preschool aged children are brought to school by their parents for a 2–3 hour evaluation and systematic observation period. It is suggested that the evaluation begin with the behavioral audiological testing while the child is still "fresh." Auditory functioning is frequently the most difficult area to gain reliable functioning data with young severely multihandicapped children.

A clinic evaluation provided in an informal setting in the "round" stimulates a flow of information among diagnosticians and parents and provides a more relaxed atmosphere for the evaluation of young severely handicapped children. If the child is placed on a floor mat in the evaluation room, surrounded by parents and team members, an informal flow of questions, responses, and interactions among diagnosticians and parents can occur as the child is observed, manipulated, and presented stimuli. The child's vision, hearing, cognition, communication (receptive and expressive), fine and gross motor skills, and adaptive behavior should be assessed. At the developmental level, there is so much overlapping and integration of skills among the domains to be assessed that this group observational procedure is very practical and time-saving. Diagnosticians in turn question and interact with parents while simultaneously observing the child from different perspectives. A practical final segment of the evaluation involves an oral motor evaluation as the child is feeding to gain an understanding of the child's oral motor functioning skills.

Following the multidisciplinary evaluation and scoring of protocols, the deaf-blind diagnostic team should conduct a conference with the parents to share evaluation results and to determine if the child appears to meet the deaf-blind identification criteria. With young low-functioning handicapped children, it may be very difficult to gain enough information from a "one-shot" evaluation period to determine the child's repeatable responses and skills. Some children become scared and cry, some fall asleep, and others react in unpredictable ways in a new situation.

In Special School District of St. Louis County, Missouri, children who appear to meet the deaf-blind criteria and those whose reactions during the evaluation were not repeatable or were questionable are enrolled in a six-week Child Assessment Program (C.A.P.). The teacher serving home-bound children enrolled in the Deaf-Blind Program makes bi-weekly visits to the child's home to further evaluate and observe the child in a safe, secure, known environment. At the conclusion of C.A.P., the teacher prepares a report regarding the child's functioning observed during the six-week period. A diagnostic conference is conducted to determine the special education diagnosis based on the multidisciplinary evaluation and C.A.P. information.

EVALUATION/RE-EVALUATION TEST BATTERY

Numerous books have been printed providing lists of tests to use with various categories of handicapped children. The sensorimotor stage functioning level continues to pose evaluation concerns, although instruments and procedures have improved considerably during the past ten years. It is suggested that the multidisciplinary evaluation team administer a variety of norm-referenced, criterion-referenced, informal diagnostic, and systematic observational instruments and procedures. A number of instruments and procedures have been found useful in evaluating deaf-blind severely multihandicapped children functioning within the sensorimotor stage of birth to 2 years (Table 5).

GENERAL CHARACTERISTICS OF DEAF-BLIND CHILDREN

McInnes and Treffry (1982) indicated . . . the deaf-blind child has one of the least understood of all handicaps. He is not a blind child who cannot hear or a deaf child who cannot see. He is a multisensory deprived child who has been denied the effective use of both of his distance senses (Preface).

According to Sontag, Burke, and York (1973), many deaf-blind students have characteristics similar to severely/profoundly mentally handicapped children, including self-stimulation and/or self-mutilation, a lack of self-help skills, a lack of communication skills, a lack of socialization skills, and numerous medical concerns.

The Deaf-Blind Resource Manual (Georgia State Dept. of Education, 1980, 2) reports that sensory deficits frequently observed among deaf-blind children include nystagmus, strabismus, congenital cataracts, sensory-neural hearing loss, and high frequency hearing loss. The manual indicates physical defects of deaf-blind children frequently include a small frail body, microcephaly, heart defects, and a lack of coordination. Additionally, deaf-blind children often display developmental delays in cognition. The manual reports that rubella syndrome deaf-blind persons frequently exhibit the following behaviors: eye poking, rocking, hand flicking, gazing at light, teeth grinding, perseveration of vocalizations or movements, delayed acquisition of self-help skills, delayed motor skills, delayed communication skills, erratic behavior, and no obvious response to environmental sounds.

Professional personnel with the Deaf-Blind Program of Special School District of St. Louis County, Missouri (1985) found that general character-

TABLE 5
EVALUATION BATTERY: DIAGNOSIS AND PROGRAMMING

1. *Vision Evaluation*
   a. *In-School Vision Evaluation* (forms in Chapter Two):
      • variety of lights, colored and white (flashlight and colored acetate sheets)
      • transilluminated toys
      • colorful and shiny toys such as windmill
      • moving toys of various sizes
      • pediatric opticokinetic drum
   b. *The Callier-Azusa Scale*,
      subtests (1) Visual Development
                (2) Visual-Motor.
   c. *Classroom Functioning*—systematic observation of visual functioning during performance of daily activities and reports of teachers.
   d. *Normal Acuity Development: Sensorimotor Stage* (Table 8)
   e. *Vision Functioning Skills Checklists* (Table 10).
   f. *Stimulation Profile: Visual* (Table 14)
2. *Hearing Evaluation*
   a. *Behavioral Observation Audiometry*—in soundproof booth with teacher and/or second audiologist
   b. *The Callier-Azusa Scale*, subtest Auditory Development
   c. *Classroom Functioning*—systematic observation of auditory functioning during performance of daily activities and reports of teachers
   d. *Auditory Development: Sensorimotor Stage* (Table 15)
   e. *Auditory Functioning Skills Checklist* (Table 21)
   f. *Stimulation Profile: Auditory* (Table 22)
3. *Tactile-Kinesthetic-Vestibular Development*
   a. *The Callier-Azusa Scale*, subtest Tactile Development
   b. *Classroom Functioning*—systematic observation of tactile skills functioning during daily activities and from teacher reports.
   c. *Tactile-Kinesthetic-Vestibular Development* (Table 23)
   d. *Tactile-Kinesthetic-Vestibular Programming Skills* (Table 32)
   e. *Stimulation Profiles: Tactile* (Table 26)
                        Vestibular (Table 27)
4. *Motor Development*
   a. Occupational/Physical Therapy Evaluations (Table 39)
   b. *Reflexes and Automatic Reactions* (Table 37)
   c. *The Callier-Azusa Scale*, Motor Development, subtests
      (1) Postural Control
      (2) Locomotion
      (3) Fine Motor
   d. *Classroom Functioning*—systematic observation of fine and gross motor functioning during daily activities and teacher reports
   e. Normal Sensorimotor Development (Table 36)

TABLE 5 (Continued)

5. *Daily Living Skills*
   a. Physical/occupational therapy evaluation
   b. *The Callier-Azusa Scale* — Daily Living Skills subtests: Undressing and **Dressing**, Personal Hygiene, Development of Feeding Skills, Toileting
   c. *Classroom Functioning* — systematic observation of self-help functioning during daily school activities and teacher reports.
   d. *Oral Motor Skills: Feeding/Eating* (Table 38)
   e. *Activities of Daily Living* (Table 40)
6. *Cognition*
   a. *Cattell Infant Intelligence Scale* or *McCarthy Scales of Children's Abilities* or *Bayley Scales of Infant Development*
   b. *The Callier-Azusa Scale*, subtest Cognitive Development or *The Oregon Project for Visually Impaired and Blind Preschool Children*
   c. *Sensorimotor Stage Cognitive Skill Development* (Table 47)
   d. *Classroom Functioning* — systematic observation of cognitive functioning during daily activities and teacher reports.
   e. Sensorimotor Cognitive Programming Skills Hierarchies (Table 50)
7. *Receptive/Expressive Language*
   a. *The Callier-Azusa Scale*, Receptive Language, Development of Speech
   b. *Receptive Expressive Language Scale* (REEL)
   c. *Classroom Functioning* — systematic observation of receptive and expressive language during daily activities and teaching reports
   d. *Development of Oral Motor Skills* (Table 51)
   e. *Receptive Language Development: Sensorimotor Stage* (Table 53)
   f. *Spoken Language Development: Sensorimotor Stage* (Table 54)
   g. *Systematic Observation Form: Expressive Language Prerequisites* (Table 55)
   h. *Systematic Observation: Functional Language Needs* (Table 56)
8. *Social/Emotional Development*
   a. *The Callier-Azusa Scale*, Social Development subtests: Interactions with Adults, Interactions with Peers, Interaction with the Environment
   b. *Classroom Functioning* — systematic observation of social functioning during daily school activities and teacher reports
   c. *Social/Emotional Developmental Skills: Sensorimotor Stage* (Table 60)
   d. *Sensorimotor Stage Social Skills Checklist* (Table 61)
   e. *Self-Awareness Characteristics Checklist: Sensorimotor Motor Stage* (Table 62)
   f. *Play Skill Development: Sensorimotor Stage* (Table 63)
   g. *Play Skills Checklist: Sensorimotor Stage* (Table 66)

istics of the majority of young (4–9 years old) deaf-blind children in their program included the following:

1. **Intelligence:** Functioning within the severe/profound mental retardation range with a mental age of 0–4 months level.

2. **Communication:** No speech. Verbal communication consists of vocalizations to indicate discomfort or pleasure.

3. **Self-Help Skills:** Totally dependent—unable to self-feed, unable to self-dress, not toilet trained.

4. **Visual Skills:** Severe visual impairment.

5. **Auditory Skills:** Moderate to severe hearing loss.

6. **Fine and Gross Motor Skills:** Severe psychomotor retardation, some form of cerebral palsy, and nonambulatory.

7. **Medical Concerns:** Seizure disorders, frequent upper respiratory health concerns.

8. **Interpersonal Relationships:** Lack of peer relationships, no spontaneous interactions. Generally appeared to recognize primary caregivers.

9. **Interactions with Environment:** No interactions with their environment; little cause-effect understanding.

10. **Other Behavioral Concerns:** Self-stimulatory behaviors, rumination, severe behavior disorders, tactile defensiveness, temper tantrums, eye gouging.

CASE STUDY SUMMARIES: PAM AND SALLY

The case study summaries of Pam and Sally (Table 6) were prepared to assist in the discrimination between deaf-blind severely multihandicapped children, and severely multihandicapped children. Sally's case study and others will be discussed throughout the next seven chapters to illustrate the discrimination process.

At the onset, Pam appeared to be appropriate for deaf-blind placement, having medical history of colobomas of both optic discs and not even a startle to sound. Current assessment revealed vision and visual-motor functioning with the right eye commensurate with developmental levels and decreased visual acuity with the left eye. The Regional Center Deaf-Blind guidelines refer to vision in the better eye (Table 1). Since Pam's vision in the better eye was commensurate with her developmental functioning (e.g., cognition, motor, communication, self-help), she did not meet the vision requirements of the Regional Center deaf-blind criteria. Evaluation revealed that Pam was functionally deaf because she did not auditorally attend to, respond to, or localize sounds, or use hearing appropriate to her developmental level. Thus, Pam met the hearing functioning portion, but not the vision functioning portion of the deaf-blind criteria.

Sally's medical history revealed a definitive medical diagnosis of markedly abnormal vision (e.g., Vision-Evoked Response Test) and mod-

TABLE 6
CASE STUDY SUMMARIES: PAM AND SALLY

Pam, 10 years, 6 months	*Sally, 4 years, 8 months*
MEDICAL: Multiple congenital anomalies of unknown etiology including colombas of both optic discs, right ear deformity, right facial paralysis, curvical spine anomalies, micrognathia, microencephaly, psychomotor retardation.	*MEDICAL:* seizure disorder, cerebral palsy
Current Concern: rumination *HISTORY:* *Vision:* 1978: R tracking all directions, reach and grasp, retrieving dropped articles, L reflexes only (continued development)	*Current Concern:* basically healthy child *HISTORY:* *Vision:* 1981: VER markedly abnormal, no fixation, no responses to light; 1983: delayed visual responses; uses eyes alternately; ashows awareness of colored lights, inconsistent fixation
Auditory: 1978: inconclusive, no startle to sound, (subsequent same results)	*Auditory:* 1981: ERA moderate sensorineural bilateral hearing loss; 1982: wore aid, inconsistent responses, not very responsive with or without aid.
Cognition: at 3 yr. 9 mo., 5–7 mos. *ASSESSMENT:* *Vision:* R spontaneously fixated light, toys, food; visually tracked < – > and in all directions crossing midline; visually discriminated pictures; demonstrated increased fine and gross motor skills and gross motor skills and judgement of depth; no large visual field defects. L decreased visual acuity due to left esotropia or congenital defect.	*Cognition:* 1981: 0–1 mo. *ASSESSMENT:* *Vision:* No visual responses to light; no opticokinetic response; no protective blink, no eye contact
Diagnosis: visual and visual motor functioning appears 18 mo.+ which is commensurate with developmental level.	*Diagnosis:* Estimated corrected visual acuity 20/100 or less in better eye and/or blindness on a cortical level.
Auditory: No definite repeatable responses up to 90 dB level. Audiometric testing suggests significant hearing loss. History of flat tympanograms but no fluid. Past has worn amplification with no observable benefits. Does not attend to, respond to, localize sounds consistently with or without amplification.	*Auditory:* Wears hearing aid. No clear or repeatable responses with or without aid. Observed responses in past have ranged from 60–90 dB HL. She does not appear to be aware of conversational speech. At 85 dB, no responses. Normal typanograms. No observable responses in classroom.
Diagnosis: Functionally deaf.	*Diagnosis:* Hearing impaired

TABLE 6 (Continued)

Pam, 10 years, 6 months	*Sally, 4 years, 8 months*
Cognition: 8–12 mo. splinter skills to 24 mos.; profound range of intellectual functioning; poor short-term memory; object permanence, shows curiosity, knows adults can help her.	*Cognition:* Newborn level, profound range. Unresponsive to environment, does not change behavior when stimulated.
Fine Motor: 24 mos.; strings beads, picks up small objects; well-coordinated hand patterns of superior pincer grasp (behavior interferes with fine motor tasks)	*Fine Motor:* 0–1 mo.; random movement; can bring either hand to mouth.
Gross Motor: 12–18 mo.; walks in toddler gait, rides a tricycle, walks up and down steps; uses locomotion to gain objects out of reach; uses motor planning to solve detour problems.	*Gross Motor:* 0–1 mo., turns head side to side in supine. Lifts head in prone.
Communication: 6–12 mos.; Seldom vocalizes; poor eye contact; inconsistently responds signed commands; cries when upset; occasionally shakes head "no."	*Communication:* 0–1 mo.; spontaneous vocalizations; inconsistently responds to high-pitched voice.
Self-Help:	*Self-Help:*
Feeding: 24 mo., independently scoops all food and drinks independently. Eats all food pureed, has narrow esophagus, picks out lumps from her mouth.	*Feeding:* eats ground table food.
Dressing: 18 mos.; assists in dressing.	*Dressing:* 0–1 mo.
Toileting: not potty trained.	*Toileting:* 0–1 mo.
Home Adaptive Behaviors: 10–12 mo. in interactions with adults, children and the environment.	*Home Adaptive Behaviors:* 0–6 mo. Interactions with adults and environment, 4–6 mo.; interaction with children, 0–1 mo.
Diagnosis: Multi-handicapped child in the areas of hearing impairment and mental retardation (profound).	*Diagnosis:* Multi-handicapped child in the areas of deaf-blind, mentally retarded (profound), physically impaired.

erate sensorineural hearing loss (e.g., Auditory-Evoked Response Test). Current evaluation revealed no visual responses and no clear repeatable responses to auditory stimuli. Thus, she met the Regional Center deaf-blind vision and hearing criteria (Table 1).

SUMMARY

The Regional Center guidelines for certifying a student as deaf-blind require a combination of visual, auditory, and educational conditions. Visual functioning must indicate an estimated visual acuity of 20/100 or less in the better eye, a chronic visual condition, cortical blindness, a field of vision of 20° or less in the better eye, or functional blindness. Hearing functioning must indicate a 30 dB bilateral sensory neural hearing loss as a minimum across the speech frequencies in the better ear with amplification, a previous chronic condition of the auditory mechanism, and/or functional deafness. Educationally, the combination of sensory deficits precludes adequately educating the child in a program for visually-impaired or hearing-impaired children.

The Regional Center diagnostic criteria does not specify a cognitive functioning range nor address additional handicapping problems of fragile health conditions and physical impairments. Deaf-blind severely multihandicapped children require different educational programming than higher functioning basically healthy deaf-blind children (e.g., rubella syndrome deaf-blind children).

A multidisciplinary evaluation is necessary to determine functioning levels of vision and hearing, fine and gross motor skills, cognitive functioning, communication (receptive and expressive), and adaptive behavior skills of daily living and socialization.

Re-evaluation procedures include a substantial amount of information regarding the child's functioning within the classroom setting and the impact of educational programming. Initial evaluation procedures for preschool children are based on a clinic evaluation and medical information. Thus, initial evaluations of deaf-blind children may result in a tentative diagnosis, pending a period of home observations and assessments in the Child Assessment Program (C.A.P.).

An evaluation/re-evaluation battery of tests should include a variety of norm-referenced, criterion-referenced, and informal diagnostic tests; developmental skills checklists; and systematic observation in the classroom. Additionally, medical professionals (e.g., optometrists and audiologists, occupational/physical therapists, pediatric nurse practitioners) will provide professional evaluations regarding vision, hearing, and physical functioning, and daily living skills.

General characteristics of young deaf-blind severely multihandicapped children include the following: (1) severe/profound mental retardation, (2) non-verbal communication except making vocalizations to indicate discomfort or pleasure, (3) total dependence regarding dressing, feeding, and toileting, (4) severe visual impairment, (5) moderate-to-severe hearing loss, (6) severe psychomotor retardation accompanied by cerebral palsy, (7) medical concerns including seizure disorders and upper respiratory health concerns, (8) no spontaneous interpersonal interactions, (9) no interactions with the environment, and (10) self-stimulatory behaviors.

Chapter Two

VISION: EVALUATION AND PROGRAMMING

The congenitally severely impaired child at any age is like a baby as far as visual development is concerned unless he is carefully stimulated and taught how to look, to note visual cues, and to make visual comparisons (Barraga, 1983, 89).

- Comprehensive Visual Evaluation
- Visual Examination
- Visual Functioning Evaluation
- Vision Diagnosis
- Visual Skills Programming
- IEP Monitoring
- Summary

CONSULTANTS:
Nancy Kennedy, O.D.
Janet Sorth, M.A.
Richard Serano, M.D.

U nder normal visual conditions, the young child learns the visual skills of fixation, tracking, focus, accommodation, and convergence through looking during day-to-day activities. The visual system is extremely important for learning because a greater quantity of information can be gained in a shorter period of time than through any other single sensory system. When the human eye is operating at maximum capacity, the 900,000 fibers of the optic nerve can transmit 430 times as much information to the brain per second as the 30,000 fibers of the human ear (Jacobson, 1951a, 1951b). "Vision is the mediator for other sensory impressions and acts as a stabilizer between the person and the external world" (Barraga, 1983, 86).

Visual impairment is a significant concern for mentally handicapped persons. Legal blindness is more than 200 times more frequent among mentally handicapped children than among nonhandicapped children (Warberg, 1986). "Twenty percent of severely visually impaired mentally retarded children show no visual perception of light or react visually to only very large objects although the eyes appear normal on examination" (Warberg, 1986, 99). "The presence of optic atrophy (OA) is twice as high among mentally retarded as among other blind children" (Warberg, 1986, 100).

The impact of a severe visual impairment permeates every phase of growth and development and retards developmental progress. A severe deficit in vision causes a delay in the acquisition of many skills, including the gross and fine motor skills of reach and grasp, eye-hand coordination; muscular control of the head, neck, and trunk muscles, eye-foot coordination; walking and playing (Scholl, 1986). The lack of visual stimulation may result in a lack of motivation to move and explore the environment.

COMPREHENSIVE VISION EVALUATION

The deaf-blind child's visual system may not function properly for a number of reasons including the following: (1) the retina of the eye does not receive light (e.g., retinal detachment, retinitis pigmentosa); (2) the retina of the eye does not receive a clearly focused image (e.g., fibrolental hyperplasia); (3) optic nerve impulses do not reach the vision center of the brain (e.g., optic atrophy); or (4) information from the eye is not processed by the brain (Blackman, 1984). A comprehensive multifaceted evaluation, therefore, is essential in determining the reason the visual system is not functioning properly and in determining the visual functioning status in order to appropriately diagnose and program for the visually impaired child.

A comprehensive vision evaluation includes information from four primary sources: (1) background medical, ophthalmological and/or neurological information from permanent school records, (2) a school-based visual examination, (3) a school-based visual functioning assessment conducted by a low-vision specialist with expertise in evaluating young severely/profoundly multihandicapped children, and (4) teacher/parent observations on the child's daily visual functioning. Information from these sources is compared to the Deaf-Blind Vision Criteria to make an appropriate diagnosis.

Visual Examination

Deaf-blind children frequently experience severe mental retardation, limited to no communication skills, limited physical and social experiences, reduced sensory stimuli, erratic behavior, and tactile defensiveness (Georgia State Dept., 1980). These innate characteristics common to deaf-blind children make it very difficult and almost impossible to visually examine the deaf-blind child under normal conditions.

Clinical examination procedures depend upon the patient to provide subjective responses or clues to assist the ophthalmologist/optometrist in making a definitive diagnosis. The clinician's lack of control of the deaf-blind child's fixation and focusing mechanisms and the child's limited or nonexistent ability to follow even basic instructions forces almost total reliance on objective findings and impressions while performing a visual examination (Seelye, 1979). The vision examination itself has four primary sections as follows: (1) external examination, (2) internal examination, (3) retinoscopy (fundoscopy), and (4) visual acuity (Seelye, 1979).

A school-based vision examination differs considerably from an office examination, due primarily to the informal nature of the school-based examination and the inability of the opthalmologist/optometrist to transport sensitive technical equipment to school. The school-based evaluation should be conducted in an unused classroom or diagnostic room so lighting can be adjusted to get responses in dim and bright room illumination. One of the best places to perform the examination of the young severely multihandicapped child is on the floor on a mat so the examiner can play with the child, easily present stimuli without undue positioning concerns, and maintain constant physical contact during the evaluation. The classroom teacher or parent or teacher assistant should be present to assist the examiner and help explain the child's reactions.

External Examination

A visual evaluation form (Table 7) helps to provide structure to the evaluation and organization of the data gathered. This form will serve as the outline for discussing the components of a visual evaluation.

TABLE 7
SCHOOL-BASED VISUAL EVALUATION FORM

Name: _____

Date: _____

D.O.B.: _____

Health History: (Past medical diagnoses, birth data, Apgar score, maternal factors, etc.)

Ocular History: (Include VEP)

I. Visual Examination
    A. External Examination (Anatomical)
        1. Oculomotor Symmetry
            a) Corneal Light Reflex Test:
            b) Strabismus:
            c) Cover/Uncover Tests:
        2. Oculomotor Skills
            a) Accommodation
            b) Convergence
            c) Binocularity
            d) Fixation
            e) Tracking
        3. Oculomotor Reflexes
            a) Frontal saccades
            b) Occipital pursuit
            c) Opticokinetic reflex
            d) Vestibulo-ocular reflex
        4. Nystagmus
            a) Pendular vs. Jerky (directional)
            b) Rotary vs. Linear
        5. Visual Fields
    B. Internal Examination
        1. Pupillary Reflexes
    C. Visual Acuity
        1. Snellen E/Schematic Picture Cards
        2. Opticokinetic Nystagmus
II. Visual Functioning Evaluation
    A. Visual Sensation
        1. Visual Awareness
            a) Protective blink reflex
            b) Responses to light
            c) Responses to colored light
        2. Functional Visual Acuity
            a) Fixation reflexes
            b) Focus
            c) Reach and grasp (visually directed)
    B. Visual Motor Skills
        1. Eye contact
        2. Tracking
        3. Convergence
        4. Accommodation

TABLE 7 (Cont'd)

---

     5. Eye-hand coordination
     6. Body awareness/visual localization
  C. Visual Perception
     1. Visual recognition
     2. Visual discrimination (size, shape, color)
     3. Visual classification
     4. Visual directionality
     5. Visual figure-ground
     6. Visual memory
     7. Visual sequencing
     8. Visual comprehension
     9. Visual-motor integration

The Health History and Ocular History

The Health History and Ocular History sections of the Visual Evaluation form are completed prior to the school-based examination from medical records and recent ophthalmological and/or neurological reports. The external examination derives basic information regarding the general appearance of the eyes, including size, shape, obvious deviations, and gross abnormalities in structure. In general, the external examination is a "screening procedure for pathologic and congenital or developmental abnormalities" (Seelye, 1979, 24).

Oculomotor Symmetry

Oculomotor Symmetry (Table 7) may be assessed by several different procedures including inspection, corneal light reflex, strabismus, and/or cover tests. "Proper alignment of the eyes allows an image of an object to project onto the most visually sensitive part of the retina, the macula" (Nelson, 1984, 24).

During the **corneal light reflex** test, the examiner holds a flashlight one to two feet away and views the reflected light from the child's cornea. "The corneal light reflex is normally located near the center of the pupils and should be symmetrically positioned in each eye. If the light reflex in one cornea is not in the same relative position as in the other, this suggests an ocular misalignment" (Nelson, 1984, 32).

Test results will provide information regarding **strabismus**, an abnormal ocular alignment due to muscle incoordination in which the eyes do not move together. Inspection is a general screening of the alignment of the eyes.

Cover tests appear to be the most accurate method of evaluating alignment; however, they require patient cooperation and good fixation in each eye (Nelson, 1984). The primary cover tests include cover/uncover, alternate cover, cover/cross-over, and prism cover tests. In using the cover/uncover test, the child must fixate an object with both eyes open while the examiner covers one eye and observes the uncovered eye for movement. The occluder (cover) is removed, and the child returns to binocular vision for a few seconds prior to covering the opposite eye. Movement of the uncovered eye indicates the presence of a manifest deviation (tropia) or **strabismus.** An inward movement of the eye toward the nose indicates the eye has an outward deviation or exotropia; an outward eye movement away from the nose implies the eye has an inward deviation or estropia; an upward deviation of the eye is hypertropia; and/or a downward deviation of the eye is hypotropia (Nelson, 1984). In the alternative cover test, the examiner moves the occluder (e.g., hand, thumb, paddle) from one eye to the other without allowing an interval for binocular viewing. If the cover tests suggest a deviation, the prism cover test is used to measure the size of the deviation (Nelson, 1984).

Occulomotor Skills

Oculomotor Skills (Table 7) include accommodation, convergence, binocularity, fixation, tracking, and the reflex eye movements of saccades, pursuit reflex, opticokinetic reflex, and vestibulo-ocular reflex (Gresty et al., 1983). **Accommodation** or the focus mechanism of the eyes makes clear vision possible at different distances. Accommodative ability appears to be present during the first weeks of life and reaches adult accuracy by nine weeks of age (Nelson, 1984).

Single **binocular** vision is dependent upon good ocular alignment in which both eyes focus simultaneously on the same object. A person maintains singular binocular vision in all directions of gaze by means of twelve extraocular muscles attached to the globe of the eye (Taylor, 1976). A visual-motor dysfunction or extraocular muscle dysfunction generally includes a dysfunction in binocularity. Eyes must **converge** for single binocular vision. Binocularity and ocular alignment are interdependent in that vergence movements of the eyes enable the child to maintain single binocular vision, while binocularly derived information is used to maintain ocular alignment. Binocular vision, along with nuances of shade and shadow, allow depth perception.

In an office setting, visual **fixation** becomes obvious by about six weeks of age (Nelson, 1984). "The ability to elicit a fixation pattern as well as the absence of oculomotor disorder in an infant is often considered evidence that central visual function is adequate" (Nelson, 1984, 19). "Target-**tracking** ability is called a smooth **pursuit** because the eyes move conjugately at a constant velocity to match the velocity of the moving visual stimulus" (Aslin, 1987, 82). To assess fixation and tracking, a red object of visual interest is slowly moved to the right and to the left. Although toys are useful in assessing visual fixation and following, the human face has been demonstrated to be a more ideal visual stimuli (Nelson, 1984). Fixation and following should first be assessed with both eyes and then with each eye separately by patching one eye. Horizontal, vertical, and oblique eye movements are made as the child rotates his/her eyes about their horizontal and vertical axes and fixates upon various stimuli (Taylor, 1976).

Oculomotor Reflexes. The saccadic system consists of six extraocular muscles that operate primarily in pairs to move the eye horizontally, vertically, or torsionally (Aslin, 1987). The **saccades** are reflex movements which transfer gaze quickly from one target to another. The **opticokinetic reflex** (OKN) is a basic target-tracking system which induces the eyes to follow relative movements of large areas of the visual world and provides the person with information about his own movements (Gresty et al., 1983; Aslin 1987).

The **vestibulo-ocular reflex** (VOR) stabilizes vision during head movements so that even though the person is running or walking, the direction of the gaze remains undisturbed (Gresty et al., 1983).

Vestibulo-ocular reflexes are assessed by rotating the child and observing the resultant effect on the eyes.

> The only true indication of visual awareness (provided that there are no other oculomotor abnormalities) is an ability to inhibit nystagmus in two situations: (1) during rotation, the normal child is able to suppress the nystagmus while looking at the examiner, and (2) when the rotation is stopped suddenly, a normal child will show only one or two beats, but a blind infant will continue to have nystagmus for several beats (Taylor, 1983, 8).

Nystagmus

Nystagmus (Table 7) is an involuntary rhythmical movement of the eyeballs. The eyes are a window to the brain and give important diagnostic clues to the presence of central nervous system (CNS) disorders (Nelson, 1984). Nystagmus usually indicates CNS disorders primarily involving the brainstem and cerebellum (Coats, 1975). It can be associated with ocular diseases and vestibular disorders as well as CNS disorders. Nystagmus often occurs as a compensatory activity in an inadequately developed or inadequately integrated nervous system caused by the failure of components of the fixation reflex (Leisman, 1976). "In an infant, the presenting manifestation of a visual defect may be nystagmus or strabismus" (Nelson, 1984, 157).

There are two basic types of nystagmus—pendular and jerky. Pendular (ocular) nystagmoid movements are of approximately equal speed in two directions like the swing of a clock pendulum, while jerky nystagmus is characterized by a slow movement in one direction followed by a rapid movement in the opposite direction (Nelson, 1984). The nystagmoid oscillations of pendular and/or jerky nystagmus may be horizontal, vertical, or rotary. "As a rule, pendular nystagmus develops secondary to poor central vision if the vision deficit has been congenitally determined or if the vision has been lost in the first two years of life" (Nelson, 1984, 158–159).

Visual Field

A visual field measurement (Table 7) is conducted to determine how well the child can see out of the corner of his eyes while looking straight ahead. Constricted visual fields indicate the possibility of mobility and visual function problems. Full visual fields are approximately 70° to 100° (Georgia State Dept. of Education, 1980). Legal blindness, a field of vision of 20° or less in the better eye, meets the vision criteria of the Deaf-Blind Guidelines. "A gross measurement of the visual field can be made by using two penlights, one for fixation and one to localize and identify within the field of vision" (Seelye, 1974, 24).

Internal Examination

A complete internal examination (Table 7) is not performed at school due to the lack of portability and sensitivity of optometric equipment. "An ophthalmoscope is used in this procedure to determine internal ocular physical health and to assess structural damage" (Seelye, 1974, 24). The direct ophthalmoscopic examination of the interior of the eye with the pupil dilated permits good visualization of the posterior pole of the retina, which includes the optic nerve, the macula, and the retina (Nelson, 1984). The field of viewing is limited, so the retinal periphery is not examined. The indirect ophthalmoscope provides a good field of viewing, but results in an inverted and reversed fundus image, so is difficult to master (Nelson, 1984).

"A wide variety of disorders involving the CNS may have ocular findings, especially of the optic nerve and retina" (Nelson, 1984, 162). Optic atrophy, irreparable damage to the optic nerve fibers, is diagnosed by objective examination revealing pale optic discs. One particularly important aspect of the internal examination concerns the future control of visual impairments such as macular degeneration, optic atrophy, cataracts, and glaucoma, and the state of genetically inherited eye disease such as retinitis pigmentosa (Georgia State Dept. of Educ., 1980). Internal examination information is usually taken from recent ophthalmology reports and/or visual-evoked response testing results.

Pupillary Reflexes

Pupillary Reflexes (Table 7) are part of an internal examination that is appropriately conducted in the school-based setting. The two major functions of the pupil are to regulate the amount of light reaching the retina and to vary the depth of focus of the eye (Solapatek & Cohen, 1987). The pupils are checked for direct, consensual, and near pupillary responses to detect any internal ocular conditions and also any abnormal conditions of the central nervous system. Direct responses are assessed by projecting light into the pupil. The pupils should contract and dilate simultaneously and to the same degree in each eye. Consensual responses are checked by projecting a light into the pupil of one eye and noting the reaction of the other. Normally, the pupil of the right eye will react consensually when the left eye is exposed to direct light, and vice versa. If one eye is blind, its pupil will not react to direct light, but will react consensually, and the pupil of the seeing eye will react to direct light but not consensually (Barens, 1946). The pupils should contract when a nearby object is observed. The reaction of the pupil is dependent upon the integrity of the retina, the optic nerve, the optic tract, and the nerve centers at the end of the optic tract which receive the impulse and then transmit it to the third nerve and to the iris (Barens, 1946).

Retinoscopy

A Retinoscopy is not conducted during a school-based examination. In this evaluation, "a battery-powered retinoscope, a lens tree, and individual trial lenses are used to neutralize the optics of the child's eye to measure objectively the refractive status and determine the need for a spectacle correction" (Seelye, 1979, 24). Refractive errors include the conditions of hyperopia or farsightedness, myopia or nearsightedness, and astigmatism. "The most common refractive error among young children is mild hyperopia" (Nelson, 1984, 40). Myopia is not common in infants, although variable myopia and astigmatism are common among premature infants (Nelson, 1984). The measurement of refractive errors in young children requires the use of drugs to dilate the pupil, to relax the sphincter muscle of the iris, and to prevent pupillary constructions. Older children can look through lenses and provide cues as to which lens improves vision.

Visual Acuity

Visual acuity (Table 7) is the most familiar measurement of central vision. It is the measurable aspect of sensation that is useful in labeling the deaf-blind child for legal identification. Visual acuity refers to the ability to discriminate details of objects at specified distances.

> In the United States, vision is usually determined at a distance of 20 feet, using standardized symbols such as those on the Snellen Eye Chart. Thus, a person with normal central vision should be able to see the series of letters on the 20/20 line at a distance of 20 feet (Wyne & O'Connor, 1979, 448).

Snellen E–Test

The Snellen E–Test is the most widely used visual acuity test for preschool children in this country (Nelson, 1984). If the visual acuities are measurable and the cognitive functioning of the child is adequate to respond to the task, visual acuity is assessed by using the Snellen Eye Chart or Snellen "E."

> The subjective testing of vision is usually first possible between two and one-half and three years of age. Children of this age can be tested most successfully by the use of schematic picture cards presented at increasing distances from the patient (Nelson, 1984, 30).

These testing procedures are not appropriate for most severely multi-handicapped children functioning within the sensorimotor stage. "An accurate diagnosis of distant visual acuity is generally not possible until approximately age three years; when the child is multihandicapped, it may be possible only years later or perhaps never" (Nelson, 1984, 239). "The assessment of visual acuity in the preverbal child depends on various clinical observations of 'visual behavior' in the young. There are no infallible methods of evaluation" (Nelson, 1984, 28). Visual acuity is developmental in nature (Table 8), maturing from birth with light perception but no acuity, no coordination, no convergence, no accommodation (Morrison et al., 1979) to normal 20/20 visual acuity by age six years (Allen, 1957).

Several techniques, including opticokinetic nystagmus (OKN), forced-choice preferential looking (FPL), and visually-evoked potentials (VEP), are providing assistance in the assessment of visual acuity with severely multihandicapped children. However, these "different sorts of tasks yield widely different estimates of visual acuity" (Banks & Dannemiller, 1987, 131).

OKN Test. If the child appears to possess normal peripheral visual apparatus and a visual acuity cannot be determined using subjective testing methods (e.g., Snellen "E," schematic picture cards), the child may be observed behaviorally for opticokinetic nystagmus (OKN). The OKN test is one of the more sensitive tests for central oculomotor pathology, but it relies on fixation (Coats, 1978). Opticokinetic nystagmus is an elicited rhythmic eye movement in response to a moving repetitive pattern. A pediatric opticokinetic drum may be used to attempt to elicit a response by rotating the drum in the child's line of vision. The OKN eye movements consist of a slow (following) phase in the direction of the pattern movement of the OKN drum and a fast (refixation) phase opposite to the direction of the pattern movement (Coats, 1975). Normal visual acuities estimated from the OKN Technique include visual acuity of 20/400 at birth, 20/400 at 2 months of age, 20/200 at 4 months of age, 20/60 at 1 year, and normal 20/20 by 20 to 30 months of age (Hoyt et al., 1982).

The OKN drum is frequently used as a routine test to evaluate a child suspected of being blind (Nelson, 1984). If no definite opticokinetic nystagmus can be elicited, the child may experience blindness at a cortical level (Mountain Plains Regional Center for Services to Deaf-Blind Children, 1985). OKN is present in full term and somewhat premature babies, but is reliably absent in blind and many brain-damaged

TABLE 8
NORMAL VISUAL ACUITY DEVELOPMENT

Age	Behavior
Newborn	Visual Acuity _____. Attends to light stimulus. No convergence, no coordination, no accommodation. Limited fixation ability so objects appear out of focus.
6 weeks	Visual Acuity _____. Aware of large objects in line of vision. Begins binocular coordination (convergence). Follows some slow-moving objects. Fixates human faces and simple targets.
2 Months	Visual Acuity _____. Looks down, not up. Fixates momentarily. Likes bright objects. Eyes coordinated fairly well. Attention to objects up to 6 feet away. Discriminates yellow, red, orange. Accomdative ability is mature.
4 Months	Visual Acuity _____. Focuses momentarily on objects. Recognizes familiar objects and people at close range. Visually controlled reach and grasp. Glances at small objects 1″ in diameter.
6 Months	Visual Acuity ___20/800___. Develops spatial relationships. Follows rapidly moving objects. Eye-hand coordination developing. Rescues toy dropped within reach. Looks at objects held close to eyes. Shifts attention from object to object.
9 Months	Visual Acuity ___20/200___. Child reaches, probes, and concentrates attention. Can see tiny pieces of paper (2–3 mm) near. Picks up 7 mm pellet. Imitates facial expressions.
12 Months	Visual Acuity _____. Binocular vision stronger. Able to focus and accommodate.
18 Months	Visual Acuity ___20/100___. Visual orientation good. Distance vision begins. Points to picture in books.
2 Years	Visual Acuity ___20/70___. Inspects objects with eyes alone. Aware of details in peripheral field vision. Visually seeks missing object or person.
3 Years	Visual Acuity ___20/40___. Possesses spatial relationship orientation. Eye-hand coordination—puzzles, form boards, crude drawing of circle.
4 Years	Visual Acuity ___20/30___. Accurate size discrimination. Eye-hand coordination more accurate.
5 Years	Visual Acuity ___20/25___. Mature eye-hand coordination. Preacademic skills—cutting, coloring, pasting.
6 Years	Visual Acuity ___20/20___. Mature visual acuity. Eyes coordinated. Depth perception good. Preacademic skills—manuscript printing.

REFERENCES: Allen, 1957; Efron and DuBoff, 1978; Stillman, 1978; Nelson, 1984; Wybar & Taylor, 1983; Barraga, 1984; Morrison et al., 1978.

infants (Taylor, 1983). "Because OKN measurements depend upon a motor response, failure to elicit a response may be due to a defect in the oculomotor system and not necessarily to the infant's failure to 'see' the stimulus" (Nelson, 1987, 22). The OKN assessment procedure lends itself to school-based behavioral assessment in determining its presence or absence.

FLP Test. A new procedure for assessing visual acuity behaviorally in young and/or severely multihandicapped children is Forced-Choice Preferential Looking (FPL). This procedure does not lend itself well to the school-based evaluation because of the equipment necessary and because it requires two or three adult observers. The FPL technique involves presenting an infant with a grating composed of black-and-white stripes equivalent to various Snellen visual acuity values and observing the smallest stripe that stimulates preferential fixation (Nelson, 1984). This procedure requires an alert and attentive child capable of fixating. Estimated normal visual acuities derived from the FPL procedure are similar to those determined using OKN until about one year of age: birth, 20/400; 2 months, 20/200; 4 months, 20/200; 6 months, 20/150; 1 year, 20/50; and 18 to 24 months, normal 20/20 visual acuity (Hoyt et al., 1982).

VEP Test. A clinical/hospital procedure for objectively measuring the young child's visual acuity is an electrodiagnostic test, Visual-Evoked Potentials (VEP). This procedure, which measures the change in electrical activity in the visual cortex in a time-locked response to a light stimulus, is used in clinical evaluations of infants with congenital cataracts, amblyopia, strabismus, refractive errors, and suspected blindness (Nelson, 1984). The child's visual acuity is inferred by delays in the standard time interval between light stimulating the retina and the occipital cortex reacting with a low voltage of electrical discharge. Normal visual acuities inferred from VEP include the following: birth, 20/100–20/200; 2 months, 20/80; 4 months, 20/80; 6 months to one year, 20/40 to 20/20. Normal 20/20 visual acuity as derived using VEP is reached between 6 and 12 months of age (Hoyt, 1982). These are significantly higher visual acuities than those determined by other methods. Thus, as research continues to perfect these techniques, OKN, FPL, and VEP, the visual acuities of infants and severely multi-handicapped children will be easier and more accurately assessed and quantified.

VISUAL FUNCTIONING EVALUATION

Environmental-specific information regarding visual functioning of deaf-blind severely multihandicapped children is crucial because these children vary widely in their daily use or nonuse of visual input. Teacher and parent information assists in providing an estimate of utilization of visual input on a daily basis. A visual functioning evaluation is a school-based procedure.

Environmental functioning information is also used to determine appropriate evaluation strategies and techniques. Parents, teachers, and therapists who are in daily contact with the handicapped child can provide the optometrist with much accurate information regarding visual functioning because they have observed the child daily in familiar and nonfamiliar surroundings and can interpret or predict the child's responses.

A visual functioning evaluation (Table 7) includes determining the child's visual abilities in the areas of visual sensation, visual motor skills, and visual perception. The Vision Status and Functioning Form (Table 9) was designed to assist in evaluating the child's functioning abilities in the environment. During re-evaluations, these questions are asked primarily of the classroom teachers, while this questionnaire is used with parents during the child's initial clinic evaluation. Question 1-5 on the Vision Status and Functioning Form (Table 9) regarding light perception is designed to be used in estimating the child's level of visual sensation awareness. Questions regarding fixation, size of objects seen, and at what distance are designed to provide estimates of visual acuity. These estimates and observations regarding daily visual functioning aid the optometrist in selection of evaluation methods, techniques, and materials. The information also assists the optometrist in deciding the appropriate degree of perseverance in attempting to elicit a response from a particular child.

Visual Sensation

Visual sensation refers to the way the retina receives light or form. Any malfunction or defect in the cornea and lens, retina, optic nerve, and tract to the occipital cortex, or the brain can reduce or eliminate sensation. Visual sensation is composed of two levels—awareness and acuity (Table 7). At the awareness level, the child may be aware of light, objects, outlines, and/or people at near and far distances. Visual awareness functioning considers visual reflexes and responses to various forms and intensities of light input.

TABLE 9
VISION STATUS AND FUNCTIONING FORM

Questions to parents to summarize their interpretation of their child's vision responses.

1. Do you feel your child perceives light? _____

2. Do you feel your child turns his/her head to or in the direction of light? _____

3. Does the child respond to colored lights? _____

4. Does the child seek out any light sources, i.e., windows, overhead lights, one light in a room, etc.? _____

5. Does the child squint or close the eyes in bright sunlight or other bright lights?

_____

6. Do you feel the child would react protectively if an object was moved quickly toward his/her eyes? _____

7. Does the child manipulate objects, wave his/her hands or an object in front of his/her face? _____

8. Do you feel the child turns for or reaches for large objects based on sight? _____

9. Do you feel the child turns for or reaches for small objects based on sight? _____

10. Does the child recognize a familiar person by sight? _____
    How far away? _____

11. Does the child make eye contact with the caregiver? _____
    How far away? _____

12. Do you feel the child sees small foodstuffs like raisins, candy, chocolate chips, etc.? _____

13. Does the child bump into objects in rolling, creeping, crawling, or walking?

_____

14. Which of your child's senses do you feel he/she learns most about his/her environment from? _____

SOURCE: Designed by Nancy Kennedy O.D., Consultant Optometrist to the Deaf-Blind Program of Special School District of St. Louis County Missouri, 1985.

Protective Blink Reflex

The Protective Blink Reflex is a natural reflex which occurs if an object is brought quickly close to one's face and is assessed to determine if the child possesses visual awareness capabilities. The first expressions of visual perception include the basic input functions of response to visual threat, fixation, and pursuit, which provide insights regarding information processing (Leisman, 1976).

Responses to Light

The child's responses to light (Table 7) are evaluated in the following areas: responses to bright vs. dim light, responses to audio/visual light stimulus, abnormal responses or reactions to light, and responses to colored light. Responses to light are evaluated to determine if visual sensation is at the awareness or visual acuity level. "The pupillary light response is not synonymous with visual awareness, but indicates functioning afferent and efferent pupillary pathways" (Nelson, 1984, 37). Visual awareness implies the stimulus is reaching the occipital cortex. Responses to light are evaluated in a semidarkened room using a penlight, reflected light, a camera flash, transilluminated (lighted) toys and shiny objects, and a flashlight with colored acetate sheets.

> Sometimes the light stimulus creates abnormal behavior such as flapping or flicking, head rolling, rocking, and other violent behavior patterns. These adverse reactions to the light stimulus can be used to determine optimal lighting standards for further evaluation procedures (Seelye, 1979, 27).

This information is also valuable in planning for maximum programming benefits.

Functional Visual Acuity

Functional visual acuity evaluation (Table 7) should be conducted in informal, unstructured settings with objects familiar to the child, including foodstuffs of various sizes such as raisins and cookies; toys, pictures, and programming materials. The child's fixational responses to large and small objects presented at near and far distances is assessed. The child's "reach and grasp" skills relating to various sizes of stimuli is quantified using the Snellen "E." The Vision Functioning Skills Checklist (Table 10) is useful in assessing visual awareness skills.

Visual-Motor Skills

Visual-motor functioning refers to the process of the brain directing and focusing the eyes and coordinating sight with movements of other parts of the body. These skills include eye contact, tracking, convergence, accommodation, eye-hand coordination, and body awareness (Table 7). The failure of a child with intact peripheral organs of vision to develop the ability to focus on an object and follow it, and to blink response to a visual threat has been referred to as cortical blindness (Leisman, 1976).

Proper and accurate evaluations of visual-motor skills are critical because higher-level visual skills such as visual perception are dependent on efficient oculomotor performance (Seelye, 1979). The Callier-Azusa Scale, subtest Visual-Motor (Stillman, 1978) is helpful in determining estimates of visual-motor developmental levels to use in comparing to overall developmental functioning. A wide variety of colored and transilluminated toys and objects are used to assess fixational and tracking skills. A penlight is very effective in assessing horizontal, vertical, diagonal, and circular tracking skills. Bright red objects may elicit a following response which a conventional flashlight will not elicit.

Convergence

Convergence is an individual's ability to follow a moving target as it proceeds toward him. Using a penlight or a toy as the target, the examiner should start about sixteen inches away from the eyes and slowly bring the target toward the bridge of the child's nose until it is only about four inches away (Efron & DuBoff, 1979, 12).

Accommodation

Accommodation is the adjustment of the eye for seeing at different distances, which is accomplished by changing the shape of the crystalline lens through action of the ciliary muscle in order to focus a clear image on the retina (Georgia State Dept. of Education, 1980). The assessment procedure is designed to determine the position and distance from the eyes that an object should be placed for the child to see it most efficiently (Efron & DuBoff, 1979). The examiner may hand the child, or present to the child, a wide variety of toys and/or transilluminated objects and note how the child holds the toy or positions his head for best vision. Eye contact with objects and persons is noted, as some children avoid eye contact with persons. Eye contact is an important prerequisite skill for eye-hand coordination and visual perception skills.

Eye-Hand Coordination

Eye-hand coordination (Table 7) can be assessed at a number of developmental functioning levels by observing the child in daily activities.

Beginning eye-hand coordination is evidenced when the child "bats at" a mobile hanging above his crib or highchair. As fine motor skills are refined, this skill can be observed by watching the child pick up small foodstuffs such as raisins. Preacademic eye-hand coordination assesses putting together puzzles, drawing, cutting, coloring, and pasting. Eye-hand coordination will generally be observed in deaf-blind severely multihandicapped children functioning at the sensorimotor stage as part of self-help skill development in self-feeding, and in teacher-initiated interactions with toys and objects as part of their daily programming.

Body Awareness

Assessment of body awareness is extremely important to deaf-blind children. This skill can be assessed by asking the child to touch a body part on cue or by finding the body part on a doll. Testing can be accomplished in a game-like setting or as part of an activity; for example, "Put your finger on your nose." Few young severely multihandicapped deaf-blind children will function on this level.

Visual Perception

Visual perception is the ability of the brain to identify, organize, and interpret visual sensory data and the mental association of the present visual stimuli with memories of past experiences (Lerner, 1985). The visual perceptual ability has been subdivided into numerous separate visual skills, including the following: visual recognition, visual closure, visual figure-ground, visual discrimination, visual directionality, spatial relationships, visual sequencing, visual comprehension, auditory-visual integration, visual-motor integration with a written response (Slingerland, 1970; Lerner, 1985). Visual perceptual skill development is highly related to academic success in the regular classroom.

Young severely multihandicapped students generally demonstrate low visual perceptual functioning levels due to severe/profound mental retardation. Fallen and Umansky (1985) indicate that visual perception problems occur in children who have spent little time in an upright position; who spend little time rolling, which elicits visual pursuit, fusion, and accommodation; who have poor muscle stability in the neck, which inhibits visual fixation; and who have poor stability in the shoulders and arms, which may cause poor reach and grasp skills. Visual perception is the highest of the visual functioning levels and is not attained with much precision by many deaf-blind students functioning within the sensorimotor stage.

At the upper limits of the sensorimotor stage of development, the primary visual perceptual skills assessed include visual recognition, visual comprehension, visual discrimination, and visual memory. At this initial visual perceptual level, the child is asked to visually recognize or identify familiar objects and pictures of objects by sight; to visually discriminate by matching common objects; to demonstrate visual comprehension of objects or concepts, and activities of normal daily programming; and to demonstrate visual memory in short-term and long-term situations.

The Vision Functioning Skills Checklist (Table 10) is helpful in assessing the student's visual perceptual functioning abilities and level. The Callier-Azusa Scale, subscale Vision (Stillman, 1978) provides information on visual-perceptual developmental functioning. The vision developmental level can be compared to cognitive and other developmental functioning levels to determine if the child's visual functioning is commensurate with overall developmental levels. A child is determined "functionally blind" if s/he does not visually track, localize, or use his/her vision appropriate to overall developmental levels" (Table 11).

VISION DIAGNOSIS

The information provided from the Vision Status and Functioning form (Table 9) provided by teachers and parents; the information from the Vision Evaluation Form (Table 7) completed during the school-based evaluation including background medical, ophthalmological and/or neurological information; and the functional evaluation information from the Callier-Azusa Scale subtests and informal assessment (Table 7) should provide considerable information to be used in determining an appropriate vision diagnosis. This information is compared to the Deaf-Blind Vision Criteria (Table 11) to determine if a child meets the vision requirements for a deaf-blind diagnosis.

Deaf-Blind Vision Criteria

The Deaf-Blind Criteria (Table 11) is primarily a legal-medical classification system requiring an estimated visual acuity. Legal blindness, central visual acuity of 20/200 or less in the better eye with correction,

TABLE 10
VISION FUNCTIONING SKILLS CHECKLIST

I. Sensation:
   A. Awareness:
   _____ Does not attend to visual stimuli.
   _____ Shows awareness to light.
   _____ Shows visual awareness to objects and people near.
   _____ Shows visual awareness of objects and people at distance.
   B. Acuity:
   _____ Shows some degree of fixation.
   _____ Glances at small objects (1″ in diameter).
   _____ Focuses eyes on own hands.
   _____ Looks intently at objects held close to eyes.
   _____ Examines objects with eyes.
   _____ Shifts visual attention from one object in visual field; two or more objects.
   _____ Recognizes faces up to 20′ away.
   _____ Sees small objects (2–3mm cookie crumbs near).
   _____ Visually locates a 7mm pellet.
   _____ Completes formboard.
   _____ Matches letters and symbols.

II. Visual-Motor Skills:
   _____ Tracks slow-moving objects (all directions).
   _____ Follows light or object moving toward and away from him (accommodation).
   _____ Focuses on object at near point (convergence).
   _____ Establishes eye contact.
   _____ Follows objects across midline.
   _____ Retrieves objects quickly and accurately.
   _____ Puts objects accurately in container (eye-hand coordination).
   _____ Catches a ball.
   _____ Builds a 3-block tower.
   _____ Demonstrates body awareness by matching body parts to those of a doll or picture.
   _____ Touches body parts on cue (body awareness-localization).

III. Visual Perception Skills:
   _____ Recognizes common objects visually.
   _____ Visually discriminates by size, shape, color.
   _____ Matches common objects (visual classification).
   _____ Demonstrates visual directionality.
   _____ Completes a pegboard, formboard, puzzle (visual figure ground).
   _____ Remembers pictures shown or follows visual directions (visual memory).
   _____ Sequences 3 objects or pictures logically.
   _____ Uses common objects purposefully (visual comprehension).
   _____ Duplicates geometric designs and letters (visual-motor integration).

REFERENCES: McInnes and Treffry, 1982; Efron and DuBoff, 1979; Stillman, 1978; Lerner, 1987.

represents a visual defect more severe than is required to meet the Deaf-Blind Vision Criteria. Partially sighted children have some usable vision with visual acuity between 20/70 and 20/200 in the better eye with correction. Thus, partially sighted children with visual acuities of 20/100 to 20/200 meet the vision criteria for deaf-blind certification. Additional visual criteria for deaf-blind diagnosis include cortical blindness, a field of vision of 20° or less in the better eye, or functional blindness (Table 11).

Functional vision, the way in which a child uses his vision, is more important than his measured visual acuity (Lowenfield, 1973). Thus, the child who does not visually track, localize, or use his/her vision appropriate to his overall developmental level is "functionally blind" (Table 11).

TABLE 11
DEAF—BLIND VISION CRITERIA

Vision:

1. Measured or estimated corrected visual acuity of 20/100 or less in the better eye, and/or a previous chronic visual condition has existed which has interfered with the visual learning mode.

2. In the presence of a normal peripheral vision apparatus as determined by an ophthalmologist, cortical blindness is determined; this blindness must be verified by reports indicating an absent opticokinetic nystagmus as appropriate to age by an ophthalmologist, a pediatrician, or a pediatric neurologist.

3. Field of vision of 20° or less in the better eye.

4. Visual acuity *cannot* be definitively measured, and the student is suspected of being blind, thus "Functionally Blind." "Functionally Blind" means that the student does not visually track, localize, or use his/her vision appropriate to the overall developmental level(s) as determined by appropriate assessment of development.

If: the measured or estimated visual acuity is better than 20/40 in one eye, there is no severe field limitation; the visual functioning appears to be appropriate to the child's developmental level as determined by appropriate developmental assessment,

Then the student shall be determined as *not* eligible.

SOURCE: Mountain Plains Regional Center, 1985.

Case Studies

Case Study: Sally

Sally's school-based Vision Evaluation (Table 12) will be used to demonstrate the use of the Visual Evaluation Form (Table 7) by the low vision specialist to note responses during the visual evaluation. The higher-functioning levels of the ocular-motor skills subtest (e.g., binocularity, accommodation, convergence) in the External Examination, and of the Visual-Motor Skills subtest (e.g., convergence, accommodation, eye-hand coordination, body awareness), and all Visual Perception subtests in the Visual Functioning Evaluation were omitted once it was determined that Sally possessed no lower level visual skills. Sally doesn't track, fixate, or make eye contact.

In determining a vision diagnosis, the vision evaluation information and previous medical information must be related to the Deaf-Blind Criteria (Table 11).

Criterion 1: Sally's estimated corrected visual acuity is 20/100 or less in the better eye. Previous VER revealed markedly abnormal visual pathways resulting in moderate-to-severe visual impairment—a chronic condition.

Criterion 2: In the presence of a normal peripheral vision apparatus, Sally's evaluation revealed no opticokinetic nystagmus.

Criterion 3: Not applicable.

Criterion 4: Visual acuity could not be definitively measured. Sally did not track, localize, or use her vision appropriate to her overall developmental level.

Thus, based on medical evidence of a poor VER and poor visual performance and the results of the current evaluation, Sally appears to meet the vision criteria #1, #2, and #4 of the deaf-blind regulations. As it is only necessary to meet one criterion, Sally meets the vision criteria for a deaf-blind diagnosis.

Case Study: Bud

Bud's visual evaluation has been completed and the results written into a formal report by the vision specialist. This vision evaluation report (Table 13) is typical of reports sent to other professionals and to parents summarizing the primary information gleaned from the vision evaluation form (Table 7).

In determining a vision diagnosis, the vision evaluation information and previous medical information were related to the Deaf-Blind Criteria (Table 7):

Criterion 1: Bud's estimated corrected visual acuity may be 20/100 or less in the better eye. Previous medical information indicates optic atrophy.

Criterion 2: Opticokinetic nystagmus was not elicited.

Criterion 3: Not applicable.

Criterion 4: Bud's visual acuity could not be definitively measured. However, he does not visually track, fixate, or use his vision appropriate to his overall developmental level. He is functionally blind.

Thus, Bud meets the Deaf-Blind Vision Criteria #1, #2, and #4.

VISUAL SKILLS PROGRAMMING

Development of the visual system in low-vision children is seldom spontaneous or automatic. The sequence of perceptual development may emerge quite unevenly and will be influenced by such factors as type and extent of impairment, mental capacity, stimulation, and encouragement to look. Teachers need to remember that learning through the visual sense can never exceed the level of perceptual/cognitive development of the individual (Barraga, 1983).

A systematic visual skill program for the visually impaired child is necessary to promote visual skill development. Visual skill programming includes progression through a number of visual functioning skill levels, including (1) sensory awareness/acuity, (2) visual-motor training and body awareness, and (3) visual perceptual training (Table 10). At the sensory stimulation level, the primary objectives are to develop visual awareness of light, objects, and other visual stimuli; and to develop visual acuity at near- and far-point.

Visual-motor training aims to coordinate sight with movement of other parts of the body through developing skills of eye contact, tracking, convergence (using both eyes together), accommodation (changing focus to see effectively at near- or far-point), eye-hand coordination (visually directed reach and grasp). Body awareness skills integrate visual, motor, and tactile skills, requiring the child to visually locate a stimulated body part and/or move body parts to assist in dressing and/or locate and touch a body part on cue. Visual perceptual training aims to develop preacademic visual processing skills such as visual discrimination of size, shape, color; visual classification; visual memory and sequencing; visual comprehension; and ultimately visual-motor integration with a written response.

TABLE 12
SALLY'S VISION EVALUATION REPORT

Name: Sally
Age: 4 years, 8 months
DOB:
Health History: Seizure disorder, cerebral palsy, developmental delay, basically healthy child.
Ocular History: Recent ophthalmological report revealed no fixation, no following with right eye, questionable fixation with left eye, no reactions to light, no OKN noted, right exotropia; optic discs were sharp.

I. Visual Examination
  A. External Examination:
    1. Oculomotor Symmetry
      a) *Corneal light reflex:*
      b) *Strabismus:* Large angle right exotropia
      c) *Cover/Uncover Test:*
    2. Oculomotor Tasks
      a) *Accommodations:*
      b) *Convergence:*
      c) *Binocularity:*
      d) *Fixation:* No direct, central, or maintained fixation.
      e) *Tracking:* No tracking in any direction.
    3. Oculomotor Reflexes
      a) Frontal Saccades
      b) Occipital Pursuit
      c) *Opticokinetic Nystagmus (OKN):* Appeared that she might have the following portion of OKN with left eye, but response could not be elicited again.
      d) *Vestibulo-ocular Reflex:*
    4. Nystagmus
      a) *Pendular vs. Jerky:*
      b) *Rotary vs. Linear:* Intermittent large wandering eye movements with fine rotary nystagmus.
    5. Visual Fields:
  B. Internal Examination
    1. *Pupillary Reflexes:*
  C. Visual Acuity
    1. *Snellen E/Schematic Picture Cards:* N/A
    2. *Opticokinetic Nystagmus:*
II. Visual Functioning Evaluation
  A. Visual Sensation
    1. Visual Awareness
      a) *Protective Blink Reflex:* No protective blink reflex.
      b) *Responses to Light:* No response to bright vs. dim light. Possible response to change in room illumination. No response to audio-visual stimuli. No response to any intensities of light.
      c) *Responses to Colored Light:* No response to colored light.

TABLE 12 (Continued)

2. Functional Visual Acuity
   a) *Fixation Reflexes:* No direct, central, or maintained fixation.
   b) *Focus:* None.
   c) *Reach and Grasp* (visually directed): No reach and grasp skills. Poor motor skill development (0–1 month).

B. Visual-Motor Skills
   1. *Eye Contact:* No eye contact with adults/children/objects.
   2. *Tracking:* No tracking.
   3. *Convergence:* N/A
   4. *Accommodation:* N/A
   5. *Eye-Hand Coordination:* N/A
   6. *Body Awareness/Visual Localization:* N/A

TABLE 13
BUD'S VISION EVALUATION REPORT

Name: Bud
Age: 8 years, 7 months

Visual History reveals that an ophthalmological evaluation report at age 2 years, 7 months, indicated a normal examination with good vision. He fixated on light, tracked light stimuli vertically and horizontally, but did not fixate on toys even when paired with an auditory stimuli. By 4 years, 7 months, Bud was functioning visually on the 5-month level. Evaluation at age 6 years, 7 months indicated Bud used his vision with a purposeful intent, fixated on objects, and reached to grasp objects. His best visual attention was toward light. He held his left hand over his left eye during fine motor tasks and eating due to experiencing double vision since his eyes did not work together. Ophtalmological evaluation at age 7 years at _____ Eye Hospital indicated optic atrophy.

Current Evaluation. Bud only on occasion blinked protectively to something brought quickly toward his eyes. He did not blink protectively to a bright strobe flash.

Bud attempted to fixate a penlight, flashlight, and a large strobe by looking in the direction of the light presented. He did not demonstrate a central, steady, or maintained response. Colored objects or light did not seem to elicit as strong a response as bright white light. He did not make eye contact or track. He did not turn for or search for objects or food based on vision. While walking in the classroom, he bumped into things. Opticokinetic nystagmus was not elicited.

Diagnosis. Estimated corrected visual acuity may be 20/100 or less in the better eye. Visual acuity could not be definitively measured, and he does not visually track, fixate, or use his vision appropriate to his overall developmental level. Bud is "functionally blind."

Visual Stimulation

Vision stimulation programs are primarily used with children who have a minimum amount of vision and/or who have not used their vision automatically for visually oriented activities or for incidental learning. Many young deaf-blind severely multihandicapped children function at the sensory stimulation level with very little visual awareness of light, objects, and other stimuli.

Vision stimulation programs should be organized from a vision developmental skills perspective (Table 10) and should be utilized systematically and consistently in classroom programming activities. Programming may include such activities as learning to determine whether a light is on, attending to an object and/or person, following a moving object with head and eye movements, and reaching for objects which are perceived through the sense of sight (Corn, 1986).

Visual Stimulation Room

The ideal situation in which to provide vision stimulation programming would be a separate vision stimulation room away from school traffic patterns in which room illumination could be changed. Many teachers use bookcases to partition off a vision stimulation corner in their classroom. The setting needs to be such that continuous incoming stimulation from the environment can be controlled for non-distracting presentation/observation of visual stimuli.

Items selected for use in a vision stimulation program should be bright, attractive, and attention-getting. They should include light stimuli of varying intensities including Christmas tree lights (blinking and non-blinking), strobe lights, spinning lights, flashlights, penlights, colored acetate sheets, Lite Brite, rotating/disco lights, and lava lights. Transilluminated (lighted) and nontransilluminated (unlighted) toys; shiny items such as tinfoil, pinwheels, and mirrors, mobiles of all types; television, and audiovisual toys should be included among the items used to gain the child's attention.

Visual-motor skills development can be encouraged by using items such as mobiles, soap bubbles, baby gyms, flashing lights, pop-up and pop-out toys, and windup toys should be available. "In selecting items for visual sensory development, three properties of objects should be considered: (1) lightness and brightness, (2) color, and (3) movement" (Van Etten, 1980, 352). The kinds of items utilized in the vision stimulation program are limited only by the teacher's imagination.

TABLE 14
SENSORY STIMULATION PROFILE: VISION

NAME:
DATE:

Type of Stimulation	Yes	No	Response Liked	Disliked	Comments: Describe child's response
T.V.: Black/White					
Color					
Patterns/Contrast					
Lights:					
Xmas Lights:					
colored					
white					
large/small					
blinking/nonblink					
Strobe (seizures)					
Tip lights					
Overhead					
Sunlight					
2 Channel/Echo					
Spinning lights					
Flash					
Penlight					
Candle					
Lite Brite					
Mirror					
Rotating/Disco					
Lava:					
silver					
blue					
red					
Mirror:					
Magnifying Glass:					
Lighted					
Without light					
Colors					
Bubbles					
Mobiles:					
Toys/children's					
Other types/contrast					
Light Catchers					
Prism					
Fishtank/Fish					
Household Pets					
Familiar Faces					

SOURCE: Author Unknown (1985). Revised and used by teachers in Deaf-Blind Program, Special School District of St. Louis County, MO.

Initially, a Vision Stimulation Profile (Table 14) is completed to determine if the student is reacting spontaneously to any stimuli. Secondly, preferred/noticed stimuli are used in programming so the child will gain an understanding of the concept. Information from other sections of the Sensory Stimulation Profile (Tables 22, 26, 27, 28, 29) provide a reinforcement menu for correct functioning on visual tasks and will provide other sensory preferences/dislikes for sensory integration training.

Case Study

Sally and Bud (Tables 12 and 13) are both functioning at the vision sensation awareness level. Sally's Individual Education Program strategies will be used to illustrate visual stimulation programming.

Sally's IEP

Vision Annual Goal: Sally will improve visual functioning.

Objective A: Sally will demonstrate an awareness of visual stimulus (i.e., toys, faces, colored lights, etc.) by a change in her behavior, such as eye movement, eye opening, startle, cry, etc. on 4 out of 5 trials on 3 consecutive data days as implemented by teacher/ assistant.

Objective B: Sally will fixate momentarily on a light or lighted object such as Christmas tree lights, strobe lights, penlights, transilluminated toys, etc. in 4 out of 5 trials on 3 consecutive data days as implemented by teacher/ assistant.

Sally's initial objective is at the lowest visual functioning level, visual awareness (Table 10). A variety of stimuli will be presented, including transilluminated and nontransilluminated toys, faces, colored lights, audiovisual, and nonaudiovisual toys. One stimuli from each category of the Visual Stimulation Profile (Table 14) will be selected and changes made as Sally shows consistent responses. Placement of the presentation of the stimuli will be noted on each trial as well as positioning of Sally for the session. Any and all responses will be accepted as correct. Sally's responses may include such behaviors as eye movement, eye opening, head movement, movement of extremities, startle, cry, smile, or a vocalization.

As Sally progresses with consistent visual awareness to light, to objects and to people near and at distances, her developmental programming will move to the more difficult visual awareness level of visual acuity skills (Table 10) and her second IEP objective will be implemented. Again, using a wide variety of visual stimuli, Sally will be encouraged to fixate for longer periods of time. Preferences noted on the Stimulation Profile can be used as a menu of rewards to reinforce correct responses.

Visual-Motor Training

The second level of visual programming involves visual-motor training (Table 10). The primary purposes of visual-motor training are to increase ocular control, improve focusing ability, and develop eye-hand coordination. Visual-motor training requires that the child is visually attentive and capable of fixating. Sally must master visual awareness skills before she can progress to visual-motor skills. Visual-motor training focuses on tracking a moving object, using the eyes together to focus at near-point (convergence), following objects across midline, increasing flexibility to focus at near and far distances, establishing eye contact, and eye-hand coordination of reaching and batting at or reaching and grasping objects. These skills will be the vision objectives on the Individual Education Program (IEP) for many deaf-blind severely multihandicapped children functioning within the sensorimotor stage.

The vision stimulation room/area provides a good setting to practice visual-motor training skills initially. Since most handicapped children do not automatically generalize skills learned in one setting to another setting, visual stimulation and visual-motor activities also need to be practiced at varying times throughout the day and in varied settings.

Visual Motor Activities

Fun focusing (Phillips & Drain, 1979, 17) is an activity for encouraging focusing on objects. The needed objects include the following: **shiny** (e.g., tinfoil, pie tins, spoons, unbreakable mirrors, jewelery, Christmas tree ornaments); **colorful** (e.g., ribbons, yarn, locks, beads, balloons, balls, foods); **patterns** (e.g., checked fabrics, doll faces, magazine picture faces); **bright** (e.g., flashlight, other lights). Begin by presenting an object 12 inches from the face; move closer and farther away until the child forms a steady gaze.

Tracking Treasure (Phillips & Drain, 1979, 19) is an activity to encourage tracking skills. Use the child's favorite toys and other objects (e.g., colorful, shiny, patterned, or bright). Present the item directly in front of child's line of vision; then slowly move object to the right, left, horizontally, diagonally. Mobiles may be good tracking stimuli.

Selective Scanning (Phillips & Drain, 1979, 20) is an activity to encourage visual scanning. Use 2 or 3 of the child's favorite toys and place them in front of his line of vision. Note whether child looks from toy to toy before making selection. If not, call the child's attention to each toy.

Body Awareness, a higher level of visual-motor skills, requires a certain degree of gross motor skill. Body awareness involves visually locating and touching a named or stimulated body part, moving arms or legs to assist in dressing, matching body parts to those of a doll or picture, examining own hands and feet, and removing a piece(s) of tape placed on a body part. Body awareness is related to locomotion and movement in space as well as tactile development. Awareness of oneself as an individual and self-concept depend on appropriate body awareness. Sally does not yet have conscious control over her body extremities, so cannot function at the visual-motor level.

Visual Perception Training

Visual perception training is a much higher level of skill development involving a cognitive interpretation of what the child has seen (attaching meaning to visual stimuli). Visual perception skills include the prereading and premathematics skills of awareness of gross differences, discrimination of details, directionality, figure-ground, and visual memory (Table 10). These visual perceptual skills are prerequisites to learning to read and to calculate.

The beginning visual perception skills involve matching common objects; using common objects purposefully; completing a form board or puzzle; and matching colors, drawings, pictures, or designs. Cognitive demands increase as the child is expected to logically sequence three objects or pictures. The student must be able to discriminate among letters and numbers; recognize the sizes and shapes of letters, numbers, words (configuration); understand left-to-right progression; focus on one word at a time on a page of words (figure ground); and remember what letters, numbers, designs, pictures look like so they can reproduce them (visual memory). The higher levels of visual perception training place high stress on visual-fine motor skills integration.

It is highly unlikely that a deaf-blind child functioning within the sensorimotor stage will progress, at most, beyond the beginning visual perception skills. The child should be able to identify an object as the same in different positions, recognize pictures of familiar objects, and begin matching identical objects and shapes to pictures.

Throughout the programming sessions, the focus should be on increasing visual efficiency. Visual learning does not occur in isolation, especially for deaf-blind children who must use tactile and motor input to verify visual information (Van Etten et al., 1980).

IEP MONITORING

An effective IEP monitoring system utilizes a data collection file folder for each student (Figure 1) with pages of IEP goals and objectives stapled to the top of the folder. To the bottom half of the folder is stapled graph paper or grids for each goal with specific skill sequences written across the top or bottom of the grid. Stapling the goals/objectives at the top of the file folder and grids on the left side facilitates access to data as pages are turned.

A child's progress toward IEP goals and objectives can be monitored frequently (daily/weekly) through the use of Vision Functioning Skills Checklists (Table 10) transferred to data collection grids (Figure 1). The student's performance can be recorded as correct trials out of ten attempts by using dated dots or bar graphs. The grid can easily be modified to record percentages or can be divided in half to record number of correct trials out of five attempts.

Frequent monitoring of the child's programming performance provides a current, accurate picture of the child's functioning level and average growth or progress rate. Awareness of the child's estimated academic growth rate allows the teacher to write a more accurate IEP for succeeding service years, and to predict skill acquisition and functioning levels for overall educational planning.

Accountability is very important in special education to teachers, administrators, parents, children, and federal-state-local compliance teams

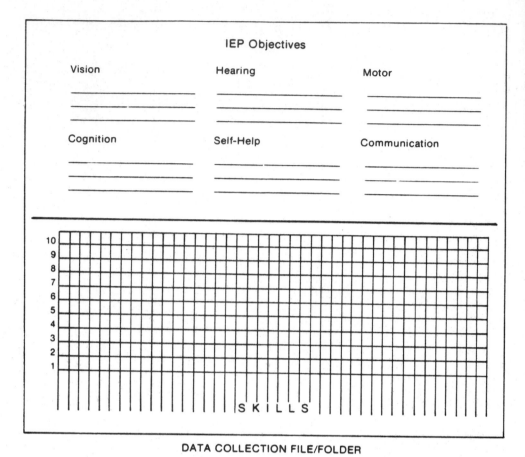

Figure 1. An efficient IEP monitoring system utilizes a data collection file folder with IEP objectives and grids with specific skill sequences for recording responses or performance.

ensuring the implementation of PL 94-142. The law mentions a number of ways to monitor a child's progress toward achieving IEP goals and objectives including checklists, charts, and graphs. The previously suggested IEP monitoring methods have been used in the classroom and found to be effective and efficient.

SUMMARY

A comprehensive visual evaluation includes a visual examination and a visual functioning evaluation. The school-based visual examination consists of an external examination, an internal examination, and determination of visual acuity. The external examination is a screening procedure for pathologic, congenital, and/or developmental abnormalities. Most internal examination procedures are not school-based procedures due to the lack of portability of optometric equipment. The purpose of the internal examination is to assess internal ocular physical health and structural condition. Young deaf-blind severely multihandicapped children's visual acuity cannot be assessed using normal subjective clinical conditions due to low cognitive functioning levels.

The major source of vision data relevant to school functioning is provided by the visual functioning evaluation which assesses the child's use of vision in his/her environment. The visual functioning evaluation consists of an assessment of visual sensation (awareness and acuity), visual-motor skills, and visual perception. Visual sensation concerns the child's awareness of light, objects, and people at near and far distances. Functional visual acuity is determined by presenting foodstuffs and common items at various distances, noting reactions, and quantifying data using the Snellen "E." Visual-motor skills include tracking, convergence, accommodation, eye contact, eye-hand coordination, and body awareness. Visual perception, the highest visual functioning level, includes the preacademic visual processing skills of visual discrimination, visual figure ground, visual memory and sequencing, visual comprehension, and visual-motor integration.

The information derived from the comprehensive visual evaluation is compared to the Deaf-Blind Vision criteria to make a diagnosis. A child meets the criteria if his vision is 20/100 with correction in the better eye and/or a previous chronic visual condition has interfered with visual learning, if the child is cortically blind, as determined by an absent optico kinetic nystagmus, if the field of vision is 20° or less in the better eye and/or if the child has been determined "functionally blind" because he does not visually track, localize, or use vision appropriate to his/her overall developmental level.

Visual skills developmental programming strategies are built around the three major levels of visual functioning: visual sensation, visual-motor skills, and visual perception. A majority of young deaf-blind severely multihandicapped children functioning at the sensorimotor stage will begin programming with visual sensation stimulation. A vision stimulation room or corner supplied with numerous light stimuli, transilluminated and audiovisual toys, shiny toys, and mobiles should enhance the acquisition of visual awareness in children. Programming strategies must be clearly delineated in the Individual Education Program of each visually impaired child, and consistently and systematically developed in the classroom. Accountability is facilitated by monitoring the IEP through daily/weekly and quarterly assessments of progress recorded on data collection charts/graphs.

Chapter Three

HEARING: EVALUATION AND PROGRAMMING

The deaf-blind are multisensory deprived: they are unable to utilize their distance senses of vision and hearing to receive nondistorted information (McInnes & Treffry, 1982, 2).

- Comprehensive Hearing Evaluation
- Types of Hearing Impairment
- Extent of Hearing Impairment
- Hearing Evaluation Areas
- Behavioral Testing Procedures
- Objective Audiometry
- Hearing Diagnosis
- Hearing Skills Programming
- Summary

CONSULTANT:
Susan Marshall, M.A., CCC–A

Auditory deficits, particularly during the developmental years, severely impact normal development in the acquisition of receptive and expressive language, in concept development particularly involving abstract problem-solving tasks, in social development and interpersonal relationships, and in school-related activities involving reading and language-based skills. Some of the most obvious disadvantages the hearing-impaired child experiences in language development stem from (1) inadequate auditory feedback from babbling and language attempts, (2) inadequate verbal reinforcement from adults, (3) inability to hear an adult language model (Hallahan & Kauffman, 1975), and (4) inadequate mother-child language stimulation interaction (Fallen & Umansky, 1985).

COMPREHENSIVE HEARING EVALUATION

Deaf-blind severely multihandicapped children are frequently very difficult to evaluate auditorally due to low cognitive and motor functioning as well as to low auditory and vision functioning levels. Without language, it is difficult to accurately assess the hearing acuity using traditional audiometric techniques. Special response techniques must be used for testing nonverbal children (Van Etten et al., 1980).

> The basic intent of any testing is to define the extent of the hearing impairment, not only in terms of decibel levels, but also in terms of the significance of the hearing loss to speech and language development, psychosocial development, and education achievement" (Sweitzer, 1979, 9).

Types of Hearing Impairment

"The ability to hear normally is a complex function which requires not only a healthy receptor, the ear, but also an intact nervous system" (Lee & Chasin, 1975, 13). The major types of hearing impairment include peripheral hearing losses (conductive, sensorineural, mixed), brainstem hearing loss, cortical hearing loss (Sweitzer, 1979), and a functional hearing loss (Lee & Chasin, 1975).

Peripheral Hearing Losses

Conductive Hearing Loss. A conductive hearing loss is due to problems in the external auditory canal and/or the middle ear, the sound-conducting apparatus (Lee & Chasin, 1975). A conductive hearing loss reduces the volume of a sound reaching the auditory nerve in the inner ear (Mercer, 1987). A conductive hearing loss may be caused by an obstruction to the external auditory canal, a drumhead perforation, tumors, excessive cerumen or earwax, external otitis or swimmer's ear, otitis media, allergies, otoscleroses, and/or congenital defects (Hallahan & Kauffman, 1978).

Sensorineural Hearing Losses. Sensorineural hearing losses are those in which the problem lies in the inner ear with the cochlea, the auditory nerve, or both (Lee & Chasin, 1975). These sensorineural impairments result in the most severe hearing losses and often result in difficulties understanding speech and in problems with balance. A sensorineural hearing loss may be caused by several hereditary conditions: viral infections such as mumps and measles, bacterial infections such as meningitis and and encephalitis, injuries such as blows to the head, anoxia (deprivation of oxygen at birth), prenatal infections of the mother such as rubella and syphilis, and acquired conditions such as excessive noise levels (Hallahan & Kauffman, 1978).

Mixed or Combined Hearing Losses. In mixed or combined hearing losses, the problem occurs both in the sound-conducting apparatus (the outer and middle ear) and in the inner ear (the cochlea and/or the auditory nerve). Central hearing losses are due to a congenital or acquired lesion affecting the auditory pathways central to the cochlear nuclei (Lee & Chasin, 1975).

Brainstem Hearing Loss

Brainstem or cortical damage may cause different kinds of processing problems, depending on the location of the brain damage. Brainstem hearing loss would indicate or suggest normal organic hearing processes within the outer, middle, and inner ear, but due to damage at the brainstem level, the message is not received within the cortex for interpretation. Cortical hearing loss indicates a normal appearing peripheral organ, but central nervous system damage at the cortex level prevents or interferes with hearing as a means of information processing.

Functional Hearing Loss

A functional hearing loss means that in the presence of normal peripheral and cortical apparatus, the child does not attend to, respond to, or localize to sounds; or use hearing appropriate to his or her overall developmental level (Mountain Plains Regional Center, 1985). A functional hearing loss is nonorganic and may be due to emotional factors and/or severe/profound mental retardation.

Extent of Hearing Impairment

The degree of hearing loss is assessed by measuring hearing thresholds (loudness) in decibels (dB) at varying frequencies (pitch) in Hertz (Hz) or the number of sound vibrations produced per second. The frequency range of the human ear is approximately 20 to 20,000 Hz. Audiologists generally assess hearing at the frequencies most important to the understanding of speech or 500 to 8,000 Hz (Mercer, 1987). The range of normal hearing is from the softest intensity that can be heard, 0 dB, to the threshold of discomfort and pain, 120 to 130 dB (Sweitzer, 1979).

Normal hearing occurs at 0 to 26 dB. The levels of hearing loss include the following: mild, 27–40 dB; moderate, 41–55 dB; moderately severe, 56–70 dB; severe, 71–90 dB; and profound, 91 dB or more (Kirk & Gallagher, 1983). A child with a mild hearing loss, for example, could hear a soft radio. Average conversational speech at a distance of 10 to 20 feet occurs at 60 dB. A child with a moderate hearing loss could understand conversational speech at a distance of 3–5 feet away and needs a hearing aid. A child with a moderately severe loss could hear an average auto, but could only understand a very loud conversation at a close distance. The child with a severe hearing loss may be able to hear a loud voice one foot from his ear, and could hear very loud music such as orchestral music and/or the noises made by a truck, train, or subway. The child with a profound hearing loss could hear an auto horn less than one foot away, and a propeller airplane engine and propellers at 15 feet away (Gillis & Kegan, 1976; Kirk, 1972).

A mild or moderate hearing loss can have a severe impact upon the acquisition of speech and language if the child has a high frequency loss. Speech is characterized by low-frequency intensity vowels and higher frequency consonants. Consonants carry most of the information for understanding speech. Thus, if a child had primarily a high frequency loss and could hear mainly vowels, s/he would have great difficulty understanding speech (Sweitzer, 1979).

Children with hearing impairments are generally classified as hard-of-hearing, or deaf. A hard-of-hearing child has a deficit in auditory acuity, but possesses some functional hearing. Deaf children have a severe-to-profound auditory loss and do not possess functional hearing (Lerner et al., 1987).

Hearing Evaluation Areas

In a formal audiological evaluation, the audiologist should attempt to ascertain the hearing status of the severely multihandicapped child by determining the following:

1. Extent of hearing impairment
   a. Degree of loss in decibels
   b. Significance of the hearing impairment to:
      (1) Speech and language development
      (2) Psychosocial development
      (3) Educational development
2. Difference in hearing between the two ears
3. Frequency characteristics of the hearing loss
4. Type of hearing impairment
   a. Peripheral

    (1) Conductive
    (2) Sensorineural
    (3) Mixed
  b. Brainstem
  c. Cortical
5. Ability to discriminate and process speech
6. Ability to adopt to and utilize amplification (Sweitzer, 1979, 9).

A comprehensive school-based evaluation includes information from medical records, behavioral observation audiometry, objective audiometry, and teacher/parent observations regarding daily auditory functioning. Information from these sources is compared to the Deaf-Blind Hearing Criteria (Table 16) to determine if the student meets the hearing criteria for certification as deaf-blind.

Behavioral Testing Procedures

All children suspected of having hearing impairments should be evaluated using behavioral testing procedures which include the following: (1) behavioral observation audiometry (BOA), (2) standard audiometry, (3) play audiometry, (4) visually reinforced audiometry, (5) tangible reinforcement operant conditioning audiometry, and (6) speech audiometry (Cox & Lloyd, 1976; Sweitzer, 1979). The type of behavioral audiometry utilized and the amount of information obtained depend on the capabilities of the student being evaluated.

Behavioral Observation Audiometry

Sound-field behavioral observation audiometry is usually the most appropriate evaluation approach to use with severely multihandicapped children functioning at very low cognitive, motor, and communication levels. "This technique is commonly used with infants and is extremely useful when testing retarded or emotionally disturbed youngsters" (Sweitzer, 1979, 9). When used with children under four months of age, chronological and/or developmental, the procedure relies on gross body changes that are primarily reflexive (Van Etten et al., 1980).

During the testing procedure, an attempt is made to obtain responses first to speech, then to warbled pure tones. If the child is not responsive to these stimuli, calibrated sound toys (e.g., bells, drums, horns, rattles) or any other interesting stimuli such as music or tapes of animal sounds, are used to elicit a response. Stimuli are presented initially at the loudest possible level so the strongest response can be observed (Sweitzer, 1979). Ultimately, the desire is to find the softest intensity which will elicit a consistent response. This level is the child's threshold of hearing or his/her hearing level.

Two audiologists should collaborate on the testing of severely multihandicapped children. Additionally, during the initial evaluation, the parent should be present, and during re-evaluation, the classroom teacher should be present to observe responses because they know the child's normal behavioral responses and can assist the audiologists in distinguishing auditory responses from random movements.

The behavioral responses frequently observed have been organized into a developmental hierarchy as follows:

Hierarchy of Responses Behavior

Startle or eye blink

Cessation of or initiation of activity

Localization
- To side with head
- To side with head and eyes
- To side and downward with sound below the ear
- Turning arc toward source of sound below or above the ear
- Turning diagonally toward source of sound below or above the ear.

Discrimination between noisemakers

Discrimination between speech sounds

(Sweitzer, 1976, 6).

The behavioral observation results can be compared to auditory developmental norm charts such as Auditory Development: Sensorimotor Stage (Table 15) to determine an estimate of functioning level. Developmental levels, not chronological age, should be compared since auditory skills develop at approximately the same rate as other areas such as cognition, motor, and communication skills. Thus, a child functioning at the 0–6 weeks cognitive level would be expected to respond to noisemakers at 50–70 dB, warbled pure tones at 78 dB, and speech at 40–60 dB by eye widening, eyeblink, arousal from sleep, or startle (Table 15). At 4–6 months functioning level, the child would be expected to turn his head toward noisemakers at 40–50 dB, warbled pure tones at 51 dB, and speech at 21 dB, assuming a listening attitude (Table 15). Normal developmental observations indicate that the 4–6 month-old child should localize to sound by turning in the direction of it, engage in vocal play by repeating sound changes, pay attention to music, and respond to tone of voice (Table 15).

TABLE 15
AUDITORY DEVELOPMENT

BIRTH
> (0–6 weeks: Speech 40–60 dB; Noisemakers 50–70 dB; Warbled Pure Tones 78 dB)
> Startles to loud sounds.
> Responds to sound by eye-widening, eyeblink, arousal from sleep.

1–3 MONTHS
> (6 weeks–4 months: Speech 47 dB; Noisemakers 50–60 dB; Pure Tones 70 dB)
> Stops activity to sound/human speech.
> Stirring or arousal from sleep due to sound.
> Smiles to caretaker's voice.
> Looks for speaker.

4–6 MONTHS
> (Speech 21 dB; Noisemakers 40–50 dB; Pure Tones 51 dB)
> Engages in vocal play by repeating sound changes.
> Localizes sound by turning in direction of it.
> Responds to tone of voice.
> Pays attention to music/sound.

7–9 MONTHS
> (Speech 15 dB; Noisemakers 30–40 dB; Pure Tones 45 dB)
> Responds to name spoken.
> Direct localization of sound to side, indirect below ear level.
> Responds to "No" by ceasing activity.

10–12 MONTHS
> (Speech 8 dB; Noisemakers 25–35 dB; Pure Tones 38 dB)
> Copies sounds.
> Identifies common sounds.

13–18 MONTHS
> (Speech 5 dB; Noisemakers 25–30 dB; Pure Tones 32 dB)
> Repeats simple words.
> Makes different response to different sounds.
> Direct localization of sound on side, up, down.

19–24 MONTHS
> (Speech 5 dB; Noisemakers 25 dB; Pure Tones 25 dB)
> Distinguishes when one sound changes.
> Follows a series of two related directions.

2–3 YEARS
> (Speech 0 dB—normal hearing acuity)
> Identifies sound.
> Responds to verbal greeting.

REFERENCES: Northern & Downs, 1984; Gard et al., 1980.

Interpretation Problems with BOA. There are some difficulties involved with relying solely on behavioral observation audiometry (BOA) with severely multihandicapped children. Their lack of response or lack of repeatable responses may not be due to peripheral hearing loss. There are many neurological problems that may cause poor motor control in which the child could not lift or turn his/her head. Other neurological problems may cause the inhibition of normal reflexive responses.

Brain damage or mental retardation may cause different kinds of processing problems, depending on the location of the damage. For example, damage to the temporal lobe may cause auditory agnosia, which is the inability to attach meaning to sound. This means that every time the child hears the sound, it is a new experience for him/her, and the sound is not meaningful. Due to these problems, a number of severely multihandicapped children may appear to have severe hearing loss with a behavioral observation audiometry evaluation when, in fact, they have functional peripheral hearing. Conversely, some children may exhibit responses to sound toys at fairly low levels, yet have a significant hearing loss.

Standard Audiometry

The ultimate goal in behavioral observation requires the child to listen to sound presented through earphones and respond by pushing a button, dropping blocks in a bucket, or by raising a hand when a sound is heard. "This procedure is preferred with most normal developing children. However, for difficult-to-test individuals and children unable to make a response, standard audiometry is of little value" (Van Etten et al., 1980, 77).

Play Audiometry

Play audiometry often requires teaching the child to play with a toy only when a sound is heard. It is not successful for severely multihandi-capped children whose low functioning in motor skills and cognitive development make playing and understanding the task almost impossible.

Visual Reinforcement Audiometry

Another form of behavioral observation audiometry is visual rein-forcement audiometry, which involves having a child play in sound-treated room. A loud sound is presented. A visual reinforcement such as a lighted moving toy is used as a positive reinforcement for the localiza-tion of a sound. With young, low-functioning deaf-blind severely multi-handicapped children, this technique is not extremely useful since many of these students have not yet developed a localization response and because they may have significant visual deficits.

Tangible Reinforcement Operant Conditioning Audiometry (TROCA)

Tangibly reinforced audiometry involves teaching a child to push a button in the presence of sound. When the button is pushed, the tone sounds, and the child receives a tangible reinforcer, such as sugar-coated cereal, coated candy, nuts, raisins, or a nonedible reinforcer (Van Etten et al., 1980, 77).

Conditioning audiometry has been developed into a very sophisticated and automated behavioral procedure with strict control over stimulus characteristics, reward schedule, and child response pattern. Actually, TROCA is used on an informal basis any time a youngster is rewarded for appropriate response behavior with a tangible reinforcement (Sweitzer, 1979).

Speech Audiometry

Speech audiometry is the assessment of the child's sensitivity for hearing speech sounds versus pure tone sounds. Any of the procedures previously described can be used to test the child's sensitivity to speech. In many ways, speech audiometry is more functional than pure tone testing (Van Etten et al., 1980, 77).

During the behavioral testing sessions previously discussed, children's reactions were determined to speech, calibrated noise toys, and warbled pure tones. Behavioral reactions to all types of noise/sounds are important in designing an educational program.

Cox and Lloyd (1976) indicate traditional speech tests are designed to gain measures of the following: speech awareness threshold, speech reception threshold, speech discrimination, and dynamic range for speech. The speech awareness threshold is the lowest point expressed in dB HL at which the child barely hears his name called or other speech stimuli 50% of the time. The speech reception threshold is the point at which the child can correctly repeat or identify 50% of a group of test items, usually two-syllable words. Speech discrimination measures the child's discrimination of a wide range of speech material including phonemes, syllables, monosyllabic words, connected discourse, and/or synthetic speech. The dynamic range for speech measures the child's range for hearing.

Objective Audiometry

Many deaf-blind severely multihandicapped children are difficult to evaluate using subjective behavioral techniques. Therefore, it is desirable, especially in questionable cases to also have objective audiometric testing results. Objective audiometry does not require cognitive or conditioned responses, but assesses the automatic responses of the child's body. The primary objective audiometry test procedures include the following:

1. Acoustic impedance
   A. Static Acoustic Impedance
   B. Dynamic Acoustic Impedance
      (1) Tympanometry
      (2) Intraaural Muscle Reflexes (acoustic and nonacoustic)
2. Brainstem-evoked response audiometry
3. Cortical-evoked response audiometry
4. Electrocochleography

(Sweitzer, 1979; Van Etten et al., 1980.)

Acoustic impedance measurements are the **only** objective tests available in the school-based setting.

Acoustic Impedance

Acoustic impedance measurements assess the effectiveness of energy flowing through the middle ear. They do not measure hearing functioning.

> The battery of acoustic impedance measurements is most effectively used as the first measurement in the clinical setting. When this battery of tests establishes the normality of function of the middle ear, it eliminates the need for measurement of bone conduction (Feldman, 1975, 88).

Impedance testing is useful with the very young or difficult-to-test child because it involves no active verbal participation. It is particularly helpful in determining the presence or absence of conductive impairments.

Static Acoustic Impedance. Acoustic impedance includes measures of static and dynamic effectiveness. Static acoustic impedance measures the difficulty with which energy flows, while acoustic admittance measures the ease with which energy flows into or through the middle ear. Static impedance helps to differentiate between normal and pathological middle ears and may identify such middle ear problems as perforated tympanic membrane, otitis media, and middle ear tumors (Feldman, 1975).

Dynamic Acoustic Impedance. Dynamic acoustic impedance measures include tympanometry and intraaural muscle reflexes. Dynamic acoustic impedance measures changes in air pressure varied across the plane of the tympanic membrane and/or changes in a steady state of impedance that occurs as a consequence of one or both intraaural muscles (Feldman, 1975).

Tympanometry assesses eardrum mobility, so can be used to detect the presence of middle ear fluid. This can be accomplished by sealing a probe tip in the ear canal. A sound is then introduced through the probe and travels along the canal until it strikes the tympanic membrane. The physical properties of the tympanic membrane determine how much of the sound wave is transmitted through the middle ear to the cochlea and how much will be reflected back to the source (Feldman, 1975). Tracings or tympanograms reflect eardrum mobility, and the presence/absence of middle ear fluid.

Tympanometry is considered very important in the assessment of multihandicapped children, although it may be difficult to assess if the child is tactilely defensive about the ears or is difficult to control. If middle ear fluid is present, audiological testing should be postponed until medical treatment resolves the condition. Once fluid develops in the middle ear, a conductive hearing loss of 30–40 dB is not uncommon. This conductive hearing loss is superimposed upon any existing sensorineural hearing loss, thus making accurate behavioral assessments impossible (Sweitzer, 1979).

The **acoustic reflex test** or measurement of intraaural muscle reflexes can be accomplished by using the same instrumentation used for tympanometry. The acoustic reflex occurs when the muscles of the inner ear, the stapedius, contract and stiffen the eardrum (Sweitzer, 1979). In a child with normal hearing, the muscles contract when presented a loud sound, apparently to protect the inner ears. "The test is conducted by delivering an intense pure tone signal to one ear and measuring the reflex (present or absent) from the opposite ear as both stapedius muscles contract, even when the sound is presented to only one ear if hearing is normal for both ears" (Cox & Lloyd, 1976, 169). The normal hearing children display considerable differences among their reflex thresholds for tones and those for noise while the child with a severe hearing loss may exhibit no differences. In normal hearing persons, the muscle contraction occurs somewhere between 70 and 100 dB HL for pure tone signals (Cox & Lloyd, 1976). "The presence of a stapedial reflex implies an intact and mobile ossicular chain. The probability of obtaining a stapedial reflex diminishes with increasing hearing loss" (Feldman, 1975, 117). Thus, acoustic reflex measurement is useful in predicting or validating significant hearing loss with severely multihandicapped children. Reflex response information contributes to identifying problems involving the auditory neural pathway (Cox & Lloyd, 1976).

Brainstem-Evoked Response Audiometry. Objective audiometry obtains results independent of a voluntary or overt response from the child. Brainstem-Evoked Response Audiometry (BSER) is an objective test which measures changes in the brainwave activity in response to an auditory stimulus. "The main reason for looking at the brainstem response may be to investigate lower levels of the auditory system" (Hood, 1975, 353). This test is generally administered while the child is anesthetized; however, researchers are experimenting with conducting the test while the child is naturally asleep or resting quietly.

Stein et al. (1981) found that most children can be successfully tested by Brainstem-Evoked Response Audiometry despite severe neurological and cerebral dysfunction, abnormal EEG, and seizure disorders. Out of 82 severely developmentally delayed youngsters in his study, 79 children had acceptable BSER results.

Cortical-Evoked Response Audiometry (CERA). Cortical-evoked response audiometry has four known components including: (1) the brainstem or early response (previously indicated), (2) the middle response, (3) the late response, and (4) the contingent negative variation (CNV) (Hood, 1975). Each type of response provides information regarding the functioning of specific regions of the auditory mechanism. The brainstem response provides information about the functioning of the subcortical regions (e.g., outer, middle, inner ear; brainstem) of the auditory nervous system (Hood, 1975).

The middle response occurs after the brainstem response and gives information regarding the primary auditory cortex and all auditory system components up to that point. The threshold of the middle response agrees well with the behavioral thresholds for the same stimuli (Hood, 1975). The late response implies that the stimulus information has reached the auditory projection of the cortex and sound/noise information has been processed. The late response is commonly used in auditory threshold testing (Hood, 1975).

The CNV response is elicited when semantic information related to the auditory stimulus has been cognitively processed. The CNV is a cortex response, but arises primarily from more frontal regions of the cortex (Hood, 1975). Thus, the brainstem, middle, and late responses are triggered by the reception of sound or noise, meaningful or not, while the CNV requires language-based information processing to elicit a response.

Electrocochleography. Electrocochleography assesses the integrity of cochlear functioning and is useful in testing individuals who cannot be tested by conventional audiometry. When a response is present, there is at least some residual hearing at the end-organ, but when there is no response at any stimulus intensity, the cochlea is nonfunctional for hearing and there is no residual hearing (Simmons & Glalthe, 1975).

Hearing Diagnosis

Information from the (1) behavioral audiometry procedures (behavioral observation audiometry and speech audiometry), (2) the objective audiometry procedures (acoustic impedance, brainstem-evoked response audiometry, and cortical-evoked response audiometry), and (3) the classroom functioning information is compared to the Deaf-Blind criteria (Table 16) to determine if hearing functioning deficits are severe enough to meet the deaf-blind criteria or if the child is functioning commensurate with developmental expectations (Table 15).

TABLE 16
DEAF-BLIND HEARING GUIDELINES

Hearing:
1. Thirty (30) dB bilateral sensory neural hearing loss as a minimum across the speech frequency in the better ear with amplification and/or a previous chronic condition of the auditory mechanism has existed which interfered with the auditory learning mode.
2. Sensitivity and middle ear functioning cannot be definitively measured and the student is suspected of being deaf, thus "Functionally Deaf." "Functionally Deaf" means that the student does not auditorally attend to, respond to, or localize sounds, or use his hearing appropriate to his/her developmental level as determined by appropriate assessment of development.

If: measured or estimated hearing acuity, with amplification, is better than 30 dB bilateral sensorineural hearing loss across the speech frequency auditory functioning is appropriate to the child's developmental level as determined by appropriate developmental assessment

Then, the student shall be determined as *not* eligible.

SOURCE: Mountain Plains Regional Center, 1985.

Difficulty Interpreting Criteria

Regarding Criterion #1 (Table 16), there are some areas which are difficult to interpret. First, it is often difficult to obtain behavioral responses with low-functioning severely multihandicapped children. In a testing situation, these children are usually unresponsive to warble tones, so it is difficult to determine if a child is aware of sounds at 30 dB across the speech frequencies. Do responses to other stimuli such as speech, noise toys, or music at 30 dB meet the criteria specifications?

Secondly, Criterion #1 does not specifically state what is considered to be the speech frequencies. Some authorities consider the speech frequencies to be 500, 1,000, and 2,000 Hz, while others consider the speech frequencies to be 500, 1,000, 2,000, and 4,000 Hz. Additionally, two children with similar audiometric results may function very differently due to how well each has learned to use their residual hearing.

The second criterion (Table 16) addresses functional deafness in which the child "does not auditorally attend to, respond to, or localize sounds, or use his hearing appropriate to his/her developmental level." Determining functional deafness involves three phases. First, developmental levels are assessed by the evaluation team using a variety of standardized, criterion-referenced, and informal scales assessing cognition, motor skills, communication, and self-help skills. Secondly, the auditory behavioral results are compared to auditory developmental norms (Table 15) to determine an auditory functioning level. Thirdly, the auditory functioning level is then compared to the developmental functioning levels, especially those of cognition and receptive communication. If the auditory functioning level is significantly less than the developmental level, the child is said to be functionally deaf. However, if the developmental functioning levels in cognition and receptive communication are approximately the same as his auditory developmental level, the child is considered to be functioning auditorally commensurate with his/her developmental level and is not considered to be functionally deaf.

Application of Deaf-Blind Criteria: Case Studies

Case Study #1

Sally, at the time of assessment, was chronologically 4 years, 7 months old (Table 17). Developmental assessment indicated cognition, communication, motor and adaptive skills at the 0–1 month level. BSER (Brainstem-Evoked Response Audiometry) revealed a moderate bilateral sensorineural hearing loss. Sally wears a moderate-gain hearing aid in her left ear. No observable responses were noted with or without the hearing aid at 85 dB in a sound field. There was no eye-blink or beginning of a localization, or even a startle. No observable responses had been noted in the classroom.

Sally was considered to meet hearing Criterion #1 (Table 16) due to a sensorineural hearing loss and no behavioral evidence to support that she was aware or responsive to auditory stimuli at 30 dB hearing level with the hearing aid.

TABLE 17

NAME: Sally
AGE: 4 years, 7 months
DEVELOPMENTAL LEVELS: Cognition: 0–1 Month
                                    Communication: 0–1 Month
                                    Motor: 0–1 Month
                                    Adaptive Behavior: 0–1 Month
    Brainstem-Evoked Response Audiometry: Moderate Bilateral Sensorineural Loss
    AID: Qualitone DAO coupled to the left ear.

AUDITORY RESPONSES

Stimulus	*Unaided/Aided Hearing Level*	*Response*
Monitored live voice	85 dB/85 dB	No Response/No Response
Squeaky Toy	85 dB/85 dB	No Response/No Response
Raggedy Ann Rattle	85 dB/85 dB	No Response/No Response
Cricket Clacker	85 dB/85 dB	No Response/No Response
Bicycle Horn	85 dB/85 dB	No Response/Possible Awareness

Case Study #2

Pam was ten years old at the time of the evaluation. Developmental functioning levels were reported as cognition, 8–12 months with splinter skills to 24 months; fine motor skills, 24 months; gross motor skills, 18–24 months; speech/language, 6 to 12 months; adaptive behavior, 18 to 24 months (Table 18). Pam was unresponsive or emitted very questionable responses at levels of 60 to 80 dB in a sound field. Comparing these auditory functioning levels to auditory developmental norms (Table 15), Pam, at the very minimum, should be responding at 40–50 dB or at the 4–7-month old level. No BSER results were available. Pam appeared to be functioning auditorally well below expectations for her developmental functioning. She did not auditorally attend to, respond to, or localize sounds, or use her hearing appropriate to her developmental level. Thus she was diagnosed as "functionally deaf."

TABLE 18
PAM'S HEARING EVALUATION REPORT

NAME: Pam
AGE: 10 years
DEVELOPMENTAL LEVELS: Cognition: 8–12 months with splinter skills at 13–24 mo.
Fine Motor: 24 months
Gross Motor: 18–24 months
Speech/Language: 6–12 months
Adaptive Behavior:
    Dressing: 18 months
    Feeding: 24 months

AUDITORY RESPONSES

Stimulus	*Hearing Level*	*Response*
Monitored live voice	80 dB	Eye Movement
Squeaky Toy	80 dB	Possible Awareness
Raggedy Ann Rattle	70 dB	Cessation
Cricket Clacker	60 dB	Eye Movement
Bicycle Horn	80 dB	Questionable Cessation
Taped Animal Sounds	75 dB	Questionable Awareness

Case Study #3

David is an example of a child who was determined to be inappropriate for placement. David was 9 years, 2 months old at the time of the hearing assessment. Developmental levels were assessed at 0–2 months in all areas, including cognition, communication, motor, and self-help skills (Table 19). On behavioral audiometry testing, David responded to noisemakers and speech at 30–50 dB (Table 19). Comparing his developmental level to auditory developmental norms (Table 15), a child of 0–6 weeks should be responding to noise toys at 50–70 dB and to speech at 40–60 dB. Conclusions reached indicated David's responses were appropriate for his overall developmental level; thus he did not meet either hearing criteria (Table 16).

However, since many previous behavioral audiometry tests for David were inconclusive, he was referred for BSER testing. It was felt that his inconsistencies to sound may have been related to change in medication for a seizure disorder. Subsequent Brainstem-Evoked Response testing indicated normal hearing bilaterally and substantiated findings that his auditory responses were appropriate for his developmental level.

TABLE 19
DAVID'S HEARING EVALUATION REPORT

NAME: David
AGE: 9 years, 2 months
DEVELOPMENTAL LEVELS: Cognition: 1 month
Motor: 0–2 months
Communication: 1 month
Adaptive Behavior: Totally dependent

AUDITORY RESPONSES

Stimulus	*Hearing Level*	*Response*
Monitored live voice	40 dB	Body-movement (arched back)
Squeaky Toy	30 dB	Body-movement (arched back)
Raggedy Ann Rattle	50 dB	Body-movement (arched back)
Cricket Noisemaker	30 dB	Body-movement (arched back)
Bicycle Horn	30 dB	Body-movement (arched back)

Case Study #4

Bud's Hearing Evaluation Report was included to illustrate format, content, and style of a hearing evaluation report (Table 20).

HEARING SKILLS PROGRAMMING

The development of hearing skills with deaf-blind multihandicapped children is seldom spontaneous and automatic. Therefore, these children need a systematic developmental program in auditory skills to reach their potential. Educational programming for the development of auditory skills follows a sequential progression of the following functioning levels: (1) awareness of sound, (2) discrimination of sound, (3) recognition of sound, and (4) comprehension of sound (Table 21).

Awareness of Sound

At the first level of developing auditory skills (Table 21), the child must demonstrate an awareness of sound by making an unconditioned or reflexive response. These responses may include startles, eyeblinks, turning head or body, cessation of activity, change in facial expressions, alerting, and any observable responses. As the awareness to sound becomes

TABLE 20
HEARING EVALUATION REPORT

NAME ____BUD____ DATE _____ D/B _____ AGE __8__ (yrs) ____ (mos)
SCHOOL _____ DISTRICT _____ GRADE DB TEST NO. __10__
HEARING THRESHOLD LEVEL IN DECIBELS ANSI 1969 AUDIOMETER ___MA 24-2__

		125	250	500	1000	2000	3000	4000	6000	8000	Threshold	Discrimina-tion Score
Right Ear	AC											
	BC											
Left Ear	AC											
	BC											
Right	A B									■	■		
Left	A B									■	■		

m = Masked   NR = No Response   NT = Not Tested   * = Live Voice
TESTER____   TEST RELIABILITY FAIR/POOR   SST_ CE_ N_ P_ PHY_ CC_ RT_
                                          SNAP_ SP_ COUNS_ O_x

COMMENTS AND RECOMMENDATIONS:
Bud was seen for a routine hearing evaluation. Bud's hearing was assessed by observing behavioral responses to various auditory stimuli presented in a sound-field. Results were not very clear and often not repeatable. Possible responses were as follows:

Stimulus	Hearing Level	Response
Monitored Live Voice	50 dB	Cessation
Squeaky Toy	70 dB	Laugh
Happy Apple	80 dB	Awareness
Cricket Noisemaker	50 dB	Possible Laugh
Bicycle Horn	70 dB	Laugh
Hand Clap	65 dB	Laugh
Hit Stick	50 dB	Possible Smile
Cymbals	70 dB	Possible Cessation
Tambourine	55 dB	Possible Smile

Impedance test for middle ear function could not be obtained due to Bud's lack of cooperation.

   Previous Brainstem-Evoked Response Audiometry six years ago indicated a bilateral severe-to-profound hearing loss. Bud has been seen at school on eleven occasions for hearing evaluations in the past seven years. Results have consistently indicated a significant hearing loss. However, during the last four evaluations during the past three years, his performance

TABLE 20 (Continued)

has indicated possible responses to speech and noisemakers from 50 dB hearing level (HL) to 80 dB HL in a sound field environment. These observed behavioral responses continue to suggest more hearing than indicated on earlier Brainstem-Evoked Response Audiometry, but are still consistent with a moderate-to-severe hearing loss.

Bud has not tolerated a hearing aid in the past due to tactile defensiveness. Therefore, he has not demonstrated an awareness of sounds at a 30 dB HL with the use of amplification and, thus meets Deaf-Blind Criterion #1.

It is recommended that the results be discussed with Bud's physician to determine if a repeat BSER would be warranted.

Licensed Clinical/Educational Audiologist

more developed, s/he may localize to sound to maintain contact with specific sounds. As the child develops and gains the knowledge that sound can be associated with an object such as a sound toy, the child can begin ear-hand coordination skills involving reaching/searching for a sound toy (Barraga, 1983). Ultimately, the child can make a conditioned response when sound is heard to demonstrate an awareness to the presence of sound.

Auditory Stimulation

Auditory stimulation programs are used primarily with children who have a minimum amount of hearing and/or who have not used their hearing automatically for auditorally oriented activities or for incidental learning. Many deaf-blind severely multihandicapped children function at the awareness level with very little auditory awareness of common sounds, music, and/or environmental sounds or noises.

Auditory stimulation programs should be organized from a hearing or auditory developmental skills perspective (Table 21), and should be implemented systematically and consistently in the classroom. Programming may include activities such as learning to recognize the presence or absence of sound, discrimination between environmental sounds and speech, localizing to stationary and moving sounds, and developing ear-hand coordination.

A separate auditory stimulation room would provide an ideal situation in which to conduct auditory stimulation programming because

TABLE 21
AUDITORY FUNCTIONING SKILLS CHECKLIST

I. Awareness of Sound
_____ Does not attend to auditory stimuli.
_____ Startles to loud or sudden auditory stimuli.
_____ Decreases or increases activity to sound.
_____ Stirs or arouses from sleep due to sound.
_____ Shows awareness to speech.
_____ Smiles to caretaker's voice.
_____ Plays with sound toys.
_____ Localizes sound by turning in direction of it.
_____ Pays attention to music/sounds.
_____ Localizes stationary sounds.
_____ Localizes moving sounds.
_____ Begins ear-hand coordination, reaching for sound toy.
_____ Attention improves for music/rhythmic sounds.
_____ Searches for sound toy.
_____ Upon hearing sound, can perform a conditioned response.

II. Discrimination of Sound
_____ Responds differently to familiar/unfamiliar sounds.
_____ Engages in vocal play by repeating sound changes.
_____ Responds to tone of voice.
_____ Copies sounds.
_____ Responds differently to aspects of speaker's voice.
_____ Makes different responses to different sounds.
_____ Distinguishes when one sound changes.
_____ Matches or discriminates between two types of noise or environmental sounds.
_____ Matches or discriminates by loudness.
_____ Matches or discriminates by pitch.
_____ Matches or discriminates by duration.
_____ Matches or discriminates by speech sounds.
Discriminates between two words:
_____ Different commands ("come" and "sit down").
_____ Different initial consonants, vowel patterns, and number of syllables (e.g., ball, lollipop).
_____ Different initial consonants and number of syllables, similar vowel pattern (e.g., cat, rattle).
_____ Different vowel pattern and syllables, same initial consonants (e.g., boat, banana).
_____ Same vowel pattern and initial consonant, different number of syllables (e.g., base, baseball).
_____ Same vowel pattern and syllables, different initial consonants (e.g., bat, cat).

III. Recognition of Sound
_____ Responds to name spoken.
_____ Responds to "No" paired with appropriate intonation by ceasing activity.
_____ Repeats simple words.

Table 21 (Continued)

_____ Identifies common sounds.
_____ Responds with gestures to "Hi, bye-bye, up" when paired with gesture.
_____ Matches same sound that is presented.
_____ Points to picture of common object when named.
_____ Responds to verbal greeting.
_____ Anticipates routine activities from sound cues.
_____ Reproduces two sounds in order presented.
_____ Recognizes intended sound source with one distracting sound source present.
_____ Sequences three sounds.
_____ Recognizes intended sound source with multiple distracting sounds.

IV. Comprehension of Sound
_____ Responds correctly when asked "where."
_____ Understands prepositions "on, in, under."
_____ Follows a series of two related directions.
_____ Follows a series of three related directions.
_____ Listens to storybooks read and request read again.
_____ Begins to understand time concepts.
_____ Understands comparatives.
_____ Sequences events verbally.
_____ Understands opposites.
_____ Receptive language preacademic/academic skills.

REFERENCES: Rudolph et al. (no date); Gard et al. (1980); Fallen & Umansky (1985).

environmental stimuli could be more controlled. At least a quiet corner of the classroom, where visual and tactile stimuli are more controlled during presentation of auditory stimuli, is required.

Auditory stimulation materials should include items of various intensities (loudness) and frequencies (pitch) of sound. Items should include common sounds, environmental sounds, and strange and unusual sounds, music, and human voices. Sound-producing items should include rhythm band instruments such as drums, bells, tamborines, xylophone, whistles, woodblocks, cymbals, maracas; musical and sound toys; wind-up music boxes and toys; records and tapes of animal sounds, environmental sounds, traffic noises, common home sounds, human voices; unusual sounds such as **Star Wars** musical track, typewriters and clocks, velcro strips, aluminum foil, and paper to crumple. Other items should be included that pair sounds with other sensory stimuli such as audiovisual toys and objects, audio/tactile toys and objects, and musical mobiles. Items included in the auditory stimulation program are limited only by the teacher's imagination.

Barraga (1983, 75) cautions: "Passive auditory stimulation from radio or television without meaningful verbal discourse with adults often results in echolalic speech or verbalizations that have no real meaning for the child and do not contribute to cognitive development." It is important when children respond to sound to give them the opportunity to interpret it fully by touching the source whenever possible or by having the sound interpreted in words (Barraga, 1983).

Initially, the **Auditory Stimulation Profile** (Table 22) is completed to determine if the child is reacting spontaneously to any auditory stimuli. Secondly, preferred stimuli are utilized in programming to encourage concept development. Information from the other sections of the Sensory Stimulation Profile (Tables 14, 22, 27, 28 and 29) are determined, and the preferences are used as a reinforcement menu for correct functioning on auditory tasks. Information from the Sensory Stimulation Profile will be helpful during sensory integration training.

Case Study: Sally

Sally's hearing evaluation report (Table 17) indicates that during the evaluation she made no observable responses to speech or noisemakers with or without the use of her hearing aid at levels of 85 dB. Therefore, her auditory programming will begin at the lowest level of auditory skills, awareness of sound (Table 21).

Sally's IEP

Hearing Annual Goal:	Sally will improve auditory functioning.
Objective A:	Sally will demonstrate a response to sound such as an eyeblink, smile, or movement when presented an auditory stimulus paired with a visual/tactile cue on 4 out of 5 trials on 3 consecutive data days as implemented by teacher/assistant.
Objective B:	Sally will demonstrate the beginning of a localization response to sound by turning her head toward the sound when presented a variety of

TABLE 22
SENSORY STIMULATION PROFILE: AUDITORY

NAME:
DATE:

Type of Stimulation	Yes	No	Response Liked	Disliked	Comments: Describe child's response
Voices:					
Children's					
Adult: male/female					
Familiar/Unfamiliar					
T.V.					
Music:					
records					
radio					
fast/slow					
loud/soft					
tolerates headphones					
Musical Instruments:					
bass drum					
xylophone					
whistle					
bells					
woodblock					
cymbals					
tambourine					
organ					
piano					
toy					
regular					
maraca					
Music boxes					
Bicycle horn					
Traffic noises					
Atmosphere:					
home					
large crowds/					
noisy					
Toys with sound					
typewriter					
tick-tock clock					
See-and-Say					
mobiles					
Pound-A–Round					
Melody Mike					
Happy Apple					
Other					
Timer					

SOURCE: Author Unknown (1985). Revised and used by teachers in the Deaf-Blind Program, Special School District of St. Louis County, MO.

sound-producing stimuli on 4 out of 5 trials on 3 consecutive data days as implemented by teacher/assistant.

At this time, we are looking for any responses to sound such as a smile, startle, or movement. In Sally's first lessons to develop auditory awareness, the teacher will pair an auditory stimulus (e.g., the sound of a maraca) with a visual stimulus (e.g., the maraca), and a tactile cue (e.g., touching the maraca as teacher shakes it to produce a sound). As Sally makes consistent responses to sound paired with a visual and a tactile cue, the cues will gradually be taken away until the auditory stimulus is presented alone.

Mercury switches attached to sound-producing items have been effective in teaching "sound-no sound" and cause-effect relationships with low-functioning deaf-blind severely multihandicapped children. The child learns that various previously random movements can be repeated to trigger a musical or sound reward.

As Sally progresses consistently in auditory awareness to sound, speech, and toys, her developmental programming will move to the more difficult auditory awareness skills (Table 21) and her second IEP objective, localizing consistently to sound, will be implemented. A wide variety of auditory stimuli will be included in her programming to encourage localization to sound.

Case Study: Bud

Bud's hearing evaluation report (Table 20) indicates that he is responding to sounds in the 50–70 dB range by pausing, laughing, or reaching out. His classroom teacher indicates that he makes little response to voice or music. Thus, Bud's auditory programming is also at the lowest level of auditory functioning—the awareness of sound level (Table 21). Since Bud attends to noisemakers, his objectives will be to expand his awareness to human voice and music.

Bud's IEP

Hearing Annual Goal:	Bud will improve auditory functioning.
Objective A:	Bud will demonstrate a response to human voice by smiling, pausing, or reaching out when pre-

	sented an auditory voice stimulus such as his teacher talking to him, TV, conversations, records/tapes, etc. on 4 out of 5 trials on 3 consecutive data days as implemented by teacher/assistant.
Objective B:	Bud will demonstrate a response to music such as a smile, pause, or reaching out when presented a music stimulus such as records or tapes of children's music, musical wind-up toys, etc. on 4 out of 5 trials on 3 consecutive data days, as implemented by teacher/assistant.

Numerous items from the auditory stimulation room previously described will be presented to Bud to encourage attending to and responding to various auditory stimuli, including music and the human voice. Reaching out is a localization action.

Additional Awareness of Sound Activities. Sound Search (Phillips & Drain, 1979, 3) is an activity to encourage localization of sound. The needed noise objects include the following: noisemakers, alarm clock, aluminum pie plate and wooden spoon, music box, hand bell, keys on a ring, wooden blocks, sandpaper blocks, coffee can with a stone in it. Using one or more of the noisemaking objects, produce a sound and encourage the child to turn to look in the direction of the sound.

Discrimination of Sound

At the discrimination level (Table 21), the child realizes there is a difference in sounds. The child can make different responses to different sounds, distinguish when sound changes, match or discriminate 2 or 3 sounds; respond to differences in loudness, pitch, duration, rhythm. The child does not necessarily know what the sound is, but can give a different response, depending on the stimuli.

Children functioning on the discrimination level may begin to engage in vocal play by repeating sound changes. They pay attention to music and other sounds and respond to tone of voice. This occurs in non-handicapped children at about 4–6 months of age (Table 15). Rhythm band instruments can be used to teach the child to repeat sounds by having the teacher play sounds or a musical pattern to be repeated by the student.

A more difficult level of discrimination of sound (Table 21) involves discriminating between two words. Initially, the words are totally different with different initial consonants, vowel patterns, and number of syllables. Gradually, the words become very similar with only one factor different such as same vowel pattern and number of syllables, but different initial consonants (word families).

Additional Discrimination of Sound Activities

Knowing Noise Makers (Phillips & Drain, 1979) is an activity to improve discrimination of sounds. Needed equipment includes 2–3 sound sources that make very different sounds (e.g., an alarm clock and a radio). A screen (e.g., cookie sheet, cardboard) is used to hide the sound sources from the child. Demonstrate, show, name, and make a sound with an object. Place screen in front of several items, produce a sound, ask child to name or point to the sound source.

Musical Matching (Phillips & Drain, 1979) is an activity to assist the child in discriminating sounds. The equipment needed is a double set of noisemakers such as rhythm band instruments. Use the "screen" again to hide sound sources. Demonstrate a sound source, name the object for the child, describe and produce the sound. Assist the child in producing the sound. Using a "screen," make a noise on one of the noisemakers. Ask the child to make the same sound.

Recognition of Sound

The third level in the development of auditory skills is the recognition of sound (Table 21). At this level, the child is beginning to gain meaning from sound. S/he actually knows what the sound is and whether it is a drum or a bell. This level begins approximately 10–12 months of age in nonhandicapped children (Table 15). Parents serve as a language mediator producing sounds for their child to imitate and label. Children generally enjoy the sounds of animals, and enjoy identifying and imitating them.

Recognition of sound skills (Table 21) includes reproducing sequences of sounds and developing the ability to attend to and to identify the sound with multiple auditory field distractions. Activities that involve the presentation of a wide variety of sounds across many situations and expecting the child to match and/or label sounds assists in recognition of sounds.

Recognition of Sound Activities

Ringing Recognition (Phillips & Drain, 1979, 2) is an activity to teach recognition of environmental sounds such as "door slam, telephone ring, knock on door, car, shut drawer, drop book on floor, mixer, toilet flush, clocks ticking and/or alarms, doorbells, vacuum cleaner." The environmental sounds should be presented to the child in as naturally occurring situations as possible. The child should respond by pointing to appropriate cards/pictures or verbally identifying the environmental sounds presented.

Comprehension of Sound

The highest level of auditory skills programming is the comprehension of sound. At this level, the child attaches meaning to the sound and acts on that understanding in some way. Comprehension of sound skills (Table 21) includes understanding cognitive prerequisite skills and relationship skills involving understanding prepositions, negatives, sequences, comparatives, opposites, and time concepts. Comprehension of speech sounds involves oral language processing while listening to a story, and the receptive language, preacademic, and academic skills.

Comprehension of sound includes selective listening, the ability to mask out meaningless or irrelevant sounds, and the ability attend to musical themes or speech that provides directions. Children can translate vocal instructions into purposeful actions. At school, children are expected to operate on many levels of auditory processing from learning to read to the complex skills of listening to a lecture and taking notes. Deaf-blind severely multihandicapped children seldom attain functioning on the auditory comprehension level, and certainly not during the sensorimotor stage.

An important aspect of auditory programming is monitoring the child's progress on IEP objectives. Monitoring the child's **auditory development** can be achieved by periodic assessment and comparing the results to Auditory Development: Sensorimotor Stage (Table 15). Auditory functioning progress (IEP objectives) can be determined using the Auditory Functioning Skills Checklist (Table 21) or through frequent systematic observations by transferring the skills to a grid and observing/recording the number of responses out of ten stimulations.

SUMMARY

Auditory functioning of severely multihandicapped children may be difficult to determine. A comprehensive audiological assessment including behavioral observation audiometry, objective audiometry, and information regarding daily classroom functioning provides a more complete evaluation of hearing abilities. Behavioral observation audiometry in a sound-field is usually the most appropriate evaluation approach to use with severely multihandicapped vision-impaired children. Behavioral responses are compared to normal auditory developmental skills charts to determine auditory developmental functioning levels.

Objective audiometry obtains results independent of a voluntary or overt response from the child. Brainstem/Cortical-Evoked Response Audiometry (BSER) is an objective audiometry test which measures changes in brainwave activity in response to an auditory stimulus providing frequency-specific hearing levels. Objective tests available to audiologists in the public school setting are acoustic impedance measurements of middle ear functioning, including static acoustic impedance, tympanometry, and intraaural muscle reflexes.

The guidelines to meet the hearing component of deaf-blind criteria include the following: (1) 30 dB bilateral sensorineural hearing loss as a minimum across the speech frequencies in the better ear with amplification, and (2) functional deafness, which means that the student does not auditorally attend to, respond to, or localize sounds, or use his hearing appropriate to his/her developmental level.

Educational programming for the development of auditory skills includes four levels of hearing functioning: awareness of sound, discrimination of sound, recognition of sound, and comprehension of sound. Most young deaf-blind severely multihandicapped children function on the awareness of sound level.

Chapter Four

SECONDARY SENSES:
EVALUATION AND PROGRAMMING

The child must be taught to tolerate, recognize, receive, discriminate, and integrate sensory input (McInnes & Treffry, 1982, 7).

- Secondary Sensory Systems
- Tactile Sensory System
- Proprioceptive-Kinesthetic System
- Vestibular Sensory System
- Integrated Sensory Systems
- Impact of Deficit Functioning
- Secondary Sensory Systems Evaluation
- Secondary Senses Programming
- Summary

Deaf-blind children have been deprived of accurate sensations and perceptions from their distance senses of vision and hearing, so they must rely on their secondary senses—tactile, proprioceptive, kinesthetic, vestibular, olfactory, and gustatory—as major sources of information. These secondary senses do not automatically over-develop to compensate for the loss of vision and hearing (Gottesman, 1971). As a result, deaf-blind severely multihandicapped children may receive little information from their environment, show little curiosity about their environment, and do not automatically act on their environment; thus, they do not learn automatically.

SECONDARY SENSORY SYSTEMS

"The patterns of sensory reception established by the infant and young child become a vital part of the child's learning style and perceptual cognitive development in the early years" (Barraga, 1983, 85).

Tactile Sensory System

The organ of the sense of touch is the skin. Tactile stimulation and sensation may originate from any external area of the body, not just the hands. The lips and hands, the most sensitive transmitters of tactile information to the brain, have large concentrations of tactile receptors (Schiffe, 1982). Touch sensitivity varies over the body surface because different parts of the body possess varied numbers of receptors (Barraga, 1983).

The tactile system is responsive not only to touch stimulation of the skin, but also to pressure, pain, and temperature (Reisman, 1987). The human skin also shows sensitivity to mechanical, thermal, electrical, and chemical stimuli (Morrison et al., 1978). There is information to indicate that pressure and touch sensitivity are present in newborn infants and that pain and thermal sensitivity develop early (Morrison et al., 1978).

Tactile stimulation is crucial to the development of a child. The majority of an infant's basic needs (e.g., feeding, bathing, dressing, diapering) involve simultaneous stimulation of various sensory modalities. As mother or caretaker touches the infant's skin to wash, dry, apply lotion or ointment and clothing, s/he talks to the child, manipulates body parts requiring muscle movements (e.g., lifts up legs) and thus provides multimodality sensory input.

> In fact, the tactual stimuli that occur between an infant and his mother have been considered the most important single aspect in the formation of a core for subsequent development in all other areas — physical, social, emotional, and intellectual (Morrison et al., 1978, 87).

Proprioceptive-Kinesthetic Sensory System

The proprioceptive-kinesthetic sensory system aids in maintaining normal muscle tone, posture, and body position, and in controlling reflexive and skilled movement (Reisman, 1987). The receptors located in the joints, muscles, and tendons are stimulated by passive and voluntary movements of various parts of the body (Morrison et al., 1978). Generally, educators refer to the kinesthetic system, while medical personnel refer to the proprioceptive sensory system.

Information from the joint and muscle receptors enables joints and muscles to coordinate a response to the pull of gravity in order to maintain balance (Morrison et al., 1978). Proprioceptive responses include changes in joint angles, muscle length, and muscle tension. "Because some muscles are always stretched, even when the body is at rest, proprioceptive impulses are continually occurring. These help in monitoring the muscle tone needed to maintain body position and posture" (Reisman, 1987, 288).

Proprioception is important in the establishment of body image because it provides sensory information which indicates the position of the body parts, the degree of activity (e.g., still or moving), and how much effort is needed in a particular movement. This information assists the child in the accomplishment of the sensory motor tasks of purposeful movements such as reach and grasp, imitation, and locomotion. "Children purposefully move their body parts in order to gain proprioceptive information" (Reisman, 1987, 289).

Abnormalities in the proprioceptive-kinesthetic sense may cause poor balance, awkwardness, or excessive swaying patterns (Morrison et al., 1978). Lee and Aronson (1974) indicate the ability to maintain upright posture depends upon the ability to interpret and respond to information about body sway. Body sway activates the vestibular system as the head moves through space, the proprioceptive-kinesthetic system due to muscle stretch and change in joint angles, and visual-proprioceptive system as the changes in the visual field give information about movement and posture (Lee & Aronson, 1974).

Vestibular Sensory System

"The vestibular system is related to the sense of motion and the position of the head in space" (Morrison et al., 1978, 79). It affects movement, balance, muscle tone, postural reactions, spatial relationships, and control of eye movements (Morrison et al., 1978; Reisman, 1987). The vestibular system develops very early and is almost completely mature at birth (Reisman, 1987). Anatomically, the vestibular system consists of the semi-circular canals and vestibule located within the inner ear, the vestibular nerve, and the otolith—a gravity detector present in the lower brainstem of all vertebrates (Morrison et al., 1978; Restak, 1984).

Vestibular system activity is initiated by fluid pressure changes with the semicircular canals reacting to body movement which stimulates the vestibular nerves to carry information to the brainstem regarding starting and stopping movements (Morrison et al., 1978). The vestibule receives information related to the head and eye movements in space, relays this information to the brain which, in turn, affects movement, balance, postural reactions, and the position of the head in space (Morrison et al., 1978). Thus the vestibular portion of the inner ear chamber is the end-organ of equilibrium (balance) and is responsible for conveying information regarding orientation to the brainstem (Wyne & O'Connor, 1979). "The vestibular system is the major contributor to sensory input in the brainstem and the cerebellum" (Morrison et al., 1978, 179).

The vestibulospinal system consists of fibers projecting to the muscles of the neck, trunk, and limbs. During normal activities, the vestibulospinal reflexes act as stabilizers and are responsible for the corrective movements that continually restore the head to its original position" (Restak, 1984, 93).

Integrated Sensory Systems as Prerequisite Abilities

For the deaf-blind child, the integrated senses, tactile-proprioceptive-kinesthetic-vestibular sensory systems become the primary source of information which must be coordinated and integrated with residual visual and auditory abilities for maximum input information to the brain. The tactile-proprioceptive-kinesthetic-vestibular systems involve touch, movement, and orientation of the body in space. The development of these integrated senses is a major prerequisite to the overall development of cognition, motor skills (prehension, mobility), communication (receptive and expressive), social and emotional development, and self-help skills (e.g., eating, dressing, toileting). In a non-handicapped child, these integrated skills develop and interact so smoothly that it is difficult to observe them individually (Table 23).

The development of cognitive skills of exploration of objects, recognition of object function, object permanence, problem-solving, matching (e.g., shapes, textures, sizes), classification, anticipation, and prediction requires tactile-proprioceptive-kinesthetic-vestibular skills for the fine-motor skills of grasping, manipulating objects, transferring objects from hand to hand, building with blocks, putting pegs in a pegboard, and stringing objects require the integration of tactile-proprioceptive-kinesthetic-vestibular abilities. These sensory integration skills are necessary prerequisites to the development of such mobility skills as the protective response, motor memory, movement in familiar and unfamiliar indoor areas, and searching techniques.

Tactile-proprioceptive-kinesthetic-vestibular integration skills are necessary communication prerequisites for the deaf-blind child to learn

TABLE 23

TACTILE-KINESTHETIC-VESTIBULAR DEVELOPMENT: SENSORIMOTOR STAGE

Age (mos.)	Behaviors
Birth	• Responds to touch and movement with total body movement. • Responds to rough-textured or cold surfaces.
1–3	• Accepts and enjoys movement and handling without startling. • Brushes or briefly touches objects. • Responds to being warm. • Responds to unpleasant-textured stimuli.
4–9	• Grabs at and attempts to pick up objects. • Reacts to tactile stimulation with nonlocalized movement. • Holds objects. • Likes and seeks new tactile stimuli. • Permits soft, smooth textures to be rubbed on hands and feet. • Permits rough textures to be rubbed on hands and feet. • Explores objects with fingers.
10–18	• Engages in sensory exploration with hands, mouth, and eyes. • Explores shape and texture of objects. • Plays in water. • Finds object placed in textual material. • Plays with soft-textured material (e.g., pudding).

REFERENCES: Stillman, 1978; Morrison et al., 1978; Schiffe & Foulke, 1982.

imitation movements (e.g., body, limb, finger), and for receptive and expressive communication (e.g., gesturing, presigning, signing, finger-spelling). In the absence of vision for joint-linguistic labeling and bonding, the integrated senses using total body activities must be used to stimulate parent and child interaction, child and child interaction, playing with or without objects, and overall social and emotional development.

Tactile-proprioceptive-kinesthetic-vestibular integrated skills serve as prerequisites for the self-help skill development areas of feeding, dressing, grooming, and toileting. The feeding skills of a deaf-blind child such as holding a bottle, detecting food textures, self-feeding finger foods, drinking from a cup, and using a spoon to self-feed—all require touch, movement, and orientation skills. Dressing skills of putting on and removing clothes, buttoning and unbuttoning, zipping and unzipping rely on tactile-proprioceptive-kinesthetic-vestibular integrated skills. Additionally, self-help skills of handwashing, grooming, and toileting require as prerequisites the skills of touch, movement, and orientation.

Gustatory and Olfactory Systems. The gustatory (taste) and olfactory (smell) systems are near distance senses. The olfactory cells located in the upper part of the nasal cavities are stimulated by minute particles of air. When the cells are stimulated, nerve impulses are sent to the brain. There are five basic aromas that can be detected including the following: flowery, fruity, spicy, resinous, and burning (Ludel, 1978). Taste areas of the mouth are mostly concentrated on the tongue. The primary tastes detected include sweet, salty, acid (sour), and bitter (Ludel, 1978). Human taste is influenced by smell, texture, and temperature of the food. These sensory systems—gustatory and olfactory—are nearly developed at birth and reach mature levels by 9 months of age (Table 24).

Smell is a near distance sensory system that serves as an ineffective substitute to the distance senses—hearing and vision. The sense of smell very quickly becomes overloaded and ceases to provide necessary discriminations. The near senses of taste and touch, in themselves, cannot compensate for the loss of effective distance senses (McInnes & Treffry, 1982).

TABLE 24
GUSTATORY/OLFACTORY DEVELOPMENT: SENSORIMOTOR STAGE

Age (mos.)	Behaviors	
Birth	Gustatory:	Prefers sweet tastes.
	Olfactory:	Responds to strong smells.
1–3	Gustatory:	Avoids bitter tastes.
	Olfactory:	Able to locate and discriminate odors. Fully developed.
3–6	Gustatory:	Avoids bitter tastes.
7–9	Gustatory:	Food preferences by taste and texture. Fully developed.

REFERENCE: Ludel, 1978.

Impact of Deficit Functioning

Tactile Defensiveness

Some deaf-blind severely multihandicapped children are tactilely defensive. Tactile defensiveness is a condition that interferes with progress in all developmental areas: cognition, fine and gross motor skills, communication, self-help skill development, and social and emotional development. "Tactile defensiveness describes the behaviors of children with impairments in the tactile and vestibular systems" (Lerner et al., 1987, 166).

Children who are tactilely defensive withdraw from being touched, hugged, or manipulated in any way. They have a very difficult time bonding with their parents as they do not cuddle nor want cuddling. Parents sometimes interpret the withdrawal and/or crying to touch as rejection of them by their child.

Tactile defensiveness interferes with fine and gross motor skills development as the child does not want to be manipulated through tasks or seek assistance in developing those skills or participate in co-active movement. Tactile defensiveness may interfere with the development of self-help skills as the child rejects being manipulated during eating (e.g., jaw control, holding a cup), rejects any hand-over-hand positions in training self-help skills. Tactile defensiveness may interfere with teaching the child to utilize residual vision and hearing if the child rejects glasses and hearing aid. Tactile defensiveness may interfere with communication skills if the child rejects learning to sign. It interferes with social development as the child avoids close contact and playing physical games (e.g., patty-cake, tickle games) to avoid being touched.

"Some children may touch or explore the environment and seek out tactile stimuli, but they must be the ones to initiate and control the stimuli" (Lerner et al., 1987, 166). For many tactilely defensive children, however, spontaneous exploration does not occur, and they withdraw into a rigid position to avoid being touched.

Case Study: Jeff

Jeff's case study (Table 25) illustrates how tactile defensiveness can interfere with development in cognition, motor skills, self-help skills, and communication.

Orientation Problems

Vision is important for the sense of orientation in space. Children who are deaf-blind have been denied full, accurate use of their major distance senses. Visual deprivation affects the accurate functioning of the vestibular system and thus affects the child's knowledge of self in space, spatial relationships, perceptual-motor integration, balance, spatial orientation, laterality, directionality, and locomotion.

Accurate perceptions and coordinations of motion and movement may be difficult for deaf-blind children to achieve. Inaccurate perceptions may cause the vestibular system to function inappropriately, either over- or under-reacting to motion. Deaf-blind children may experience

TABLE 25
CASE STUDY: TACTILE DEFENSIVENESS

Name: Jeff
Age: 5 years, 4 months
Health: Medical diagnosis of cerebral palsy

Cognitive Evaluation. Current psychological evaluation indicates that Jeff is functioning within the profoundly mentally handicapped range of intelligence with a mental age of less than six months. He does not manipulate objects, but visually inspects them. He appears to continue to look at a spot where a moving object was last seen (beginning concept of object permanence).

Muscle Tone and Range of Motion. Jeff's muscle tone is generally floppy underneath stiffness, probably caused by his active movement into stiff patterns, especially in trunk and legs, from his avoidance of touching. Touching and handling usually cause fussing and posturing into a position of retracted arms and stiff trunk and legs with feet tightly pointed up. Range of motion is passively within normal limits except for stiffness in his trunk.

Gross Motor Skills. Jeff appears to be functioning at the 4–5 month level in gross motor skills. He prefers lying on his back in his stiff position. He log-rolls to either side and onto his stomach. While on his stomach, he can lift his head, but will not prop on his forearms. He can move from one place to another with a wiggling movement. Head control is good in all positions and when moving from one position to another. Jeff does not tolerate a standing position when using a prone stander. If he could tolerate handling without fussing and posturing in a stiff position, he would probably display better motor skills such as: better sitting balance, more purposeful upper extremity movement, protective extension in the arms, etc.

Fine Motor Skills. Jeff functions at the 0–1 month level in fine motor skills. He holds his arms retracted and up, with hands fisted, avoiding bringing his hands to midline or batting, and he resists being manipulated in these skills.

Feeding. Jeff appears to be functioning at the 6-month level in feeding skills. He does not need to have his table food ground if it is held at the sides of his mouth for chewing. Tongue thrust is much improved, no longer pushing food from the mouth. He still uses suckling to consume food in the middle of the mouth. Tactile defensiveness has decreased at the face to allow for jaw control as necessary. Jeff can sometimes maintain an independent grasp on a spoon and assist in bringing it to his mouth, although he misses his mouth. He tolerates having his hand held on his cup. When drinking, he retracts his lips from the rim of a cup and does not assist in pulling liquid out of the cup. Therefore, liquid is lost while drinking.

Communication. Jeff functions communicatively at the 3–4 month level. He cries or whines when frustrated or uncomfortable. He will sometimes smile when approached by a familiar person or during an activity he finds pleasurable. He usually does not vocalize when alone. He will sometimes respond to speech stimulation from caregiver by making sounds or noises. His primary vocalizations are whines or cries to indicate displeasure for handling or a particular activity. Jeff shows an interest for signs by visually attending and responds correctly to signs such as "eat" and "drink." He is beginning to display an understanding of the sign for "up" by lifting his head and shoulders in anticipation of being picked up. As yet, he has not responded or attended to signs such as "stop" and "go" because he does not enjoy the activities connected with these signs and is usually fussing throughout these work periods.

difficulty in perceiving slow, smooth movements such as spinning on a slow-moving merry-go-round. Accurate vestibular functioning is a prerequisite to balance and mobility. Movements required for learning to sit, stand, and walk may cause nausea and unpleasantness in the deaf-blind child.

Jeff (Table 25) also experiences vestibular malfunctioning. When placed on a carpeted hanging swing, he fusses not only in response to the new texture, but to the movement, regardless how slight. He prefers to lay very stiff, making no movement. Progress in locomotion will be slight unless programming can reduce aversion to tactile stimuli and increase toleration for proprioceptive-kinesthetic-vestibular stimulation.

Additional Secondary Sensory Dysfunctions

Tactile, kinesthetic, and vestibular dysfunctions may interfere with the development of bilateral integration, lateralization, form and space conceptualization, eye-hand coordination, speech and language (Connolly, 1984, 318). Morrison et al. (1978) indicates proprioceptive-kinesthetic dysfunctions may interfere with spatial relationships, body image, and motor planning. If movement development and sensory input are distorted, the development of spatial concepts and body image will be delayed or distorted. The child who demonstrates poorly developed body image will frequently demonstrate awkwardness or clumsy, uncoordinated movements, excessive swaying patterns. Motor planning will be hindered by deficits in spatial-temporal perception, body image, tactile, proprioceptive, or visual perception. The child may be unable to cross the midline, have poor eye-hand/eye-foot coordination, problems with balance, and muscle tone. Persistent primitive reflexes may also interfere with motor planning.

SECONDARY SENSORY SYSTEMS EVALUATION

Tactile Evaluation

Evaluation of tactile skills requires much systematic observation, data collection, and clinical teaching. The hierarchial sequence of tactile skill development (Table 23) reveals integration of tactile and motor skills from general reactions at birth with a total body response to tactile stimulation to specific tactile-motor integration skills as in discrimination or recognition of an object by exploring it with hands and fingers. The Callier-Azusa Scale, Tactile subtest (Stillman, 1978) also provides helpful information in determining a developmental functioning level.

An informal clinical teaching procedure to determine the child's reactions to a wide variety of tactile preferences or dislikes and the type or degree of sensory response elicited involves using the Sensory Stimulation Profile: Tactile (Table 26). Clinical teaching will expose the child to a wide variety of soft, rough, and smooth textures and indicate reactions to pressure in firm or light tickling. Responses will be elicited to various temperatures, cold or warm stimulants, miscellaneous resting surfaces, and to vibration. The child's most sensitive areas (e.g., hands, feet, face, trunk, etc.) will be determined during activities such as massage, bath, dinner.

McInnes and Treffry (1982) emphasize the importance of not only determining the level of tactile development—alert to, tolerate, utilize, integrate—but also to determine the factors of stimulation such as type, level, duration, and strength. It is extremely important to determine functioning levels when tactile information provides one of the primary inputs of information to the brain for the deaf-blind child.

Proprioceptive-Kinesthetic Evaluation

The primary purpose of the proprioceptive-kinesthetic evaluation is to determine coordinated joint action and coordinated muscle action in various skills, postures, and movement transitions (Stengel et al., 1984). This assessment is an integral part of a Motor Evaluation. (See "Motor Function and Joint Range of Motion" in Chapter Five.) The Southern California Sensory Integration Tests (Ayres, 1972) are frequently utilized in assessing sensorimotor level skills. The physical therapist is the primary evaluator of functioning in the secondary sensation areas.

Vestibular Evaluation

Few formal tests exist within the public schools to determine vestibular functioning. Since vestibular functioning impacts the gross motor skills of locomotion, balance, and spatial orientation, it is usually assessed during gross motor evaluation by the physical therapist.

Lee and Chasin (1975) indicate that a medical vestibular examination

TABLE 26
STIMULATION PROFILE: TACTILE

NAME:
DATE:

Type of Stimulation	*Yes*	*No*	*Response* *Liked*	*Disliked*	*Comments: Describe child's response*
Cold					
weather					
ice					
snow					
foods					
Warm					
bath					
elec. blanket					
air/hair dryer					
heating pad					
foods					
Miscellaneous					
rest surfaces—					
clothed:					
floor					
carpet					
tile					
rest surfaces—					
naked:					
floor					
carpet					
tile					
Vibration					
Sensitive areas					
hands					
feet					
face					
other					
Massage					
Touch					
without warning					
washing face					
washing hair					
combing hair					
Reactions at bath time?					
Reactions at dinner time?					
Food textures					
1.					
2.					
3.					

SOURCE: Author Unknown (1985). Revised and used by teachers in the Deaf-Blind Program, Special School District of St. Louis County, MO.

utilizes nystagmus, gait, and past-pointing as indicators of vestibular functioning. Nystagmus is elicited using the opticokinetic drum. (See "OKN TEST" in Chapter Two.) Gait testing requires the child to walk with eyes open and eyes closed, first in normal and then in tandem fashion. "The patient with poor bilateral vestibular function will demonstrate a broad-based gait with eyes open and severe difficulty in walking with eyes closed" (Lee & Chasin, 1975, 24). In testing past-pointing, the child is asked to touch his own nose with his index finger and then reach out and touch the examiner's finger, first with eyes open and then with eyes closed. Consistent past-pointing (over-shooting) the examiner's finger to one side may indicate vestibular hypofunctioning and/or central nervous system disorders (Lee & Chasin, 1975). This type of vestibular evaluation is not usually possible with deaf-blind severely multihandicapped children functioning within the sensorimotor stage because many are nonambulatory and/or unable to follow the past-pointing directions.

Vestibular functioning in infants is assessed by using rotational and postrotational nystagmus tests (Morrison et al, 1978). The Southern California Post Rotary Nystagmus Test (Ayres, 1975) is frequently used by placing the child seated on a scooterboard or rotary-nystagmus board, rotating the child with eyes closed, and observing the elicited nystagmus.

> When the child's eyes are opened, nystagmus is seen with the quick component to the right and the slow one to the left. Directions are reversed on stopping rotation. Depending on the speed of rotation, the nystagmus may normally last 20 or 30 seconds (Paine & Oppé, 1966).

Informal evaluation can be conducted using the Sensory Stimulation Profile: Vestibular (Table 27) which will provide valuable information regarding the child's reactions to balance, motion, and orientation in space using various stimuli. Vestibular functioning has not been task-analyzed separately from motor skills.

Gustatory and Olfactory Evaluation

The gustatory and olfactory sensory systems are best evaluated using clinical teaching activities and during feeding. The Sensory Stimulation Profiles: Gustatory (Table 28) and Olfactory (Table 29) provide much useful information regarding these senses. Gustatory evaluation assesses the child's preferences in food temperatures, food preferences, seasonings, food textures. The examiner should also note the presence of any food

TABLE 27
STIMULATION PROFILE: VESTIBULAR

NAME:
DATE:

Type of Stimulation	Yes	No	Response Liked	Disliked	Comments: Describe child's response
Hanging swing					
Platform swing					
Washbasket — up and down					
Washbasket — turn-table					
Ball					
prone					
sitting					
Merry Molehill					
supine					
prone					
sitting					
Scooterboard					
prone					
sitting					
Bolster					
Rocking Horse					
Orange Tub					
Swinging in arms					
Rocking in arms					
Comfy Babe					

SOURCE: Author Unknown. (1985). Revised and used by teachers in the Deaf-Blind Program, Special School District of St. Louis County, MO.

allergies, amount of assistance needed, and preferred eating positions.

The olfactory evaluation considers aroma stimulation reactions to scents such as perfume and shaving cream, mouthwash/toothpaste, vinegar/Vicks, spices and seasonings such as fruits, cinnamon, lemon juice/honey.

Case Study: Sally

Sally's evaluation in secondary sensation indicates functioning at the newborn level (Table 30). Currently, most of her responses are reflexive in nature.

Case Study: Bud

Bud's secondary sensation evaluation report indicates functioning at the 10–12 month level (Table 31). This information indicates that Bud

TABLE 28
SENSORY STIMULATION PROFILE: TASTES (GUSTATORY)

NAME:
DATE:

Type of Stimulation	Yes	No	Response Liked	Response Disliked	Comments: Describe child's response
Allergies					
Temperature					
room temp.					
warm					
cold/ice/ice cream					
Food preferences					
sweets					
liquids					
solids					
fruits					
veggies					
table					
baby food					
Seasonings					
spicy					
sweet					
salty					
sour					
mild vs. strong					
Texture					
crunchy					
mushy					
sticky					
jello/ice cream					
pudding					
table food					
baby food					
Amount of Assistance					
self feeds					
needs assistance					
Feeding position					
upright					
reclining					
adapted chair					
high chair					
Favorite foods					
Behaviors before eating					

SOURCE: Author Unknown. (1985). Revised and used by teachers in the Deaf-Blind Program, Special School District of St. Louis County, MO.

TABLE 29
SENSORY STIMULATION PROFILE: SMELLS (OLFACTORY)

NAME:
DATE:

Type of Stimulation	Yes	No	Response Liked	Response Disliked	Comments: Describe child's response
Perfume/After-shave familiar/unfamiliar					
Shaving cream					
Listerine/mouthwash/toothpaste					
Vinegar					
Vicks					
Spices/seasonings					
peppermint					
vanilla					
strawberry extr.					
banana					
other					
curry					
garlic					
onion					
chili powder					
ginger					
cloves					
nutmeg					
cinnamon					
lemon juice					
coffee					
honey					

SOURCE: Author Unknown. (1985). Revised and used by teachers in the Deaf-Blind Program, Special School District of St. Louis County, MO.

possesses a concept of tactile stimulation, vestibular stimulation, olfactory and gustatory stimulation.

PROGRAMMING: SECONDARY SENSES

Where there is no information supplied to the brain, there can be no learning (Schmit, 1979). Sensory stimulation is a process of awakening the senses, stimulating them to become active pathways of information to the brain. In the case of deaf-blind severely multihandicapped children, sensory stimulation serves to develop the secondary senses and to encourage residual use of vision and hearing senses as avenues for developmen-

TABLE 30

SECONDARY SENSATIONS EVALUATION REPORT

Name: Sally
Age: 4 years, 8 months
Date:

Sally appears to be functioning at the 0–1 month level in tactile skills development. She responds to touch and movement with total body movement. When her cheek is touched during mealtime, she begins the suckling pattern with her lips. She has a withdrawal reaction to foot stimulation. She responds to rough textures and cold surfaces. The results of the Stimulation Profile indicate that Sally enjoys movement; therefore, movement will be used as a reinforcement for other desired behaviors.

TABLE 31

BUD'S SECONDARY SENSATIONS EVALUATION REPORT

Bud was administered the Oregon Project Skills Inventory for Visually Impaired and Blind Preschool Children. His performance indicates functioning at the 10–12 month level with splinter skills at the 13–15 month level.

Tactile Stimulation

Bud alerts to tactile stimulation and responds to the touch of a familiar person. He examines objects tactilely with his hands and searches tactilely for an object removed from direct contact. Bud recognizes family members using tactile cues. He feels and explores objects with his mouth and eats different textured foods.

Vestibular Stimulation

Bud enjoys vestibular stimulation. His favorite toys are those that involve movement such as the rocking chair and rocking horse. He uses integrated sensory skills of tactile-kinesthetic-vestibular sensations to explore his environment. He crawls from place to place, pulls himself up to stand, and is learning to walk.

Higher-level splinter skills include exploring another child tactilely as an object; examining liquid and semisolid foods with his hands, enjoying tickle games.

Olfactory and Gustatory Stimulation

Bud is aware of olfactory and gustatory stimulations. He smells objects as part of his exploring pattern. He continuously sucks his thumb.

tal programming. The heightened secondary senses, coupled with residual vision and hearing, provides multimodal information input to the brain.

The primary purpose of stimulation program activities is to assist the child to compensate for overwhelming sensory deprivation. The role that vision and hearing should play in learning must be assumed by tactile-proprioceptive-kinesthetic-vestibular sensations and systems. These systems are so interwoven and interdependent that it is difficult to task-analyze them and discuss them as separate entities. The Tactile-

Kinesthetic-Vestibular Sensory Programming Skills (Table 32) and the results of the Stimulation Profiles: Tactile and Vestibular (Tables 26 and 27) provide information that is useful in classroom programming. Programming involves progression through three levels of skill areas including (1) awareness and attention, (2) recognition and discrimination, and (3) orientation in space (Table 32).

Awareness and Attention

At the awareness and attention level, the child alerts to tactile stimulation of various types and learns to tolerate tactile stimulation activities. The child progresses from responses to touch and movement with total body movement to localized responses. Early skills involve stimulation administered by the teacher with no exploratory behaviors on the part of the child. Skills toward the end of this level involve movement on the part of the child as s/he begins to affect their environment. The child learns to attend to textures, temperatures, vibrating surfaces, and varied stimuli.

Stimulation Activities

Van Etten et al. (1980) suggested conducting tactile sensory development activities in a corner of the room covered with carpet squares of various colors sewed together. Tactile sensory development materials should include the following kinds of items: **smooth** (i.e., nylon cloth, felt, plastic), **rough** (i.e., sandpaper, terry cloth, net, sand, brushes of various textures and sizes), **soft** (i.e., powder puff, flannel, sponge, foam rubber, satin, cotton balls, fur, stuffed toys), **hard** (i.e., wood, metal, concrete, glass), **big** (i.e., rocks, dowels, balls), **little** (i.e., rocks, dowels, balls), **heavy** (i.e., rocks, weights, bean bags), **light** (i.e., feathers, sponge balls, soapsuds, yarn balls), **cold or cool** (i.e., water, blow dryer, ice), **warm or hot** (i.e., water, blow dryer), **sticky** (i.e., peanut butter, honey, glue, syrup, tape), **slick** (i.e., silk cloth, lotion, fingerpaints, powder) (Van Etten et al., 1980, 349). Other materials include various textures, consistencies of food such as bananas that can be involved in manipulating, squeezing, and mashing (Appell, 1986).

Massage. A very successful activity at the awareness and attention level of tactile-kinesthetic-vestibular programming is massage. This intervention technique assists parents and teachers in establishing contact with deaf-blind severely multihandicapped children functioning within the sensorimotor stage.

TABLE 32

TACTILE-KINESTHETIC-VESTIBULAR SENSORY PROGRAMMING SKILLS

I. Awareness and Attention
   _____ Responds to touch and movement with total body movement.
   _____ Responds to rough-textured surfaces.
   _____ Responds to cold surfaces.
   _____ Responds to being warm.
   _____ Responds to unpleasant textured stimuli.
   _____ Responds to weight and pressure.
   _____ Accepts and enjoys movement and handling without startling.
   _____ Reacts to tactile stimulation with nonlocalized movement.
   _____ Likes and seeks new tactile stimuli.
   _____ Holds objects placed in hands.
   _____ Permits soft, smooth textures to be rubbed on hands and feet.
   _____ Accepts water on face.
   _____ Permits rough textures to be rubbed on hands and feet.
   _____ Brushes or briefly touches object.
   _____ Engages in sensory exploration with hands, mouth, and eyes.
   _____ Explores objects with fingers.
   _____ Explores shape and texture of objects.
   _____ Plays in water.
   _____ Plays with soft-textured material (e.g., pudding).
   _____ Grabs at and attempts to pick up object.
   _____ Reaches out to explore immediate environment with hand, arm, foot, leg.
   _____ Tolerates manipulation during motor, feeding, dressing, etc. activities.
   _____ Attends to items moved by mechanical assistance or limited personal assistance.

II. RECOGNITION AND DISCRIMINATION
   _____ Finds object placed in textural material.
   _____ Recognizes familiar object by touching.
   _____ Responds to tactile stimulation by moving stimulated limb.
   _____ Discriminates and matches objects by touch (seen and unseen).
   _____ Touches objects in textural sequence.
   _____ Selects object from sequence of textures.
   _____ Tactilely matches different textures.
   _____ Tactilely matches objects by size.
   _____ Sorts 2 kinds of tactilely dissimilar objects.
   _____ Determines limb position with eyes closed.
   _____ Localizes tactile stimulus to specific body part (e.g., touches part, removes tape).
   _____ Ranks objects tactilely (e.g., softest to roughest).
   _____ Searches for dropped/lost object within arm's reach.
   _____ Matches 3 or more textures to same number of samples.
   _____ Matches textures when number of textures and samples are not equal.
   _____ Responds appropriately to one consistent tactile message.
   _____ Uses one tactile symbol appropriate with a situational cue.
   _____ Discriminates 5–10 different tactile messages/symbols.

TABLE 32 (Continued)

III. ORIENTATION IN SPACE
——————— Moves hesitantly around environment; may become easily disoriented.
——————— Reaches out to contact wall/door with hand/foot while walking.
——————— Travels (walks) by following along wall.
——————— Uses permanent fixtures in room to determine location.
——————— Uses textured markers/cues in room to determine location in room.
——————— Locates object dropped when standing.
——————— Locates object dropped when moving.
——————— Appears to have a knowledge and sense of self in space (e.g., balance during locomotion).
——————— Understands directionality related to self.
——————— Shows knowledge of laterality.
——————— Demonstrates knowledge of position in space (e.g., doesn't bump into people or things during locomotion).
——————— Has developed "motor memory."
——————— Demonstrates perceptual-motor (gross) integration by kicking large ball.
——————— Demonstrates eye-hand coordination by stringing beads, etc.
——————— Reveals spatial orientation during movement through space—walking, running, scooter board, tricycle.
——————— Propels a toy.
——————— Uses spatial orientation to explore environment.
——————— Identifies and labels spatial relationships (e.g., far/near, in/out, front/back, top/bottom, first/last, over/under).

REFERENCES: Brown et al., 1979; Lerner et al., 1987; Stillman, 1978; Frost, 1972; Rudolph et al., Undated.

TABLE 33
TACTILE-KINESTHETIC-VESTIBULAR STIMULATION ACTIVITIES
Awareness and Attention Level (Nonambulatory/Passive Student)

Hands/Feet Activities	*Body Activities*
• Rub with blanket/towel • Rub with smooth/rough, soft/hard, light/heavy, cool/warm, sticky/slick textures • Warm/cold blow dryer	• Lying in a hammock that wraps around the body • Lying on a carpeted surface • Roll child up in a blanket and unroll • Bathe child in small swimming pool • Lying on vibrating pad • Massage • Rubbing body/trunk with baby powder

REFERENCES: Lerner, 1987; Appell, 1986.

The normal bonding process which develops between mother and infant is disturbed in children with sensory impairments. The child with sensory impairments such as tactile defensiveness, abnormal muscle tone, and motor deficits may be less able to cuddle and make adjustments to parent or caregiver interaction, leaving parents and caregivers feeling inadequate and rejected.

The child is positioned in a comfortable position on a floor mat to begin the massage. The teacher or parent should use olive oil or food oils instead of baby oil in case the child puts his/her hand into their mouth. Massage is accomplished by making long, smooth movement strokes from the thigh to the foot, and from the shoulder to the hand. Shorter strokes are made from the elbow to the hand. The teacher or parent supports the child's foot in their palm as they stroke gently from the knee to the foot.

Massage has many benefits. It helps to promote attachment/bonding between the caregiver and child. Massage helps to relax tense children and may make them easier to feed and alleviate some digestive problems that make them fussy. The tactile input helps to keep children more alert and aware. The teacher/parent should use this as a special communication time, talking to the child, encouraging responses and vocalizations.

Recognition and Discrimination

Between the developmental ages of 10 and 18 months, the child (Table 23) enters the recognition and discrimination phase of tactile-kinesthetic-vestibular sensation programming (Table 32). Movement is required at this level of functioning. The child begins to use kinesthetic-vestibular sensation as s/he begins to explore the environment. "Motor integration can occur only when the infant and young child use the motor system in responding to the sensory stimulation" (Barraga, 1983, 85). Early fine-motor skills of reach and grasp enable the child to explore his/her environment.

Movement appears to stimulate cognitive development as the child begins to have an impact on his/her environment. Exploration through movement assists the child in understanding causality, object function, and object permanence. The child's cognitive functioning improves to allow matching and classification of objects by size, shape, textures. The child's beginning ideas about body image allow him/her to respond by localizing the part or limb stimulated. The child learns to sort similar and dissimilar objects; rank objects from softest to roughest as he develops cognitively.

At the recognition and discrimination phase, the child can begin to learn tactile precommunication skills (receptive language) such as learning tactile symbols and cues and the appropriate response.

Recognition and Discrimination Activities

Texture Tub Activities (Phillips & Drain, 1979, 10) assist the child in refining discrimination skills. A plastic basin or container is partially filled with one or more of the following textures: popcorn, rice, macaroni, cornmeal, sand (wet/dry), oatmeal, gravel, water (soapy and clear), dry beans. Using small toys or objects such as spoons, measuring cups, squeeze toys, balls, paper cups assist the child in playing. "Pour the material over the child's hands and assist the child in scooping, filling, and dumping containers with the material." Bury objects partially and totally, encouraging the child to find them.

Sand/Water Play Areas (Bailey & Wolery, 1984) suggest providing a sand/water "tub" center with varying activities and schedules; for example, Monday—water, Tuesday—sand, Wednesday—water with food coloring, Thursday—beans and noodles, Friday—water with soapsuds. They suggest providing a variety of textured materials (i.e., macaroni, salt, noodles, shells, dried beans, leaves, styrofoam) and tools (i.e., cans, sponges, shovels, floating and sinking objects, boats, toy mixers and beaters, funnels, squeeze bottles, straws, and buckets). Object permanence can be encouraged through partially or completely burying objects under the dry materials or water. Motor coordination is encouraged through digging, pouring, lifting. Means-ends is facilitated through experiences with tool use (e.g., beaters, cups, funnels, etc.).

Orientation in Space

The highest functioning level of the integrated secondary sensory skills, tactile-kinesthetic-vestibular, is orientation in space (Table 32). At this level, the child is moving within his/her environment and gaining a knowledge of himself/herself in space, directionality, laterality, balance, and perceptual-motor integration skills.

Children begin developing a concept of their "body image" by using the hands to find the feet, shoulder, and other body parts. Body image

TABLE 34
TACTILE—KINESTHETIC-VESTIBULAR STIMULATION ACTIVITIES
RECOGNITION AND DISCRIMINATION LEVEL
(AMBULATORY/ACTIVE STUDENT)

Hand Activities
- fingerpainting with fingerpaints and shaving cream
- fingerpainting with pudding or cereal
- building a tower with finger jello cubes or frozen jello cubes
- squeezing and mashing bananas
- reaching for toys inside a carpeted barrel
- playing with sand/water
- playing with playdough and clay
- digging for objects in buried sand
- manipulating heavy/light (rock/feather) objects
- manipulating sticky items (honey, peanut butter, syrup)
- touching/manipulating various items: rough/smooth; soft/hard; big/little; cold/warm; slick
- peanut butter play dough
- texture tub activities

Body Stimulation Activities
- rolling on a carpet surface
- rolling up in a blanket and unrolling
- playing inside carpeted barrel
- massage
- sitting in barrel of beans (diaper only) letting beans roll from shoulder to leg

Feet Stimulation Activities
- walking barefooted in grass, sand, leaves.

REFERENCES: Lerner, 1987; Appell, 1986; Phillips & Drain, 1979.

helps to stabilize the child's orientation in near space (Barraga, 1983). The hands must become a highly sensitive avenue for information input through exploration and manipulation. The child must be encouraged and provided the freedom to safely explore the environment.

Two important skills which can be learned by children as they locomote throughout the home and classroom include (1) the use of the total body as it moves through space to encounter stationary objects, and (2) the use of the hands to explore objects that are stable or that move with contact (Barraga, 1983).

Proprioceptive-kinesthetic-vestibular movements provide the child with much information regarding his environment. "Without the ability to see and imitate the body movements of others, the blind child must experience the movement in his muscles before a specific action can be perceived or verbal instructions from others understood" (Barraga, 1983, 41).

Vestibular abilities such as balance and orientation in space become important. The purpose of materials chosen for proprioceptive-kinesthetic-vestibular sensory development is to encourage movement. Increased movement facilitates exploration, and the development of tactile exploration increases the likelihood that students will attempt to move in an effort to reach attractive objects (Van Etten et al., 1980).

Orientation in Space Activities

Textured markers can be used as cues to help the child determine his/her location in a room as s/he uses some form of locomotion (i.e., scooting, crawling, walking) to explore the environment.

Movement toys of all kinds provide many opportunities for the child to practice balance and orientation in space activities.

TABLE 35
TACTILE-KINESTHETIC-VESTIBULAR ACTIVITIES
ORIENTATION IN SPACE LEVEL
(AMBULATORY/ACTIVE STUDENT)

Hand/Feet Activities	*Body Activities*
• Hitting a punching bag	• Trampoline games
• Hitting a tether ball	• Playing with inner tubes
• Throwing items through space (balls, bean bags)	• Rolling/tumbling on mats
• Kicking large balls	• Rocking on a hobby horse or in a rocking chair
• String beads	• Pulling toys/wagon
• Crawling backward to a target	• Moving on a scooterboard
• Rock on hand and knees	• Swinging on a swing
• Jumping on air mattress, trampoline, or inner tube	• Riding on a merry-go-round
• Passing objects	• Sliding down a slide
• Pushing heavy objects	• Riding a tricycle
	• Using a skateboard
	• Locating object dropped when standing/moving
	• Crawling in & out of boxes
	• Angels in the snow
	• Wheelbarrows
	• Tumble tubs
	• Spinning
	• Sitting on and rocking a bolster

REFERENCES: Van Etten et al., 1980; Lerner et al., 1987; Morrison et al., 1978.

Gustatory/Olfactory Stimulation

Gustatory Stimulation

The purpose of the gustatory stimulation program is to encourage the child to eat a wide variety of foods of various textures. The stimulation program can be integrated naturally with mealtime or as a separate skill activity at other times throughout the day. The decision must be made with each child in mind so as not to interfere with his nutritional program. The major types of food utilized in the development of gustatory skills include strained, thickened, semisolid, lumpy, firm, chewy, crispy, sticky, sandwiches, combination foods (Van Etten et al., 1980).

For many low-functioning children who have poor oral motor skills, providing a variety of textures is nearly impossible as all of their foods must be ground. At this stage, varying tastes and temperatures will continue to provide stimulation. As oral motor skills improve to the chewing stage, more variety in texture can be achieved by adding crunchy foods to their diet.

Gustatory Stimulation Activities. Fingerpainting (tasting) with different puddings and instant cereals is enjoyable; add raisins, chocolate chips, and shredded coconut for texture (Appell, 1986). **Building** with finger jello cubes (and tasting) or stacking frozen jello cubes can enhance gustatory abilities. Tasting warm sweet jello provides taste and temperature variation experiences.

The child's awareness of taste can be increased by using a wide variety of foods of different tastes and textures in his/her diet. Examples of a variety of tastes in foods include the following: **sweet foods** (i.e., sugar, fruit, ice cream, honey, syrup), **sour/tangy or bitter foods** (i.e., grapefruit, lemon, dill pickle, buttermilk, yogurt, vinegar), **salty foods** (i.e., salt, boiled peanuts, potato chips, saltine crackers), **bland foods** (i.e., white bread, cooked rice, cooked noodles, mashed potatoes) (Phillips & Drain, 1979). **Soft/smooth-textured foods** include mashed potatoes, ice cream, tomato soup, applesauce, yogurt, while **crunchy foods** may include potato chips, cornflakes (cereals), granola, toasted bread crumbs, raw carrots. Contrasting temperature foods may include the following: **cold foods** (i.e., ice, cold orange juice, ice cream, Kool-aid, popsicles) and **hot/warm foods** (i.e., soup, mashed potatoes).

Olfactory Stimulation

Olfactory stimulation occurs naturally as a part of the gustatory stimulation program. Some of the aromas utilized in programming should include onion, garlic, peppermint, rose oil, numerous spices, perfumes, soaps (Van Etten et al., 1980, 356). Olfactory and gustatory stimulation can be involved in manipulating/squeezing/mashing scented foods such as oranges, lemons, and bananas.

Olfactory Stimulation Activities. Fingerpainting with different flavored puddings and cereals to which spices have been added to enhance flavor can stimulate olfaction. Higher-functioning children can be assigned the task of matching scented stickers to corresponding pictures of fruits, vegetables, etc. or matching the scented stickers to actual foods (e.g., banana-scented sticker to real banana or picture of banana).

Case Study: Sally

Sally is functioning at the beginning awareness and attention level of tactile-kinesthetic-vestibular development programming skills (Table 32). Her IEP goal is to "alert to" tactile stimulation and begin to act on her environment. Using information from the Sensory Stimulation Profile (Tables 26, 27, 28, 29), a wide variety of textures, temperatures, and tactile stimuli can be used to encourage her to alert to tactile stimulation.

Sally's IEP

Secondary Sensation Goal: Sally will alert to tactile stimulation.

Objective A: Sally will demonstrate "alerting to" by making a movement such as an eyeblink, smile, startle, or cry after receiving tactile stimulation (e.g., a variety of textures, temperatures, and/or tactile stimuli) on 4 out of 5 trials on 3 consecutive data days as implemented by teacher/assistant.

Objective B: Sally will be able to briefly touch or brush an object after being presented a wide variety of object stimuli including objects with different textures, temperatures, and vibrations on 4 out of 5 trials on 3 consecutive data days as implemented by teacher/assistant.

Consistent repeatable responses to tactile stimulation will indicate Sally is aware of and pays attention to tactile stimulation. The list of awareness and attention skills (Table 32) should provide many opportunities and suggestions for activities as well as the Stimulation Activities (Table 33) in planning Sally's activities. Consistent responses should lead naturally to integrating tactile stimulation with a motor response as Sally also progresses motorically. Using a wide variety of tactile stimuli, Sally will be encouraged to reach for or briefly touch objects.

Case Study: Bud

Bud has mastered all of the skill competencies at the awareness and attention level (Table 32) and is concurrently functioning at the recognition and discrimination level, and due to locomotion development, is also functioning at the orientation in space level. His IEP goal is to improve functioning in recognition and discrimination, and in orientation in space abilities. The improved functioning in recognition and discrimination aims to improve abilities in precommunication tactile skills. Currently, he can sign two one-word statements—"eat," "drink."

His second objective aims to begin developing a knowledge of body image so he can assist with dressing and ultimately dress himself. Body awareness will also assist Bud in locomotion as he continues to learn to walk and move through space. He currently enjoys several orientation-in-space activities involving rocking on the hobby horse and in a rocking chair. However, since he is just learning to walk, he moves hesitantly around in the classroom and becomes disoriented, easily losing his balance.

Bud's IEP

Secondary Sensation Goal: Bud will improve tactile recognition and discrimination skills, and orientation in space skills.

Objective A: Bud will improve tactile recognition and discrimination skills by searching for and finding an object (e.g., ball, cup, truck) placed in textural material (e.g., sand, beans, rice) on 4 out of 5 trials on 3 consecutive data days as implemented by teacher/assistant.

Objective B: Bud will improve tactile recognition and discrimination skills of body image by responding to tactile stimulation of the body part (e.g., arms, legs, fingers) by moving the stimulated body part on 4 out of 5 trials on 3 consecutive data days as implemented by teacher/assistant.

Objective C: Bud will improve orientation in space skills by reaching out to touch the wall or near permanent furniture when he begins to lose balance rather than sitting down on 4 out of 5 incidents on 3 consecutive data days as implemented by teacher/assistant.

The list of recognition and discrimination skills and orientation in space skills (Table 10) and activities (Tables 34 and 35) should provide many opportunities and suggestions to vary Bud's programming activities.

Program/progress monitoring should include two areas—developmental skills and programming skills. Periodic assessment using Tactile-Kinesthetic-Vestibular Development: Sensorimotor Stage (Table 23) provides age-based functioning levels. Frequent systematic observation using Tactile-Kinesthetic-Vestibular Sensory Programming Skills (Table 32) or transferring those skills to a Data Collection Grid assist in monitoring the child's progress toward IEP objectives.

SUMMARY

Deaf-blind children deprived of accurate perceptions through their distance senses must rely on the secondary senses (tactile, proprioceptive-kinesthetic, vestibular, olfactory, gustatory) to provide most of their sensory input information. The tactile system is responsive not only to touch stimulation of the skin, but also to pressure, pain, and temperature. The proprioceptive-kinesthetic system receives information from joints, muscles, and tendons which aids in maintaining normal muscle tone, posture and body position, and in controlling reflexive and skilled movement. The end organ of the vestibular system, within the inner ear, receives information regarding the sense of motion and the position of the head in space, which affects movement, balance, muscle tone, postural reactions, spatial relationships, and control of eye movements. The gustatory (taste) and olfactory (smell) systems are the near distance senses and are ineffective substitutes for the distance senses of hearing and vision.

These secondary senses do not, however, automatically develop to a high level of precision to compensate for deficient vision and hearing.

For maximum input information to the brain, the secondary sensation information needs to be integrated with residual auditory and visual stimulation input.

The development of the tactile-kinesthetic-vestibular senses is a major prerequisite developmental skill for deaf-blind children. Adequate tactile-kinesthetic-vestibular skills are required for the initial development of cognition, motor skills, communication, social/emotional, and self-help skills. Some deaf-blind severely multihandicapped children are tactilely defensive. This is a condition that results when children experience impairments in tactile and/or vestibular systems that interfere with the progress of all developmental skill areas.

The vestibular system enables one to detect motion and orientation in space. Vision is important for orienting in space. Inaccurate functioning of the vestibular system affects the child's orientation in space (balance, laterality, directionality) and fine and gross motor skill development.

Sensory stimulation programming aims to develop the secondary senses and to encourage residual use of vision and hearing as active pathways of information to the brain. Three levels of secondary sensory programming include (1) awareness and attention, (2) recognition and discrimination, and (3) orientation in space. At the awareness and attention level, severely handicapped children learn to respond to tactile stimulation and begin movement that affects their environment. At the recognition and discrimination stage, the child begins to use kinesthetic-vestibular sensation as s/he explores the environment. At the orientation in space level, the child learns to move confidently within his/her environment.

Chapter Five

MOTOR DEVELOPMENT:
EVALUATION AND PROGRAMMING

Human learning begins with motor learning (Lerner et al., 1987, 164).

- Normal Sensorimotor Development
- Abnormal Sensorimotor Development
- Sensorimotor Evaluation
  Gross and Fine Motor
  Reflexes and Automatic Reactions
- Muscle Tone, Strength, and Function
  Joint Range of Motion
  Posture
  Sensory Integration
  Gait
  Respiratory Function
  Activities of Daily Living
- Sensorimotor Development Programming
- Summary

CONSULTANTS:
Mary Garavaglia, P.T.
Susan Pope, M. Ed.

NORMAL SENSORIMOTOR DEVELOPMENT

"Normal sensorimotor development is an important basis for all other forms of development" (Haynes, 1983, 15). A reciprocal developmental relationship exists among the motor and sensory skills as they integrate to facilitate the development of cognition (thinking). "For the very young infant with a yet undeveloped cerebral cortex, movement is thinking" (Ward, 1981, 100). The development of intentionality during the sensorimotor stage is highly dependent on vision to control the beginning stages of reach and grasp. Vision and motor development interact to develop concepts of action causality.

Motor development is related to maturation. It follows a cephlocaudal (head-to-feet control) and a proximal (center of body) to distal (extremities) direction. Motor development follows a sequential pattern, but the rate varies from child to child. "No two human beings develop at exactly the same pace or reach the various developmental stages at precisely the same time" (Fallen & Umansky, 1985, 199). Maturation, directionality, and sequencing of patterns are all basic principles of motor development.

"There are several levels of motor system functions. They range from innate reflex motor behavior of the newborn infant to complex motor acts" (Lerner et al., 1987, 157–158). "The behavioral repertoire of the newborn infant consists only of reflexes that are innate and automatic responses (sucking, rooting, Moro)" (Ward, 1981, 101). "Reflexive movement is gradually replaced by voluntary movement. This change from reflexive to voluntary or purposeful movement is considered the beginning of cognitive development (learning)" (Healy & Stainback, 1980, 13). The process of replacing reflexive movement with voluntary or purposeful movement goes through several major stages: (1) **trial and error period** (repeated motor action to duplicate something pleasurable previously experienced), (2) **more complex processes** (manipulating and exploring objects and environment), and (3) **motor planning** (involves thinking before making a motor response) (Healy & Stainback, 1980).

Normal motor development progresses within a two-year period from the newborn reflexive stage with no conscious motor control to the two-year-old who is walking, using motor planning, using the pincer grasp to scribble and build, using reflexes that will continue a lifetime, and in general coordinating sensory and motor skills as s/he develops independence in moving through space. Table 36 presents a summary of normal sensorimotor development.

Reflex Development

Reflexes and automatic responses or reactions are the basis for posture and movement. Reflexes can also be an indication of central nervous system development and brain maturity (Ward, 1981). The first several months of life are characterized by involuntary reflexive responses to stimuli. The reflexive motor behaviors of a newborn infant include

TABLE 36
NORMAL SENSORIMOTOR DEVELOPMENT

| Age (mos.) | Reflexes | Gross Motor | | Fine Motor |
		Postural Control	Locomotion	
0–1	*Brainstem level* • Moro, grasp, ATNR, STNR, rooting, sucking, Babinski, walking, neck righting	• Lies with flexed arms and legs. • No posture in trunk. • No head control.		• Reflex grasp of objects.
1–3	*Brainstem level* • Moro, grasp, ATNR, STNR, rooting, sucking, Babinski, walking, neck righting, labryinthine righting. • Decreased influence of grasp reflex.	• 1 mo. — Prone holds head and chin up. • 2 mo. — Prone holds head and chest up. • 3 mo. — Head control complete in prone. • Sits supported in infant seat. • Bears little weight in legs.	• Prone — rolls from side to side. • Rolls from prone to supine as a unit.	
4–6	*Brainstem level* • STNR, TLR *Midbrain Level* • Landau, Amphibian *Automatic Reactions* • Labyrinthine, optical righting, body righting, protective extension of arms, equilibrium reaction in prone, protective extensor thrust.	• Sits with support, upper trunk erect (4 mo.). • Sits on adult's lap with rattle. • Sits on highchair and grasps dangling object (6 mo.). • Bears weight on legs and bounces when supported under arms. • Head control in supine. • Movement — flexion and extension coordinated.	• Rolls from back to side. • Rolls from stomach to back, rotating independently. • Moves by rocking, rolling, twisting, or pushing with feet. • Amphibian crawls forward or backward.	• Voluntarily holds object. • Reaches purposefully to touch. • Picks up 1 toy at a time. • Hand to mouth behavior. • Plays with hands at midline. • Purposeful reach and grasp (6 mo.). • Voluntarily releases object (6 mo.). • Ulnar palmar grasp (little finger, ring finger & palm), 6 mo.

TABLE 36 (Continued)

Age (mos.)	Reflexes	Gross Motor		Fine Motor
		Postural Control	Locomotion	
7–9	*Midbrain Reflexes* • Landau, Amphibian, *Automatic Reactions* • labryinthine, optical righting, body righting acting on the body, protective extensor thrust, protective extension of arms, equilibrium reactions in prone, supine, and sitting.	• Sits alone—arms free to play (7 mo.). • Stands with help (8 mo.). • Stand holding furniture. • Pushes up on hands and knees, rocks back and forth. • Assumes sitting position from lying on back by rotating around trunk. • Body images and motor planning.	• 4-point crawls. • Scoots forward on bottom.	• Transfers object hand to hand. • Hand and palm grasp (7 mo.) *palmar grasp.* • Moves fingers with some control. • Radial-digital grasp (8 mo.) (thumb, index and middle finger). • Scissors grasp (9 mo.). • Grasps and purposefully drops objects.
10–12	*Midbrain Reflexes* • Landau, Amphibian *Automatic Reactions* • Labyrinthine; optical righting; body righting; equilibrium in prone, supine, sitting, quadrapedal, standing; protective extensor thrust.	• Pivots on bottom while sitting. • Pulls to stand by using furniture (12 mo.). • From sitting position squats to play. • Pulls from sitting to standing by rotating trunk segmentally.	• Walks when led (10 mo.). • Cruises around furniture. • Bear-crawls (using (using feet instead of knees as support). • Walks with one hand held. • Walks 3–5 steps alone; falls.	• Pincer grasp (thumb and one finger). • Bangs 2 objects together. • Pokes and probes with index finger. • Reaches out both arms to catch ball. • Drops objects into container and dumps. • Uses arms and hands to hold large object. • Suppination.
13–18	*Automatic Reactions* • Primitive reflexes integrated (brainstem).	• Stands alone using body rotation (14 mo.). • Stands arms free to play.	• Climbs stair steps (13 mo.). • Walks alone, toddler gait (15 mo.), falls often.	• Places object on table without dropping. • Uses stick to beat drum.

TABLE 36 (Continued)

Age (mos.)	Reflexes	Gross Motor		Fine Motor
		Postural Control	Locomotion	
	• Optical righting; body righting; protective extension of arms; equilibrium reaction in prone, sitting, supine, crawling and standing, quadrapedal.	• Sits down bending knees from free standing position in one motion. • From standing, squats to play. • Seats self in small chair. • Climbs into adult chair. • Rolls ball.	• Walks, arms lowered to waist (18 mo.). • Walks up stairs with help.	• Opens and closes simple containers. • Uses thumb for pressing. • Places objects in container. • Turns 2–3 pages in a book at a time. • Marks with crayon (fist hold). • Puts rings on stick.
19–24	*Automatic Reactions* Labyrinthine, optical righting, body righting acting on the body, body righting acting on the head; equilibrium reactions in prone, supine, sitting, quadrapedal, standing, protective extension of arms.	• Squats to pick up object & re-erects. • Gets down from adult chair. • Kicks large object (beach ball). • Step-jumps from bottom stair. • Kneels on both knees & rises to standing. • Throws ball overhand. • Squats from standing to play.	• Walks pulling, pushing or holding toy. • Climbs up & down stairs on all fours. • Runs stiffly. • Walks up & down stairs holding rail one step at a time. • Walks heel-toe gait. • Runs forward well, problems turning corners.	• Strings beads using both hands. • Plays with clay (rolls, pounds, squeezes, pulls). • Puts pegs in pegboard. • Scribbles. • Pours from one container to another. • Turns knobs. • Unscrews lids. • Builds 6–7 block tower.

REFERENCES: Fallen & Umansky, 1985; Bailey & Wolery, 1984; Stillman, 1978; Healy & Stainback, 1980; Morrison et al., 1978; Lerner et al., 1987.

sucking and swallowing, rooting, Moro, startle, Babinski, grasp, walking (Lerner et al., 1987). Shortly after birth, the infant also displays the reflex patterns of neck righting, asymmetric tonic neck reflex (ATNR), symmetric tonic neck reflex (STNR), tonic labyrinthine reflex (TLR) (Table 37).

The neonatal reflexes of sucking (e.g., stroking the lips or around the mouth to elicit a sucking pattern) and rooting (e.g., stroking the side of the cheek to stimulate head turn) are reflexes to facilitate nursing (a survival mechanism). The Moro reflex is a primitive protective reaction to a sudden backward movement or jarring of the head in which the child responds with instant extension of his/her trunk, arms, legs (Table 37).

TABLE 37
REFLEXES AND AUTOMATIC REACTIONS

Reflexes (Brainstem Level)			
Reflex	*Stimulus*	*Response*	*Age*
Sucking	Stroking lips or around mouth.	Sucking is stimulated.	0 to 3 mo.
Rooting	Downward stroking of the cheek.	Head turns to side stroked.	0 to 3 mo.
Moro	Sudden backward movement or jarring of the head.	Body responds with instant extension of trunk, arms, legs.	0 to 4 mo.
Startle	Rapid movement toward face or loud movement.	Total body flexion (clenched fists, rapid movement of arms and legs into flexion.	0 to 3 mo.
Babinski	Stroking on sole of foot.	Big toes bend upward, toes fan out.	0 to 4 mo.
Grasp	Pressure applied on palm.	Fingers curl in closed position.	0 to 6 mo.
Walking	Touch sole of foot in upright position.	Legs are lifted upward, alternating like walking.	0 to 5 mo.
Neck Righting	Child on back, turn head to side.	Body rotates as a whole (log roll) in same direction as head.	0 to 6 mo.
Asymmetric Tonic Neck Reflex (ATNR)	Child on back, head midline, arms & legs extended, turn head to one side.	Arm & leg on side that head faces extend, opposite limbs flex.	0 to 6 mo.
Symmetric Tonic Neck Reflex (STNR)	Head moved up away from body or down (in prone over tester's knee or suspended in air).	Move head down—arms bend & legs extend. Move head up—arms extend & legs bend, back arches, head pushes back.	0 to 6 mo.
Tonic Labyrinthine Reflex (TLR)	In prone (on stomach). In supine (on back).	Prone: Present-dominance of flexor in arms, legs, hips. Supine: If present, increase in extensor tone in trunk/arms/legs.	0 to 4 mo.
Reflexes (Midbrain)			
Landau	Hold child in prone, adult's hand under trunk.	Will hold head up to some degree.	4 to 12 mo.
Amphibian	Lifting one side of hip while in prone position.	Arm & leg lifted side draw together, limbs of opposite side extend.	6 mo. to life

TABLE 37 (Continued)

Automatic Reactions			

Righting Reactions	*Stimulus*	*Response*	*Age*
Labyrinthine	Tip child forward, backward, or sideward, blindfolded, over tester's knees.	Head remains upright.	2 mo. to life
Optical Righting	Held in space, prone, supine, to either side over tester's knees.	Rights head automatically.	2–6 mo. to life
Body Righting: Acting on the Body	Supine position, turn head to one side.	Segmental turning—shoulder, trunk, pelvis, then legs.	7 mo. to 3 yrs.
Acting on the Head	Feet on ground or lay on either side on hard surface.	Rights head in space—brings into alignment with trunk of body.	4 mo. to 5 yrs.

Equilibrium Reactions	*Stimulus*	*Response*	*Age*
In Prone	Prone on tilt board, tilt to one side.	Head bends, body arches toward raised side; arms & legs straighten and come out from midline of body.	4–6 mos. to life
In Supine	Supine (back) on tilt board, tilt to one side.	Head bends, body arches toward raised side; arms & legs straighten and come out from midline of body.	7–10 mos. to life
In Sitting	Sitting—push to one side.	Side: Head moves to raised side, arms & legs straighten out from midline.	8–12 mos. to life
	Sitting—push backward.	Backward: Head, shoulders, arms move forward, legs straighten.	
In Quadra-pedal	On hands & knees—tip gently to one side.	Arm & leg on raised side straighten out from midline, opposite arm extends from midline as protective reaction.	10–12 mos. to life

TABLE 37 (Continued)

Automatic Reactions			
Equilibrium Reactions	*Stimulus*	*Response*	*Age*
In Standing	Standing position—pull outward on either arm.	Pull arm: Opposite arm & leg straighten outward & head rights itself.	12–18 mo. to life
	Hold under armpits & tilt backward.	Hold under armpits: Head, shoulders, arms move forward & feet point upward, bending at ankles.	

Automatic Reactions			
Supportive Reactions	*Stimulus*	*Response*	*Age*
Protective Extensor Thrust	Suspend child in air by ankles, move head quickly toward the floor.	Arms extend in direction of fall to protect head, fingers spread apart.	6 mo. to life

REFERENCES: Healy & Stainback, 1980; Fallen & Umansky, 1985; Bailey & Wolery, 1984; Lerner et al., 1987; Morrison et al., 1978.

The startle response indicates that the infant's neurological system is not mature enough to screen out such an overload of stimuli so that the sudden or loud stimulus courses, as a total shocking stimulus, to the young nervous system which, in turn, responds with a total body response in flexion (Morrison et al., 1978, 91).

The Babinski, grasp, and walking reflexes (Table 37) have no particular survival purpose for the infant, but indicate the immature and gross nature of his/her responses to stimuli (Morrison et al., 1978). These neonatal reflexes are integrated as the infant matures and disappear around 4 months of age (Table 37).

Reflexes which also occur in the newborn infant and indicate the pull of gravity on his/her immature system include ATNR, STNR, TLR, and neck righting (Table 37). These brainstem level reflexes should be inhibited by about six months of age to give the child more control of his/her body against gravity. The asymmetric tonic neck reflex (ATNR) occurs when the head is turned to one side, stimulating the arm and leg on the side the head faces to extend and the arm and leg on the opposite side to flex. The symmetric tonic neck reflex (STNR) occurs when the head is bent forward or backward. When the head is bent forward, the arms bend and the legs extend, but when the head is bent backward, the arms extend and the legs bend (Table 37). The tonic labyrinthine reflex (TLR) occurs as gravity affects the child in supine (on his back) or in prone (on his stomach). When the child is placed in supine, s/he extends the arms and legs, arches the back, and pushes the head back (Table 37). In prone, the child flexes his arms and legs and rests his head on his chest.

Reflexes emerging about 4–6 months of age which indicate a maturing central nervous system include the Landau and the Amphibian (Table 37). The Landau reflex is stimulated by holding the child in prone (on stomach) with the adult's hand under the trunk, and the child responds by holding the head up to some degree. This reflex response is incorporated by 12 months into similar purposeful behavior movements. The Amphibian reflex emerges about six months of age and continues throughout the lifetime. While in prone, if the individual lifts one side of his hip, the arm and leg of the lifted side draw together and the limbs of the opposite side extend. Thus, by six months of age, the immature reflex movements should be inhibited by emerging righting and equilibrium reactions giving the child more control over his environment.

Automatic Reactions

Automatic reactions begin emerging in the normal infant by about six months of age (Table 37). "Automatic reactions make the postural adjustments that assist in maintaining balance during movement, maintain the body in alignment with itself, and provide support when you are knocked off balance and/or falling" (Bailey & Wolery, 1984, 309). Automatic reactions include righting reactions, equilibrium reactions, and supportive reactions (Table 37). Reflexive patterns of movement, present at birth, must be inhibited by the development of righting and equilibrium reactions.

Righting Reactions

The righting reactions involve the tendency to keep the top part of the body uppermost and to maintain the head and body in their proper relationship to each other (Healy & Stainback, 1980, 15). Righting reactions (Table 37) including labyrinthine, optical righting, body righting acting on the body, and body righting acting on the head assist in maintaining body alignments to keep the head faced toward the front of the trunk with the eyes and mouth horizontal to the floor (Bailey & Wolery, 1984; Healy & Stainback, 1980; Fallen & Umansky, 1985).

"Righting reactions also provide the infant with the new component of rotation within the body axis (twisting of the trunk) as a means of accomplishing this alignment" (Haynes, 1983, 15). By about 9 months of age, the righting reactions are fully integrated; thus, the infant can rotate between shoulders and pelvis in prone to the sitting position, independently. Body righting acting on the body and body righting acting on the head are incorporated by ages 3–5 years, while the labyrinthine and optical righting continue to be present throughout life (Table 37).

Equilibrium Reactions

"The equilibrium reactions are balance reactions that use the righting reactions and modify them further. They take the form of either noticeable movements or infinitesimal changes in muscle tone, which must be felt rather than seen" (Haynes, 1983, 15). Equilibrium reactions include balance reactions in prone, supine, sitting, quadrapedal, and/or standing (Table 37). When the center of gravity is changed due to moving the body or its supporting surface, the equilibrium reactions cause the trunk and limbs to engage in compensatory movements in order to maintain balance (Bailey & Wolery, 1984). "The equilibrium reactions are the highest level of reaction and indicate an ability to adapt or move the body against gravity. This ability to adapt and balance in space begins at about 6 months of age and continues through life" (Healy & Stainback, 1980, 15).

Supportive Reactions

"Supportive reactions are movements of the legs and arms that assist in preventing and breaking falls" (Bailey & Wolery, 1984, 309). Protective Extensor Thrust (Table 37), or the Parachute Reflex, in which the child stretches out his/her arms to break a fall must be present before any attempt is made to teach the child to walk. This automatic reaction or reflex indicates activity at the midbrain level and is controlled by the cortex.

Gross Motor Development

Reflex development, postural development, locomotion, and fine motor skills development have an interactive developmental growth process. The immature brainstem level reflexes including ATNR, STNR, TLR, and neck righting (Table 37) are normally inhibited by six months of age, allowing the child to have more control over gravity by performing such motor tasks as rolling and sitting with support (Table 36).

Emerging about six months of age are the righting and equilibrium reactions which assist the child with postural control and balance during movement (Table 37). Righting reactions provide the infant a rotation movement, twisting the trunk, which allows the development of postural skills such as segmental rolling, rocking on hands and knees, assuming a sitting position, and locomotion skills of crawling and scooting (Table 36). Equilibrium reactions in prone, supine, sitting, quadrapedal, and standing assist the child with postural control and movement within the environment. Emerging about six months of age is the supportive reaction of protective extensor thrust or the parachute reflex, a midbrain level reflex which allows the child to break a fall during the unsteady months of learning to walk and run and in moving between various postural positions (Table 36).

In addition to the progressive postural and locomotor development, three other interrelative developmental processes including body image, spatial-temporal relations, and motor planning affect gross motor development. Body image starts to form in infancy with awareness and purposeful use of the hands, and the child develops as s/he learns about the body parts, how they move, and how much space it uses (Morrison et al., 1978). Body image and motor planning begin the interactive process at about 7 months of age when the child is able to pull up his legs and watch himself play with his toes, and rehearse mentally what he wants to do (Morrison et al., 1978). "He gradually becomes aware of spatial concepts through the process of experiencing his own body moving in space. Spatial relationships are among the first visual tasks to start and the last to fully develop" (Morrison et al., 1978, 98). "In motor planning, the child must have developed basic motor patterns, a sense of body image, and spatial relations in order to cognitively plan appropriate motions" (Morrison et al., 1978, 98).

The normal gross motor development of a 10-to-18-month-old child relies on good postural control, body image, and motor planning which allows the child to move from sitting to standing to squatting to kneeling, etc. during play (Table 36). Within 3 months, the average 15-month-old child progresses from walking alone with a toddler gait to walking with a lowered arm gait requiring more control and equilibrium movements.

The postural movements of the 19–24-month-old child are quite sophisticated, allowing movement between positions with relative ease during play. The average two-year-old walks pulling or pushing a toy, runs forward well, and walks up and down stairs holding the rail, one step at a time (Table 36). Thus, in the short span of two years, the normal child has progressed from a reflexive infant with no postural control and no locomotion skills to a fairly independent child, movement-wise, with good postural control, good locomotion skills of walking and running with relative ease, a sense of body image, and a sense of spatial relationships.

Fine Motor Development

"Prehensile skills—reaching, grasping, and manipulating—gradually develop as the grasp reflex is inhibited" (Fallen & Umansky, 1985, 205). Fine motor skills develop in a relatively predictable fashion. Hand and finger development includes the progression from pronation (palm up) to supination (palm down), from proximal shoulder joints to distal finger joints, and from ulnar (little finger side of the hand) to radial (thumb side of the hand) (Bailey & Wolery, 1985; Fallen & Umansky, 1985).

"Initially, infants exclusively use pronation; however, as they develop, they also acquire the ability to supinate the arm, greatly increasing the number of functional behaviors" (Bailey & Wolery, 1984, 323). Young infants are flexed and cannot extend their arms or use their hands well, but as they mature, they gain control of their extremities and, thus, develop from proximal to distal control.

The reflexive grasp observed in the 0-to-2-month-old infant is involuntary in nature and requires no thought or motor planning by the child. The 3-to-6-month-old child is making volitional movements as s/he reaches to touch or grasp, picks up something and mouths it, and voluntarily releases the objects, using the ulnar palmar grasp to hold an object with the little and ring fingers against the palm (Table 36).

Fine motor development occurs rapidly during the 7-to-9-month period as the child moves from the hand and palm grasp (7 months) to the radial digital grasp (8 months) using the thumb, index, and middle finger to grasp an object to the scissors grasp (9 months) using the thumb and side of the index finger to grasp an object (Table 36). The 7-to-9-month-old child can grasp and purposefully drop objects and transfer an object from one hand to another.

The 10-to-12-month-old child can use the pincer grasp (thumb and first finger) to pick up small items such as raisins while resting his/her arm on the table (Bailey & Wolery, 1984). The year-old child can bang two objects together, use his/her fingers individually, poke and probe with his/her index finger, and drop objects in a container (Table 36). "The child's ability to use these grasps is refined throughout the preschool years. The strength, speed, and coordination of these grasp patterns increase as children grow older" (Bailey & Wolery, 1984, 324).

The 18-month-old child can place objects on a table, use a stick to beat a drum, open and close simple containers, use his/her thumb for pressing, turn 2–3 pages of a book at a time, mark with a crayon, and put rings on a stick (Table 36). The two-year-old child is refining fine motor skills. S/he strings beads using both hands, plays with clay (rolls, pounds, squeezes, pulls), puts pegs into a pegboard, scribbles with a large crayon, pours from one container to another, turns knobs, unscrews lids, and builds a 6–7-block tower (Table 36).

Sensory Integration

According to Healy & Stainback (1980, 30), sensory integration involves the ability to process and channel stimuli received from the environment, which enables the child to produce a situationally appropriate motor response. A damaged central nervous system (CNS) may prevent the adequate channeling and processing of sensory stimuli and limit the child's ability to execute motor skill responses.

Ayres defines sensory integration as the ability to organize sensory information for functional use in producing an adaptive response (Lunnen, 1984, 301). Sensory integrative therapy is directed toward improving the brain's capacity to perceive, to remember, and to plan motor activity. Sensory integration and adaptive motor responses are the basis for facilitation of learning (Connolly, 1984).

Oral Motor Development

"The development of normal oral motor patterns for feeding, respiration, phonation, speech and language is a complex process influenced by reflexes, muscle tone, positioning, sensory integration, and behavior" (Lunnen, 1984, 293). Normally, oral motor skills follow a sequential acquisition pattern from reflexive behaviors at birth to good oral motor control by the end of the first year (Table 38).

Oral motor development is concerned with the coordination of sucking,

TABLE 38
ORAL MOTOR SKILLS: FEEDING/EATING

Age	Behavior
0–2 mos.	• Reflexes present: bite, rooting, suck-swallow
2–4 mos.	• Coordination of sucking, swallowing, & breathing • Lip control: mouth poises for nipple • Rooting reflex is gone
4–5 mos.	• Lip control: brings lips together at rim of cup • Tongue control: elevates to move food off roof of mouth • Tongue projects after spoon/nipple is removed (tongue thrust)
5–6 mos.	• Reflexes: tongue thrust decreasing, gag reflex diminished, bite reflex gone • Sucks liquid from cup • Lip control: makes smacking noises with lips; good lip closure • Tongue control: tongue reversal after spoon removal • Jaw control: pre-rotary chewing; moves mouth up and down, swallowing is completely voluntary
6–7 mos.	• Lip control: pulls food off spoon with lips; keeps lips closed while chewing; good control • Good tongue control
7–9 mos.	• Jaw control: bites cracker; enjoys chewing
9–10 mos.	• Tongue control: lateralization inside mouth begins; protrudes tongue purposfully; licks food off spoon • Drooling ceases • Jaw control: lateral movement of jaw
10–11 mos.	• Tongue control: lateral motion of tongue inside or outside mouth; lifts food from lower lip
11–13 mos.	• Reflexes: integrated • Lip control: good • Tongue control: good • Jaw control: chews well

REFERENCES: Copeland et al., 1976; Stillman, 1978; Fallen & Umansky, 1985.

swallowing, and breathing not only during eating, but also during prespeech vocalizations and speech. (Oral motor skills related to speech production, see "Oral Motor Prerequisites," Chapter 7.) The primary oral motor skills involved in the eating behaviors of sucking, swallowing, biting and chewing include tongue control (e.g., elevation, reversal, protrusion, lateralization), lip control (e.g., closure, manipulation), and jaw control (e.g., chewing, lateral movement).

ABNORMAL SENSORIMOTOR DEVELOPMENT

"Young children who lack normal motor experiences or who have delays in motor development are deprived of the foundation of the early learning process" (Lerner et al., 1987, 156–157). Atypical sensorimotor development impedes progress in all other developmental areas because early learning has a motor basis. Characteristics of sensory motor dysfunction in young children include the following: (1) remnants of primitive reflexes, (2) poorly developed righting and equilibrium reactions, (3) tactile deficits or sensitivity, (4) poor development of position, body image, or spatial relations, (5) defective or primitive motor planning ability (Morrison et al., 1978).

Atypical Sensorimotor Development

Motor impairments may manifest themselves as atypical motor stages or motor dysfunctions. The child whose motor milestones (Table 36) are different from the established norm may demonstrate one of the following atypical patterns: (1) stage skipping—skipping a regular stage to achieve a mature motor pattern earlier than expected, (2) stage deviation—remaining at an immature stage indefinitely due to failure to make significant progress, (3) partial stages—acquiring partial skills and not fitting into a particular patterns, and/or (4) stage lag—lingering at an early stage of skill development longer than expected, then passing quickly through several stages to a mature pattern (Lerner et al., 1987, 168–169). Deaf-blind severely multihandicapped children are frequently identified with the atypical motor pattern of stage deviation in which they remain at an immature stage indefinitely.

Motor dysfunctions may be categorized as deficits in muscle tone, muscle control, and muscle strength (Lerner et al., 1987, 169). Variables commonly associated with abnormal motor development include (1) inadequate integration of primitive reflexes, (2) sensory deprivation, and (3) lack of sensory integration (Healy & Stainback, 1980). Sensorimotor development may be delayed or impeded by a variety of sensory and motor impairments including impaired vision, impaired hearing, brain damage, and mental retardation.

Visual Impairment

In visually handicapped children, some stages of motor development are prolonged while the acquisition of others will be delayed. Sitting or standing can be achieved at a normal age, but crawling and walking are likely to be delayed and may need systematic programming during the initial stages of skill acquisition (Ellis, 1986).

During the sensorimotor stage developmental process, severely restricted vision may affect motor skill acquisition in numerous ways including the following: (1) delay visually directed reach and grasp because the infant does not see interesting objects within reach; (2) delay acquisition of the cognitive structure of object concept because parents are unable to use visual-linguistic marking of objects; (3) delay prelinguistic communication because the child does not automatically learn a gestural system; (4) delay acquisition of the concept of causality due to lack of reach and grasp, and reduced exploration; (5) delay locomotion skills of crawling and walking due to problems with balance, righting reactions, and equilibrium reactions; (6) reduce sensory-motor integration abilities which will hamper acquisition of concepts of spatial relationships, body image, and motor planning; and (7) impede generalization abilities.

Hearing Impairment

While communication problems of the hearing impaired are the obvious primary areas of concern, a lack of appropriate communication severely hampers all aspects of development. Cognitive skill acquisition is delayed due to a lack of verbal encoding for memory storage and a lack of or delay in symbolic representational thought. Deaf children tend to be egocentric and experience more emotional problems than nondeaf children. The lack of symbolic representational thought severely affects the development of play skills. Hearing-impaired children are often clumsy and awkward in their movements because the cause of their deafness may also have affected the vestibular or balance mechanisms of the inner ear (Morrison et al., 1978).

Mental Retardation

Research has consistently found mentally handicapped people to be inferior to non-handicapped subjects on measures of physical development, gross-motor, and fine-motor abilities (Anwar, 1986). A definite relationship exists between the severity of mental retardation and the severity of motor skill deficiencies (Fallen & Umansky, 1985). Since retardation represents a diffuse neurologic insult, most children who are severely or profoundly retarded also have serious physical handicaps (Lunnen, 1984). In severe retardation, even automatic movements may be carried out with a certain degree of inefficiency (Anwar, 1986). Although mentally retarded children generally lag behind their normal peers in motor skills, they appear to have a higher potential in this area than in other developmental areas (Fallen & Umansky, 1985).

Abnormal Reflexes and Automatic Reactions

Abnormal Reflex Development

Normal reflexive movement is gradually integrated as righting, equilibrium, and supportive reactions allow and encourage purposeful and voluntary movement, body image, spatial relations, and motor planning. The brainstem level reflexes (Table 37) should be integrated by six months of age. If this fails to occur, these primitive reflexes interfere with more purposeful movement.

The systematic tonic neck reflex (STNR) may occur in both the arms and legs. The STNR prevents a child from bringing his/her hand to mouth by extending or bending the arms. The child with persistent STNR may have difficulty in creeping as the arms will tend to collapse (flex) if the head goes down, and flexion of the lower extremities may be impossible if the head remains tilted forward (Healy & Stainback, 1980). The STNR also may interfere with the sitting posture if a downward head movement causes leg extension.

The asymmetric tonic neck reflex (ATNR) prevents a child from visually examining an object in his/her hand because the "fencing" position doesn't allow the child to bring both hands to midline simultaneously. Persistent startle (flexion reaction) and Moro (extension reaction) reflexes will result in the child being unable to voluntarily control arm movement and specifically unable to keep hands at midline.

Since the tonic labyrinthine reflex (TLR) in prone causes the head to rest on the chest and in supine, the head pushes back, many visual problems including visual pursuit, visually directed reach and grasp, and use of visual perceptual cues may be caused by TLR remaining a dominant reflex. "There is clinical evidence that retarded preschoolers demonstrate the TLR beyond the stage of development in which it is normally expected" (Morrison et al., 1978, 51). Tonic labyrinthine reflexes persisting beyond the normal stage of development may create an abnormal distribution of muscle tone which interferes with balance, the ability to raise the head, roll over, crawl, pull to sitting, etc. (Healy & Stainback, 1980).

Abnormal Automatic Reactions

Righting reactions (Table 37) begin to appear between two and four months of age. Righting reactions interact with each other to establish normal head and body relationships in space (Morrison et al., 1978). Righting reactions enable the child to roll over, stand up, and walk. Poorly interpreted or absent righting reactions cause problems in balance and ambulation. If body righting is absent, the flexibility necessary for most gross and fine motor movements is not present (Healy & Stainback, 1980). When neck righting is present beyond six months of age, the body rotates as a whole, which interferes with segmental rolling. If head righting is not present, the child may have difficulty developing balance. Abnormal head positions may interfere with general vision and with eye-hand coordination (Healy & Stainback, 1980). If labyrinthine righting reactions are not present, the child will be unable to raise his/her head to a normal position.

If equilibrium responses are impaired, the child may be unable to react quickly to changes in position, which may cause imbalance and a lack of flexibility in movement. Poor balance results in poor posture, difficulty performing fine motor tasks, and clumsy walking patterns (Healy & Stainback, 1980). Without the supportive reaction of protective extensor thrust, the child could fall from a sitting and/or standing position and be severely injured.

The reflexes and automatic reactions (righting, equilibrium, and supportive) have been studied as prognosticators for ambulation (walking). Nonambulators frequently have the following characteristics beyond six months of age: no protective extensor thrust, persistent asymmetric tonic neck reflex, Moro reflex, neonatal neck/body righting, and no rotational abilities.

Abnormal Muscle Tone

"Muscle tone refers to the potential a muscle has for action" (Lerner et al., 1987, 159). Passive muscle tone is the muscles' resistance to being

moved. Muscle strength or active muscle tone is the power of spontaneous or directed muscle movement. "Muscle tone is basic to many other
sensory-motor functions such as posture. It also reflects the amount of
proprioceptive input available to the central nervous system" (Morrison
et al., 1978, 14). Muscle tone has a range from high muscle tension and
tightness (hypertonic) to low muscle tension and flaccidness (hypotonic)
(Bailey & Wolery, 1978).

"All muscle action is controlled by the specialized centers of the brain"
(Lerner et al., 1987, 160). Abnormalities in motor development are often
a result of brain damage to motor centers. Muscle tone abnormalities
generally involve deficit muscle tone, muscle control, and/or muscle
strength. Muscle tone deficits generally involve hypotonicity (loss of
muscle tone) or hypertonicity (tight muscles). Deficits in muscle control
may appear as tremors (rapid, jerky, involuntary movements of the arms
and/or legs). Involuntary muscle vibrations impair the child's balance
and coordination" (Lerner et al., 1987, 169). Muscle weakness (paresis or
plegia) may be categorized according to the part(s) of the body affected.
The most common categorizations of muscle weakness include the
following: hemiplegia (right or left side of body affected), diplegia (two
limbs affected, generally legs), quadriplegia (all four limbs affected),
paraplegia (only the legs affected) (Denhoff, 1976).

Cerebral Palsy

Cerebral palsy is a condition that is a result of damage to motor areas
of the brain. This condition is suspected when a reflex seems unusually
strong or continues to be exhibited at a late age. Some of the early
indications of cerebral palsy are feeding problems including refusal or
difficulty in sucking, lack of head control, tight contracture (bending) of
the limbs, inability to grasp. Later problems include the inability to roll
over, to sit up, or to walk. The type of cerebral palsy is determined by the
location of damage to the brain. Cerebral palsy is frequently categorized
according to muscle tone deficits (spastic, rigid, and atonic) and muscle
control deficits (athetosis, ataxia, tremor, and chorea) (Wynn & O'Connor,
1978).

> *Spasticity* is characterized by increased muscle tone, stereotyped and
> limited patterns of movement, decrease in active and passive range of
> motion, tendency to develop contractures and deformities, persistence
> of primitive and tonic reflexes, and poor development of the postural
> reflex mechanism (Campbell, 1984, 409).

There are three primary types of spastic cerebral palsy including spastic hemiplegia, spastic diplegia, and spastic quadriplegia. Spastic heimplegia, the most common type of spastic cerebral palsy, affects one entire side of the body including face, neck, trunk, and extremities with abnormal muscle tone and movement (Campbell, 1984). Spastic diplegia, while affecting the whole body, exhibits greater involvement in the trunk and leg muscles. The spastic quadriplegic child exhibits hypertonicity in all extremities, head, neck and trunk, reducing the ability to move against gravity to very slight (Campbell, 1984). **Rigid cerebral palsy,** a very rare condition, is characterized by constant muscle tension in which the limbs are stiff and hard to bend.

Atonic cerebral palsy involves a condition of hypotonicity in which muscles are completely relaxed or flaccid. In a severe hypotonic condition, children take on a ragdoll appearance. Floppy children cannot control or coordinate their muscles, nor assume a stable posture. The atonic child characteristically assumes a frog-like position, both while awake and asleep. This posture, coupled with poor tone and a lack of voluntary movement, can lead to hip dislocation or other deformity (Haynes, 1983). The initially hypotonic infant may experience a change in muscle tone as s/he begins to develop in which the hypotonia is replaced by intermittent extensor spasticity (Haynes, 1983).

Cerebral palsy involving muscle control deficits include athetosis, ataxia, tremor, and chorea. **Athetosis** is characterized by jerky, involuntary, slow, irregular, and twisting movements. Involuntary movements occur when deliberate, voluntary exertion is made. In "pure athetosis," the postural tone varies between hypotonic and normal with involuntary slow and writhing movements (Haynes, 1984).

There are several types of athetosis; however, characteristic of all are fluctuations in muscle tone, resulting in almost constant uncoordinated movement. Major problems occur most frequently in the hands (fingers and wrists), then in the lips and tongue, and least often in the feet. The abnormal tone may prevent head control, resulting in an inability to control eye movement in focusing, tracking, etc. The abnormal tone may cause the tongue to thrust and the mouth to open, which interferes with chewing and swallowing and makes feeding difficult. Abnormal tone can also interfere with the respiratory control essential to the production of speech (Haynes, 1984). Involuntary motions and facial contortions inhibit the ability to smile or otherwise use body language to communicate (Haynes, 1984). Ambulation, if present, exhibits a very unusual gait, and frequently the child moves forward by means of a bunny-hop because of the stability it provides.

Ataxia is characterized by "awkwardness of fine and gross motor movements, especially lack of coordination and awkwardness in the movements required for balance, posture, and orientation in space" (Hallahan & Kauffman, 1978, 385). Ataxia is seldom seen in pure form, but is usually accompanied by athetosis, spasticity, or both. The ataxic child is unable to contract appropriately the opposing muscle groups needed to achieve stability and fluid movement (Haynes, 1984). These children tend to lock themselves into a few secure positions; thus movement generally involves primitive patterns of flexion and extension. Righting and equilibrium reactions may be absent or seen only part of the time; thus, the ambulating child is awkward, appears to be dizzy, and falls often (Haynes, 1984).

Tremor cerebral palsy and **chorea** are rare types of cerebral palsy. Tremor is characterized by small and rhythmic involuntary movement of the flexor and extensor muscles in the arms, fingers, and legs. Chorea involves dramatic rapid, jerky movements primarily in the arms and legs.

The cerebral palsied child frequently experiences secondary handicapping conditions in the areas of speech, hearing, and vision. Speech defects are of a neuromuscular nature and include voice disorders, rhythm disorders, and articulation disorders. Research indicates the two common hearing disorders associated with cerebral palsy are high-frequency deafness and central or cortical deafness (Marks, 1974). Additionally, cerebral palsied children appear to have higher incidences of visual disorders than normal children, including retrolental fibroplasia, nystagmus, and strabismus (Bobath, 1980).

Abnormal Joint Range of Motion

Joint range of movement depends on muscle length, bony alignment, and soft tissue flexibility. A joint can be restricted in its natural course of movement by tight muscles, misalignment of the bones, and soft tissue contractures.

Samilson's (1981) research indicated the incidence of hip subluxation or dislocation among the severely involved, neurologically immature, developmentally retarded individuals was 28%; and postures that predisposed to dislocation were hip flexion, adduction, scoliosis, and pelvic obliquity.

Static and dynamic joint deformities are a major concern of physical therapists. Static joint deformities develop as a result of prolonged positioning, while dynamic joint deformities are caused by imbalanced muscular forces (Bridgford, 1984). One of the most common dynamic deformities associated with unopposed voluntary muscle function is hip dislocation. Prolonged joint malalignment during weight-bearing can also produce static deformities. Initially, both types of joint deformity are supple, but become fixed or rigid as skeletal and connective tissue structures change in response to prolonged abnormal positioning.

Abnormal Gait

The ability to walk presupposes standing balance, and all of the reflexes and integrative mechanisms required in standing because they are utilized in walking (Paine & Oppé, 1966). Walking also requires alternate integration and timing of a number of associated movements which include alternately supporting the weight of the body and moving forward (Paine & Oppé, 1966).

Many mentally retarded children walk in a crouched posture due to the delay in motor maturation and balance, which can lead to fixed flexion deformities of the hips and knees (Lunnen, 1984). Mentally retarded children frequently walk with a wide base of support and arms held in a high guard position similar to the initial locomotion pattern adopted by young children learning to walk (Lunnen, 1984). Toe-walking, a typical gait pattern of severely and profoundly retarded children without cerebral palsy, may be due to sensory dysfunctions such as vestibular dysfunction accompanied by tactile defensiveness (Lunnen, 1984). Foot problems are common with mentally retarded children and often result in flat feet and the inability to establish a good heel-toe pattern (Lunnen, 1984). Gait problems resulting in abnormal medial rotation at the hip may be caused by abnormal muscle patterns of activity during gait (Campbell, 1984).

Different gait patterns are characteristic of a diversity of neurological and orthopedic abnormalities (Paine & Oppé, 1966). In the abnormal gait of cerebellar ataxia, the child walks on a wide base, staggering and lurching irregularly to either side, or swaying forward or backward, similar to the gait pattern with alcoholic intoxication (Paine & Oppé, 1966). The gait of spastic paraparesis is characterized by walking with a stiff, shuffling type of gait, scraping the toes, but also adducting the lower extremities so as to bump the knees against one another or to cross one foot in front of the other in a scissors gait (Paine & Oppé, 1966). Writhing contortions of the trunk and neck, a tendency to throw the head backward or from side to side, grimacing of the face, and grotesque and often writhing movements of the extremities are characteristic of athetoid cerebral palsies (Paine & Oppé, 1966, 147).

Abnormal Oral Motor Functioning

Severely handicapped children experience considerable difficulty often fatal as a result of poor oral motor function which may cause aspiration of food and/or pneumonia, a chemical reaction to aspiration of food and/or malnutrition (Lunnen, 1984). Many cerebral palsied children, especially athetoid, have a history of oral motor dysfunction including feeding problems, persistent primitive oral reflexes, drooling, and respiratory problems. Of particular concern is the hypoactive gag reflex which may contribute to aspiration or choking during feeding (Harris, 1984, 182).

Eating and feeding dysfunctions can be caused by a wide variety of neuromuscular and/or environmental conditions. Poor oral motor development may manifest itself as problems in sucking, swallowing, biting, chewing, jaw control, tongue control, and/or lip control. Difficulties in sucking, swallowing, biting, and chewing are indicators of neuromuscular or structural impairment (Fallen & Umansky, 1985).

Oral motor development may be negatively affected by immature reflexes such as tongue thrust and persistent ATNR, and by abnormal tone, either hypertonic or hypotonic, as it affects head and neck control. Adequate head and neck control are crucial to the alignment of the oropharynx and larynx which affects the speed and ease of the flow of liquids and food. Muscle tone, and the strength and endurance of the neck and trunk, affect the amount of energy expended during eating and the duration the child can sustain it (Blaskey, 1984).

Children suffering severe head injuries frequently require nasogastric tube feeding due to impaired swallow, gag, and cough reflexes. Severely handicapped, medically fragile, at-risk infants who have impaired suck, swallow, and gag reflexes often require nasogastric tube feeding. Prolonged nasogastric tube feeding often results in deprivation of oral sensation and, therefore delays the return or development of normal reflex responses for swallowing and preventing aspiration (Blaskey, 1984).

Eating/feeding problems may be caused by conditions or circumstances within the environment or physical setting. Some severely multihandicapped children become upset and refuse to eat due to excessive noises, bright lights, and/or interruptions during the feeding period. Children may develop dysfunctions due to allergies to certain foods. Various textures such as lumpy or changes in temperatures of the food may cause the child to reject food.

SENSORIMOTOR EVALUATION

Physical and occupational therapeutic evaluations determine the status of the child's motor development and any motor abnormalities. Therapeutic evaluations by physical and occupational therapists may not be performed without a prescription from the child's physician. A thorough therapeutic evaluation includes determining functioning abilities in the following areas: (1) motor development, (2) reflex development, (3) muscle tone, (4) muscle strength and function, (5) joint range of motion and muscle length, (6) posture, (7) sensory integration and processing, (8) gait, (9) respiratory status, and (10) activities of daily living (Table 39).

Motor Development Evaluation

Gross and Fine Motor Skills

The motor development evaluation is concerned with determining the child's progress toward normal developmental milestones in gross and fine motor skills. Normal gross motor developmental milestones include postural and locomotion abilities including the following: sitting with support (3 months), rolling over (4–6 months), sitting without support (7 months), pulls to sitting position (7–9 months), creeping (7–9 months), pulls to standing position (12 months), walking (12–18 months), and running (18–24 months) (Table 36). Normal fine motor developmental milestones include the following: Reflex grasp (0–3 months); purposeful reach and grasp (6 months); voluntary release (6 months); ulnar palm ar grasp (6 months); palmar grasp (7 months); radial-digital grasp (8 months); scissors grasp (9 months); pincer grasp (10 months); reaches out both arms to catch a ball (12 months); uses thumb for pressing (12–18 months); marks with crayon (12–18 months); strings beads, scribbles, builds block tower (19–24 months) (Table 36).

TABLE 39
PHYSICAL AND OCCUPATIONAL THERAPY EVALUATION

I. Motor Development
   A. Gross Motor Skills
   B. Fine Motor Skills
II. Reflex Development
   A. Brainstem Level
   B. Midbrain Level
   C. Automatic Reactions
      1. Righting Reactions
      2. Equilibrium Reactions
      3. Supportive Reactions
III. Muscle Tone
   A. Hypotonicity
   B. Hypertonicity
   C. Intermittent Tone
IV. Muscle Strength and Function
V. Joint Range of Motion and Muscle Length
VI. Posture
VII. Sensory Integration
VIII. Gait
IX. Respiratory Status
X. Activities of Daily Living
   A. Eating
   B. Toileting
   C. Dressing
   D. Grooming

Gross and fine motor skill development is generally assessed using a checklist of normal developmental motor sequences such as those Table 36. The **Callier-Azusa Scale** (Stillman, 1978), Motor Development subtests Postural Control, Locomotion, and Fine Motor Skills are useful in determining the developmental functioning level of deaf-blind severely multihandicapped children.

Documentation of degree of developmental motor delay is important for several reasons: (1) to qualify the child for placement in a special education or developmental disabilities program, (2) to justify the receipt of physical therapy services, and (3) to serve as a baseline measure in documenting change as a result of intervention (Harris, 1984, 179).

McInnes and Treffry (1982, 141) recommend caution in the use of developmental scales with deaf-blind children. "It must not be assumed that because he can perform tasks which are used in various developmental scales to indicate levels of development, he can perform all the tasks which normally preceded a particular level on the scale."

Reflex Development and Automatic Reactions Evaluation

A comprehensive reflex assessment is essential because the often extensive brain damage may be manifested in the persistence of primitive reflexes that interfere with normal development and predispose to asymmetries in muscle tone, sometimes leading to serious deformity (Lunnen, 1984, 288–289).

Primitive (brainstem) Reflexes

"The reflexes that originate in the brainstem affect changes in muscle tone throughout the body" (Morrison et al., 1978, 120). One significant screening that can be done with infants is to check for the absence of basic reflex patterns, righting, and equilibrium reactions. The appearance of brainstem level reflexes beyond six months of age indicates a delay in integration of the reflexes into normal movement patterns (Table 37). These immature reflexes (e.g., sucking, rooting, Moro, startle, Babinski, grasp, walking) can be tested by activating the stimulus and observing for the response (Table 37).

Neck righting is a primitive reflex that should be integrated by about 6 months of age (Table 37). In testing for neck righting, place the child on his/her back and turn the head to the side; if the reflex is present, the body will rotate as a whole (log roll) in the same direction as the head (Morrison et al., 1978).

The most significant brainstem level reflexes include the asymetric tonic neck reflex (ATNR), the symmetric tonic neck reflex (STNR), and the tonic labyrinthine reflex (TLR). The **ATNR** is tested by placing the child in supine (on back), with head in midline and arms and legs extended; then turn the child's head to one side (Table 37). If the reflex is not present and has been integrated into normal movement, there will be no reaction of the child's limbs on either side, but if the reflex is still present or poorly integrated, the arm and leg on the side the head faces will extend and the limbs on the opposite side will flex (Morrison et al., 1978, 120).

To test the **STNR,** the child is placed prone over the tester's knees and the head is moved up away from the body or moved down (Table 37). If the reflex is present, when the head is moved up away from the body, the arms will extend and the legs will flex, or when the head is moved down, the arms will extend and the legs will flex. If the symmetric tonic neck reflex has been integrated, there will be no change in the muscular tone of the arms and legs (Morrison et al., 1978).

The **tonic labyrintine reflex** can be tested by placing the child on his back. There should be no increase in extensor tone in the body if this reflex is absent; if present, there is an increase in extensor tone in trunk, arms, and legs (Morrison et al., 1978). TLR can be tested in prone; if reflex is present, there is a dominance of flexor tone in the arms, legs, and hips. If absent (normal), the child can assume and maintain a flexible pattern with head, arms, and legs off the floor (Morrison et al., 1978).

Midbrain Reflexes

The midbrain reflexes, Landau and Amphibian, can be tested by activating the stimulus and observing the response (Table 37). The **Landau** emerges about 4 months of age and should be integrated by 12 months. If the reflex is present, a child held in prone with the adult's hand under the trunk will hold his/her head up. The **Amphibian Reflex** emerges about six months of age and continues in effect throughout a lifetime. While in prone, if present, lifting one side of the hip will cause the arm and leg of the lifted side to draw together and the limbs of the opposite side to extend (Table 37).

Automatic Reactions (Righting Reactions)

Righting reactions interact with each other to establish normal head and body relationships in space. Righting reactions enable the child to roll over, stand up, and walk. Poorly integrated or absent righting reactions cause problems in balance and ambulation (Morrison et al., 1978, 125).

Labyrinthine righting emerges about 1–2 months of age and continues through life (Table 37). Labyrinthine righting can be assessed by blindfolding the child and alternately placing him/her in prone, supine, and on either side over the tester's knees. When the reflex is present, the reaction allows the child to raise the head to a vertical position; if not present, the child is unable to raise his/her head to a normal position (Morrison et al., 1978).

Optical righting emerges about two months of age and continues through life. To assess, use the same procedures as with labyrinthine righting, but use no blindfold (Table 37). If the reaction is present, the child rights his/her head automatically.

Body righting can be tested by placing the child in supine (on back) and turning the head to one side; if reflex is present, the body will turn segmentally—the shoulder, trunk, pelvis, then legs (Table 37).

Body Righting Acting on the Head emerges about four months of age and continues until five years. To test, hold the child vertically, placing his/her feet on the ground, or have the child lie on either side on a hard surface. If the righting reaction is present, the child will right his head, bringing it into alignment with the trunk of the body (Table 37).

Automatic Reactions (Equilibrium Reactions)

Equilibrium Reactions emerge prior to one year of age and continue through life.

Combined with righting reactions and other reflexes, equilibrium reactions make it possible to overcome the effects of gravity. The role of equilibrium reactions is to maintain the head and body against gravity in whatever posture the righting reactions bring the child (Morrison et al., 1978, 128).

Equilibrium reactions can be tested by tipping the child forward, backward, sideward in prone, supine, sitting on hands and knees, and standing (Table 37) "An absent or partial response is considered abnormal" (Morrison et al., 1978, 128).

Supportive Reactions

The **protective extensor thrust** emerges about six months of age and continues through life. To assess, suspend the child in the air by ankles or pelvis and move the child's head quickly toward the floor; if the reaction is present, the child will extend his arms, fingers spread apart, in the direction of the fall to protect the head (Table 37).

Muscle Tone Evaluation

Muscle tone is basic to many other sensorimotor functions such as posture. Muscle tone can be assessed by observing the infant and child in various activities requiring the use of muscles. Tone is evaluated in active and passive modes. Active tone is the power and adaptability of muscles during spontaneous movement, while passive tone refers to the resistance of the muscles when movements are imposed by the examiner (Wilson, 1984).

Muscle tone ranges from hypotonia (muscle weakness) to normal to hypertonus (muscle tightness). Children with normal tone can make quick and immediate postural adjustments during active movement, while in passive, the body parts can resist displacement and rapidly follow changing movements imposed by the examiner (Wilson, 1984).

Hypertonicity

Severe hypertonus is revealed as an unusual tightness in muscles and a stiffness in movements. It can be observed as stereotypic movements which prevent varied, differentiated movement. When rolling or crawling, the legs of the hypertonic child are not flexed appropriately and extensor movements dominate (Morrison et al., 1978). In hypertonic children, the rotational components of movement which normally emerge in prone-on-elbows, prone-on-hands, all fours, and standing fail to develop (Stengel et al., 1984).

Activities that require a response to the pull of gravity cause the hypertonic child to become tense and poorly coordinated (Morrison et al., 1978). In hypertonic children, if ambulation is achieved, they almost always walk without a heel strike. The fine skill patterns are impaired by high tone including isolated finger movement, thumb opposition, well-articulated speech, and efficient eye control (Stengel et al., 1984). The physical therapist uses systematic observation and trained hands in evaluating muscle tone.

Hypotonicity

Severe hypotonia, which may result from muscle weakness and impaired sensorimotor integration, is a common characteristic of the severely mentally retarded population when cerebral palsy and other defined neuro-musculoskeletal problems are excluded (Lunnen, 1984). Children with severe hypotonia have no resistance to imposed movement and inability to resist gravity (Wilson, 1984). Young hypotonic children may exhibit weak and inefficient sucking patterns with incomplete mouth closure; early hand-to-mouth behavior is accomplished by head turning rather than antigravity arm movement; and their arms and legs may be flat on a surface in a froglegged position (hips widely abducted and knees flexed) (Stengel et al., 1984; Morrison et al., 1978). They are frequently referred to as "floppy," or ragdoll-like. Low abdominal muscle tone can cause the belly to protrude and the lower ribs to flare out (Stengel et al., 1984). Head lifting often takes the form of "stacking" (Stengel et al., 1984).

Hypotonia interferes with acquisition of those motor skills requiring muscle strength, agility, and speed. The hypotonic child may have difficulty reacting to stimuli; sustaining the head, trunk, or limbs in a given position for any extended period of time; voluntarily changing positions; engaging in weight-bearing activities (Healy & Stainback, 1980).

Low muscle tone affects the development of skill patterns of the trunk and proximal joints. In older children, hypotonicity may be indicated by joints that may be hyperextended in order to compensate for lack of solid muscle tone (Morrison et al., 1978). "Unless severely affected, children with low tone will go on to develop motor milestones, albeit at a slower rate, in spite of diminished underlying postural competence. The movements and postures, however, have an immature appearance due to wide bases of support and lack of trunk rotation" (Stengel et al., 1984, 52).

Intermittent Tone

Dystonia is occasional and unpredictable resistance to postural changes or imposed movements. During active movement, tone may alternate between unpredictable resistance and normal adjustment, while during passive movement, tone may alternate between unpredictable resistance and complete absence of resistance (Wilson, 1984). The child with inter-mittent tone may have difficulty initiating active movement or sustaining posture (Wilson, 1984). When purposeful movement is attempted, the changes in tone may result in a loss of control over the movement involving both gross and/or fine motor skills (Healy & Stainback, 1980).

It is not rare to find that for one child, parts of his/her body may demonstrate appropriate muscle tone while other parts are either unusually hypertonic or hypotonic (Morrison et al., 1978). Young children who are at risk for cerebral palsy frequently experience abnormalities in muscle tone (Wilson, 1984).

Muscle Strength Evaluation

"It is very difficult to test muscle strength with any objectivity in the severely and profoundly retarded. One must extrapolate muscle capabili-ties from observation of general motor activity and posture" (Lunnen, 1984, 289). Normally, assessment of muscle strength involves determin-ing the relative strength of muscle groups in gravity-eliminated posi-tions and against gravity (Blaskey, 1984). Young or sensorimotor stage severely profoundly retarded children may be nonambulatory and may initiate little spontaneous activity. Thus, determining the strengths of individual muscles may be difficult because muscle endurance may be impaired from prolonged inactivity (Blaskey, 1984).

A muscle weakness is called paresis, while a total inability to move is called plegia (Lerner et al., 1987). Hemiplegia refers to a muscle weakness or paralysis on one entire side of the body including the face, neck, trunk, and extremities; diplegia refers to involvement in trunk and lower extremities; while quadriplegia involves total body involvement (Campbell, 1984). Thus the physical therapist uses systematic observation, active and passive movements, and postural control in assessing muscle strength.

Motor Function Evaluation

The quality and functioning level of a child's movement provides clues to his/her level of consciousness, cognition, sensation, sensorimotor integration, and neuromuscular status (Blaskey, 1984). An analysis of motor function is conducted by systematically observing a child's movements and comparing them to normal developmental expectations (Shepherd, 1984). In infants and nonambulatory severely multihandicapped children, motor function is evaluated by observing the following: (1) spontaneous movement and posture as the child lies in supine and prone positions and is handled, cuddled, and talked to, and (2) motor behavior during the testing of reflexes and reactions (Shepherd, 1984).

Observing ambulatory children during play and daily activities as they move in and out of various positions assists in identifying the influence of muscle tone, sensation, muscle strength and endurance, sensorimotor integration, and cognition on motor control (Blaskey, 1984). It is important to note whether movement occurs spontaneously or only in response to stimulation. The level of consciousness of the child determines whether the movement will be purposeful or random. Deficits in sensorimotor integration, impaired cognition, and decreased level of consciousness affect the functional use of motor patterns available (Blaskey, 1984).

Joint Range of Motion and Muscle Length Evaluation

Evaluation is conducted to determine the mobility of each joint as well as the length of key muscle groups. Problem areas can be identified by the physical therapist by observing spontaneously assumed postures in supine lying, sitting, and standing. These observations in combination with a gross assessment of passive range of motion can be used to identify the presence of clinically significant conditions including torticollis (twisted neck with inclined head); scoliosis (lateral curvature of the spine); pelvic obliquity (pelvis neither perpendicular nor parallel); obvious leg length discrepancy; and hip, knee, and ankle contractures (Bridgford, 1984).

A realistic goal for physical therapy is mobility that allows stable joint alignment for standing, sitting, and transfers.

Posture Evaluation

"The body must have good alignment of segments with respect to gravity and be evenly balanced to avoid strain and facilitate movement" (Morrison et al., 1978, 115). Good postural alignment helps to prevent back and limb deformities. The head, chest, and pelvis need to be aligned to give a midline. If well aligned, the body has symmetry. "One of the most obvious indications of good posture is the alignment of the child's body as he stands erect. Inadequate posture is observed in a protruding abdomen and/or buttocks, bent knees, and poorly aligned back as indicated by the spinal curve" (Morrison et al., 1978, 115–116).

Posture should be assessed in sitting, standing, and movement. Normal postural reactions include the following: (1) the ability and mobility to move antigravity (normal prone extension, supine flexion, right and left sidelying, lateral flexion), (2) the ability to right the head and trunk appropriately when the body moves or is moved, (3) appropriate synergistic fixation of proximal parts to dynamically stabilize distal parts (dependent on normal trunk control), and (4) the ability of the whole body (head, trunk, extremities) to respond appropriately and with coordination when the center of gravity is disturbed (equilibrium reactions) (Stengal et al., 1984, 56).

The postural reactions of equilibrium, righting, and protective extension are primarily responsible for a child's ability to gain and to maintain mobile posture against the force of gravity and the freedom of movement necessary to develop highly skilled activities. These reflexes were discussed earlier (Table 37). Assessment of older or higher functioning sensorimotor stage children can be conducted naturally as the child is encouraged through play to assume as many postures requiring resistance to the force of gravity as possible.

Abnormalities in posture may be due to structural defects, poor muscle tone, dominance of primitive reflexes, contracted muscles, and abnormalities in the kinesthetic-vestibular sense. Postural abnormalities may manifest themselves as poor balance in sitting, standing, raising or lowering self; standing on one leg; awkwardness or excessive swaying; lack of eye-hand coordination; and problems in midline crossing (Morrison et al., 1978).

Sensory Integration Evaluation

Sensory integration is usually assessed during the vision and hearing and secondary senses evaluation. Disorders that are identified by Ayres as exemplary of sensory integrative problems include vestibular system dysfunctions, tactile defensiveness, somatosensory (body awareness) dysfunctions, and visual perceptual disorders (Connolly, 1984). Sensorimotor integrative dysfunction may be caused by brain damage or sensory deprivation, either real or internal (Morrison et al., 1978).

Gait Evaluation

The physical therapist's gait evaluation should include the observation of a number of areas including the following: (1) position of the body as a whole, (2) muscle tone, (3) reciprocal, coordinated movements of the arms and legs, (4) maintenance of the head in midline, (5) focal point of the eyes, (6) stability of the hips, (7) heel-toe pattern, (8) size and speed of the steps, (9) degree of separation of the feet, (10) walking barefooted, walking with shoes, and walking with any customary braces or apparatus, (11) asymmetry of foot falls, (12) soles and heels of shoes, (13) ability to climb stairs, and (14) characteristic gait patterns (Lunnen, 1984; Campbell, 1984; Paine & Oppé, 1966). Electromyographic recordings during locomotion can determine patterns of muscle activation that are not identifiable with visual observation (Campbell, 1984). Systematic observation for the presence of characteristic abnormal gaits such as those evidenced by cerebral palsy types, toe walking, crouched posture, and immature walking postures and patterns provide clues to the particular neurological and orthopedic problems experienced by the child.

Respiratory Function Evaluation

"Respiratory problems are common in the multi-handicapped retarded child and can interfere with phonation, feeding, and general good health" (Lunnen, 1984, 295). Respiratory problems are frequently a result of a combination of the following conditions: (1) improper positioning, (2) weakness or spasticity in the respiratory muscles, (3) incoordination of oral motor and respiratory movements with frequent aspiration, (4) increased saliva production and inefficient means of clearing the throat, (5) allergies causing respiratory symptoms (Lunnen, 1984, 295).

The child's breathing pattern, ability to nose or mouth breathe, and state of congestion should be determined. Mouth breathers experience problems coordinating respiration and feeding, and have a tendency to aspirate food. Aspiration and aspiration pneumonia are significant causes of death among the mentally retarded (Lunnen, 1984). Noisy respiration is frequent, but the physical therapist needs to differentiate upper airway congestion from pneumonia.

Activities of Daily Living: Evaluation

Activities of daily living, frequently referred to as self-help skills, include eating, dressing, grooming, and toileting. Children functioning within the sensorimotor stage continue to function within the early stages of development in these areas (Table 40). The highest level of development attained is in the area of eating in which the child chews appropriately, feeds himself finger foods, and is learning to use equipment/utensils (straw, cup, spoon) by the age of two years. By the end of the sensorimotor stage, the child is learning to care for toileting needs (Table 40), but is not potty trained. The sensorimotor stage dressing skills include taking off the shoes and socks, but the child is unable to dress or completely undress himself. The sensorimotor stage child is totally dependent on others in the area of grooming, but is beginning to show an interest in tooth brushing (Table 40).

Activities of daily living are generally assessed by comparing the child's typical behaviors/skills to a norm list (e.g., Table 40) and/or using more formal assessment instruments such as the **Callier-Azusa Scale** (Stillman, 1978), Daily Living Skills subtests—Undressing and Dressing, Personal Hygiene, Development of Feeding Skills, and Toileting.

TABLE 40
ACTIVITIES OF DAILY LIVING: SENSORIMOTOR STAGE

Age (mos.)	Eating	Toileting	Dressing	Grooming
3– 6	• Holds bottle. • Begins to swallow from cup. • Sucks some solids from spoon. • Basic chewing begins.			
6– 9	• Brings bottle to mouth and holds alone. • Feeds self cookie. • Sucks food from spoon. • Uses scissor grasp to pick up foods.			
9–12	• Controls drooling. • More control over lips, tongue, & jaw. • Feeds self finger foods.	• Pays attention to acts of elimination.	• Holds out arm for sleeve.	
12–18	• Chews appropriately. • Grasps spoon & shows some use. • Holds cup by handle & lifts to mouth for sip.	• Indicates when elimination has occurred. • Dry following nap. • Begins to sit on potty.	• Takes off shoes & socks. • Tries to put on shoes.	
18–24	• Sucks using straw. • Begins to chew food with mouth closed.	• Daytime urination control (age 2). • Requires assistance with clothes & wiping.	• Finds large armhole. • Shows preference for for certain clothes.	• Attempts to brush teeth, modeling adult.

REFERENCES: Caplan, 1971; Fallen & Umansky, 1985; Stillman, 1978; Lerner et al., 1987.

Oral Motor Functioning Evaluation

The physical therapist's evaluation of oral motor functioning of severely multihandicapped children is an important prerequisite to developing an appropriate training program. The oral motor evaluation should occur during a typical feeding situation with attention to the following areas: (1) positioning, (2) special equipment, if needed, (3) type, texture, and temperature of food, (4) basic diet, (5) oral reflexes (e.g., rooting, sucking, swallowing, gag, bite, Babkin), (6) muscle tone, (7) tactile sensitivity of cheeks, lips, tongue, (8) jaw stability and facial musculature balance, (9) feeding behaviors (e.g., sucking, taking food from spoon, drinking from cup, biting and chewing, self-feeding) (Lunnen, 1984; Fallen & Umansky, 1985).

Sensory evaluation of the face, lips, gums, tongue, soft palate, and posterior pharyngeal wall may identify hypo- or hyper-sensitivity to touch. Perioral and intraoral hypersensitivity may result in a tonic bite and a gag that will interfere with the jaw opening to get food into the mouth (Blaskey, 1984). The reflex gag and cough are evaluated in all severely multihandicapped children. Blaskey (1984) indicates a reflex gag normally elicited on the posterior third of the tongue may be hypersensitive if it is elicited in the middle-to-anterior third, and may be diminished if it can only be elicited on the soft palate or posterior pharyngeal wall.

Swallow can be evaluated by placing a small amount of water in the side of the mouth with a straw. An audible swallow, multiple attempts to swallow, delayed initiation of swallow, or inadequate laryngeal excursion indicate incoordination and possible aspiration (Blaskey, 1984).

Adaptive Equipment and Environmental Conditions

The physical therapist needs to evaluate all aspects of daily living for the severely handicapped child. Transportation to and from school and necessary safety equipment to facilitate that transportation including appropriate wheelchairs, ramps, and bus chair lifts are a concern. The physical therapist must observe and evaluate procedures used in handling, positioning, feeding, and toileting the child to ensure safety and the best educational strategies to promote proper motor development.

> A child should have a variety of positioning alternatives that are comfortable, enable him or her to interact maximally with the environment, and provide the support necessary for the activity intended, but still stimulate independent mastery of the necessary postural stabilization (Lunnen, 1984, 296).

Adaptive equipment must be considered to determine needs during various daily activities, and to determine specific equipment to normalize abnormal developmental areas (e.g., tone, reflexes, posture), and to encourage gross and fine motor skill development. "Especially for the multihandicapped, nonambulatory child, the proper use of adaptive equipment can be one of the most important aspects of a therapeutic program" (Lunnen, 1984, 296).

Case Study Evaluation Reports

Case Study: Sally

Sally's sensorimotor evaluation report illustrates the functioning abilities of a nonambulatory deaf-blind severely multihandicapped child whose overall functioning is at the 0–1 month level (Table 41).

Case Study: Bud

Bud's sensorimotor evaluation report reveals the functioning abilities of an ambulatory child functioning within the 10–12 month range with splinter skills at the two-year level. He ambulates behind a pushcart and/or cruises along a wall with nudging. He uses the pincer grasp to pick up small objects, uses both hands at midline, and transfers an object from one hand to the other. Bud's oral motor skills are adequate for eating regular table food. He is learning self-feeding (Table 42).

SENSORIMOTOR DEVELOPMENT PROGRAMMING

At the sensorimotor functioning level, all learning involves motoric action—at first random, then purposeful. Thus, motor skill programming is not considered in isolation. Previously discussed programming in the areas of vision, hearing, and secondary senses all involve integration of sensory stimulation and motoric output. Cognitive skill development of causality, means-end, and imitation which are prerequisites to higher levels of learning and communication are learned through active involvement on the part of the child.

"Mentally retarded individuals characteristically have a short attention span and require extensive repetition for learning; therefore, consistency of treatment with frequent opportunity for practice and reinforcement is crucial" (Lunnen, 1984, 298). Mentally handicapped children also experience short-term memory problems and fail to generalize automatically; thus consistent repetition and practice are necessary all through the day in varied settings with varied caregivers/teachers to facilitate learning of carefully task-analyzed skills.

Therapeutic intervention involves teaching parents and school caregivers handling and positioning techniques, adapting equipment and the environment, and providing programming activities to promote motor development and sensory integration.

TABLE 41
SALLY'S MOTOR DEVELOPMENT EVALUATION REPORT

Case Study: Sally

Age: 4 years, 8 months

1. *Motor Development*

Sally was evaluated using the Callier-Azusa Scale and the Physical Therapist's Evaluation. Her overall functioning level was 0–1 month level.

Gross Motor. Sally has gross spontaneous movement in all extremities. She has a withdrawal reaction to foot stimulation. She has emerging head control. When supported prone, she can prop on her elbows and momentarily hold her head vertically. She can lift her head repeatedly when positioned in kneeling in the prone stander. When supine, she will turn her head (more right than left). Head control is poor. She has no rotational or functional trunk control. She turns her trunk and head when rotated at the hips to either side. Sally moves either arm randomly.

Fine Motor. Fine motor movement is limited to a fisted hand posture. Sally can bring either hand to her mouth using head turning and elbow bending.

2. *Reflexes and Automatic Reactions*

Reflexes. Sally has primitive reflexes which should have evolved into more complex reactions by six months of age. She has persistent asymmetrical tonic neck reflex (ATNR), neonatal neck righting, and extensor tongue thrust. She has tilting reactions emerging in prone.

Automatic Responses. Sally's righting reactions are poor. She has no equilibrium or supportive reactions.

3. & 4. *Muscle Tone/Muscle Strength and Function*

Sally has atonic cerebral palsy. She lies on her back in a frog-legged position. Her hamstring muscles are tight due to her legs being externally rotated when sitting or lying. Sally's muscle tone has been very changeable this year. She is either hypotonic (floppy) or appears hypertonic with an asymmetrical tonic neck reflex notable, especially in the legs. She postures her right leg in flexion and the left leg in extension.

5. *Joint Range of Motion*

Sally has hypotonicity and laxity (extra joint movement) within all joints. She has no joint restrictions.

6. *Posture*

Sally cannot maintain alignment. She does not have fixed deformities.

7. *Gait*

Sally is nonambulatory.

8. *Sensory Integration*

Sally is deaf-blind, functioning at the awareness level.

9. *Respiratory Status*

Sally breathes shallowly, using her ribs. She can nose or mouth breathe. She has a hypersensitive gag and does not readily aspirate food or drink.

10. *Activities of Daily Living*

Sally's daily living/self-help skills are at the 0–1 month developmental level, compatible with other developmental skills.

TABLE 41 (Continued)

Feeding/Oral Motor Function. Sally is fed ground table foods and drinks from the rim of a cup while positioned in her orthokinetic wheelchair. Muscle tone/sensation for oral structures appear decreased. Her tongue moves forward and back in a suckling pattern with food/drink staying within the central groove of her tongue. Sucking increases with consecutive sips of a drink. Lip closure is poor, so some spillage occurs when drinking from a cup. Her mouth is frequently open, gums hypertrophied, and drooling is present. She has some problems coordinating, sucking, swallowing, and breathing. Sally's gagging appears to be her way of clearing food from her airway since no coughing has been observed. She uses minimal tongue lateralization with biting on a food stimulus placed between teeth.

Dressing, Toileting, Grooming. Sally is totally dependent on caregiver in these self-help areas.

Handling Programming

Handling involves the touching, lifting, and/or manipulating of the child from position to position (Healy & Stainback, 1980). Handling techniques involve promoting head and trunk control and the proper way to carry the child. Learning to handle a child means knowing where to hold the child and how they will respond.

The hypotonic (floppy) child should be given firm support to maintain the head and body in a symmetrical position. A floppy child should never be pulled to sit by pulling on the arms. A hypotonic child needs firm shoulder support to facilitate head control. Rotation of a floppy child to a sitting position allows the child to use his/her neck muscles to stabilize his/her head. Firm support at the pelvis can promote trunk control. The floppy child should be supported so s/he can use his/her own muscles. The floppy child should be handled slowly and in a quiet environment to avoid overstimulation of the startle reflex (Morrison et al., 1978).

The hypertonic (spastic) child will get very stiff if s/he does not move frequently. Slow rotary (twisting) movements will decrease spasticity. A tight arm or leg will loosen up if slowly extended and rotated at the same time. Spasticity will get worse if you pull on the hands or wrists and let go quickly. In dressing a spastic child, cup the shoulder or elbow and push the arm through a sleeve rather than pulling the arms through by the hand or fingers. In trying to help a hypertonic child move or hold still, it is best to put your hands around the joints because the control is greater.

TABLE 42
BUD'S MOTOR DEVELOPMENT EVALUATION REPORT

Name: Bud
Age: 8 years, 7 months
1. *Motor Development*
    Gross Motor. Bud was administered *The Oregon Project Skills Inventory for Visually Impaired and Blind Preschool Children* and evaluated by the physical therapist. His gross motor skills functioning level was at the 11-month level with splinter skills at the 15-month level.
    Bud can roll from his stomach to his back and pull to a sitting position when grasping an adult's fingers. He maintains a sitting position without support, extending his arms to protect himself from falling. He moves to his stomach from a sitting position, and from his stomach to a standing position. He assumes a crawling stance and crawls on his hands and knees. Bud stands with minimum support from an adult and steps sideways holding onto a stationary object. He pulls himself to standing, lowers himself from standing to sitting, and walks with minimum aid.
    Bud rarely maintains static positions, usually moving about the classroom via four-point crawl or bunny hop. He prefers "W" sitting, but will sit with legs forward. He will pull up to stand via half-kneel when given hand assist, but when pulling to stand along furniture by himself, he relies on upper extremities and trunk, not using the half-kneel position. He ambulates well behind a small pushcart. Bud will cruise along a wall with nudging, both directions. He has shown improvement walking with one hand held, right better than left, while maintaining opposite hand on wall. He does not do well consistently; performance depends on behavior. He requires maximum support with stairs. Bud crawls over and around objects in the classroom. He seats himself with assistance in a small chair and uses the rocking horse.
    Fine Motor. Bud's fine motor skills functioning is at the 10-month level with splinter skills at the 14-month level.
    Bud can pick up an object using a palmar grasp, reach and grasp bright or sound-producing familiar objects in front of him, hold an object and examine it tactilely, squeeze objects, bang objects against a hard surface, and release objects. He uses both hands at the midline, transfers an object from one hand to another, and use a pincer grasp to pick up an object. He reaches with one hand from a crawling position, and can dump objects from a container. Splinter skills include pulling out large pegs from a pegboard and removing objects from a container one at a time.
2. *Reflexes and Automatic Reactions*
    Bud demonstrates upper extremity protective responses forward and to the side. He relies on excessive trunk flexion/extension to maintain balance.
3. *Muscle Tone*
4. *Muscle Strength and Function*
5. *Joint Range of Motion*
6. *Posture*
    Bud maintains sitting without support, uses a four-point crawl, and maintains balance moving among various positions, has adequate standing posture, and walks behind a pushcart.
7. *Sensory Integration*
    Bud is deaf-blind. He is consistently using tactile cues for locomotion and daily activities.

TABLE 42 (Continued)

8. *Gait*
   He uses a learner's gait pattern with arms extended for balance and to tactilely find location.

9. *Respiratory Status*
   No apparent concerns.

10. *Activities of Daily Living*
   Bud's performance on self-help skills indicates functioning on the 11-month level with splinter skills to the 26-month level.
   Feeding. Bud's oral motor skills are adequate for eating regular table foods. He tactilely feels for the spoon with his right hand. He needs hand-over-hand assistance for scooping, but usually brings spoon to his mouth independently. He signs "drink," picks up his cup and drinks independently, but releases it in midair. He has taste and tactile preferences with food. He picks up bite-sized foods. He does not consistently bite off an appropriate size from a sandwich.
   Dressing. At the two-year level, Bud independently on cue takes off an unfastened hat, pulls off socks, takes off shoes when laces are untied and loosened, and takes off shirt, jacket, or coat when unfastened. He assists while being dressed by pushing his head through the neck opening of a pullover shirt, putting his arms through the sleeves, and putting his legs through the pant legs. He assists while being diapered by raising his body.
   Toileting. He urinates in potty almost every time he is placed on it, but must be placed on potty every 50–70 minutes or will wet his diaper. Bowel movements are usually in potty, rarely in diaper.
   Grooming. Bud has no independent grooming skills.

Positioning Programming

The physical therapist assists the classroom teacher in planning and implementing appropriate positions and activities to promote more normal muscle tone, reflexes, and reactions. Positioning involves the arrangement of body parts to maximize normal postural alignments (Healy & Stainback, 1980). Proper positioning of a child also promotes comfort and avoids decubitus, promotes respiratory drainage, and provides different environmental experiences. Due to the advantages of frequent position change, the child should be repositioned every half hour.

A major objective of proper positioning is to assist the child in maintaining postural symmetry (Finnie, 1979). The neck, shoulders, hips, and knees are important focal points controlling the amount of muscle tone. During handling and positioning, these focal points should be supported. Providing support at the neck, shoulders, hips, and knees helps the child to relax and normalize tone.

The safety travel wheelchair is a very good system for providing support. Head straps, H straps across the chest; scoliosis adductor and abductor pads provide good alignment for activities, feeding, and transportation. In the wheelchair, the child should be positioned to insure hips are back and in the middle of the chair, feet are flat on the footrests, knees apart, and seat belts around the hips—not stomach.

In other seating arrangements, feet should be on the floor or on a box or stool, and the body symmetrical. An inner tube, a foam piece, and a wedge can be used to provide good support for a hypotonic child. Chairs without legs are good seating arrangements for children with tight knees. When sitting on the floor, do not allow the child to sit in the "W" position. Sitting in the "W" position and bunny hopping are detrimental because they discourage the development of extension, abduction, and external rotation, which are important components of a normal walking pattern (Haynes, 1983).

Lying a child on his/her stomach with a roll or wedge under his/her arms is an excellent position for practicing head control and helping to control arms. Positioning can be used effectively to inhibit primitive reflexes (Bailey & Wolery, 1984). The effects of ATNR (Table 37) can be reduced by encouraging midline rather than side activities and/or by having the child lie comfortably on his/her side, supported by bolsters or small pillows if necessary to maintain a straight body (Morrison et al., 1978).

The hypotonic (floppy) child should not be permitted to sleep or lie in the frog-like posture because deformities can occur from this position. Haynes (1983) suggests preventing the frog-like posture by allowing the child to lie in a hammock or on a partially inflated air mattress or sidelying between two long bolsters.

The hypotonic child requires positioning that will insure symmetrical alignment of the head and body in lying, sitting, and standing. These children usually require head, back, and side support in all positions. In order to insure stability of position, seat belts, foot straps, shoulder straps, and head straps are useful.

The hypertonic child needs to be secured in a symmetrical position to inhibit extreme muscle tone from pulling parts of the body out of alignment. Seat belts, foot straps, and rolled seats are helpful in maintaining knee and hip flexion, and back supports and side bolsters aid in maintaining a straight spine.

Adaptive Equipment Programming

Adaptive equipment has become an integral part of therapeutic, educational, and home management programs for severely handicapped children with central nervous system (CNS) dysfunction (Lunnen, 1984). Adaptive equipment is used for a variety of reasons including the following: (1) to provide greater opportunities for independence, (2) to prevent contractures and deformities, (3) to encourage active movement and greater variety of movement, (4) to reinforce normal movement components such as alignment, weight shift, and postural alignment, and (5) to provide mobility and encourage exploration (Lunnen, 1984). Basic types of adaptive equipment include the wedge, the bolster, the prone board, and modified chairs (Bailey & Wolery, 1984).

The Wedge

The wedge is a very versatile, sloped piece of equipment usually made of foam rubber, or wood covered with padding. "The wedge is used to normalize tone, increase neck strength, and facilitate working at midline rather than to the side" (Bailey & Wolery, 1984, 313). The foam rubber wedge is usually used with hypertonic children, while the solid wooden wedge is used with hyptotonic children (Campbell et al., 1977).

In using the wedge, the child is generally positioned prone (on stomach) on the wedge with feet at the lower end and head toward the higher end in such a way that the shoulders and arms are over the front end with elbows resting on the floor. The joint compression from partial weight-bearing on the elbows tends to stimulate the shoulder muscles to contract and makes it easier for the child to lift his/her head to see people and things, and to extend the upper spine against gravity (Haynes, 1983).

The wedge is frequently used in combination with other equipment to provide appropriate positioning. The wedge may be used as a foot rest for proper positioning of legs and feet. Two wedges may be combined to provide positioning to encourage better respiratory functioning and postural drainage.

The Bolster

The bolster is a rolled pillow, or carpet roll secured with tape to prevent unrolling. It is used in numerous ways to support a child and provide better positioning. A bolster is frequently used to modify chairs to provide better positioning.

In prone, a bolster can be placed under the child's chest with elbows resting on the floor to provide similar benefits as the wedge in stimulating muscle contraction and head lifting.

Prone Board

A prone board promotes increased stability in the upright position by encouraging weight bearing on the hips and legs in proper alignment, thus freeing the hands for fine motor activities (Haynes, 1983). The prone board not only encourages weight bearing, but also improves digestive functions and cardiac conditioning. A child can initially be placed on the prone board kneeling to build up muscles and weight bearing abilities, and eventually be placed on it in a standing weight-bearing position—a prerequisite to walking.

Modified Chairs

Therapists frequently modify chairs for the physically handicapped child to promote a symmetrical sitting posture. Bolsters are very effective in individually adapting chairs.

Bolsters are frequently used in individually adapting highchairs and rocking chairs. A barrel chair, cut out and padded, helps to provide adequate support for a spastic child who needs to decrease muscle tone in order to sit well.

Motor Activities Programming

Activities have a multiplicity of purposes including (1) inhibiting abnormal or immature reflexive patterns, (2) normalizing postural tone, (3) promoting righting, balance, coordination, and sensory stimulation, and (4) promoting movement. The physical/occupational therapists play a major role in determining the appropriate activities for each child.

Activities Inhibiting Reflexive Patterns

Lying on the side is the position of choice to counteract the effect of gravity and the stimulation of the asymmetric tonic neck reflex (ATNR) and symmetric tonic neck reflex (STNR) (Morrison, et al., 1978). Creeping in a circle pattern pushing a toy car encourages inhibiting remnant ATNR; scooterboard activities encourage integration of tonic neck reflex (TNR) and optical righting reactions (Morrison et al., 1978).

Righting, Balance, and Coordination Reactions Activities

Righting reactions are stimulated in a number of ways. Rolling encourages head turning and developing body righting reactions. Somersaulting stimulates the integration of righting reactions by providing vestibular stimulation.

"The ability to be able to sit is dependent on head control, trunk control, and balance" (Morrison et al., 1978, 143). Sitting balance can be stimulated by placing the child on a bolster or ball with some chest support and rocking it back and forth. To encourage the development of an internal balance mechanism, the seated child should be given a toy to play with so s/he does not use his/her hands for support (Morrison et al., 1978).

Tilting surfaces are used to promote balance reactions in prone, supine, sitting, kneeling, or standing. Tilt boards, swings, and therapeutic balls can be used to encourage balance reactions. Physical therapists frequently assist students with developing trunk rotation skills, propping on elbows, sitting balance, and protective reactions using the therapeutic ball.

Facilitating fluent motor skills requires practicing changing positions and moving from one position to another without loss of balance. Coming to a sitting position and coming to a standing position are movement skills that need to be practiced by physically handicapped children.

Balance beam walking can help the ambulatory child with poorly integrated righting reactions to develop equilibrium because this activity fosters coordination of muscle reactions, motor planning, and spatial relationships (Morrison et al., 1978). Twist board activities aim at normalizing poorly integrated righting reactions and helping the child develop balance, trunk rotation, and bilateral coordination through vestibular stimulation (Morrison et al., 1978).

Barrel activities provide a variety of benefits including the following: (1) rolling inside the barrel provides vestibular stimulation, (2) balancing on top stimulates labyrinthine, optical righting, and equilibrium reactions, (3) rolling over the barrel can stimulate the automatic reaction of protective extension, and (4) pushing the barrel stimulates good postural tone (Morrison et al., 1978).

Gross Motor Skills Activities

Nonhandicapped children follow a normal developmental sequence of gross motor skills (Table 36). The appropriate gross motor skills for the early childhood years develop balance, strength, flexibility, endurance, locomotor skills, throwing, catching, kicking, self-help care, and body image skills (Fallen & Umansky, 1985).

Handicapped children usually follow the same developmental sequence of skills but at a slower pace than nonhandicapped children. "Teachers may need to encourage the development of basic gross motor skills, facilitate the acquisition of more advanced motor attainments, or improve the accuracy or speed of already acquired movements" (Bailey & Wolery, 1984, 317).

The development of gross motor skills in deaf-blind severely/profoundly multihandicapped children involves specific programming by the physical therapist to inhibit immature reflexes; to encourage righting, balance, and protective reactions; to make specific modifications regarding muscle tone and joint range of motion; to encourage the development of muscle strength and weight bearing; to assist postural development; and eventually to promote locomotion. Adaptive equipment is frequently required to facilitate development of gross motor skills in severely multihandicapped children.

A wide variety of toys and equipment is generally used to assist with gross motor skill development including various sizes of chairs, tables, rocking chairs, swings, rocking horse, slides, mats, walking boards, trampolines, air mattresses, stairs, tricycles, scooterboards, tumble tubs, bolsters of various sizes, barrels, twist boards, tilt boards, spinning toys, balls of various sizes, and rhythm band musical instruments.

Children learning to sit should practice sitting on a wide variety of equipment and on the floor. Small toys of interest (e.g., musical, lighted, moving) encourage children to play or explore the toy with their hands while simultaneously developing trunk strength to promote balance. Learning to roll a ball and to play rhythm band instruments also facilitates sitting.

A wide variety of small toys placed in various locations about the room can encourage exploration by the crawling child. Transilluminated (lighted) and audio toys may be used to assist in localization. Crawling through a cardboard box or tunnel (e.g., several opened cardboard boxes placed end to end) can be enjoyable.

Push and pull toys encourage children learning to walk. A variety of lightweight balls, bean bags, cotton or felt balls stuffed with nylons, and large balloons may be used in developing throwing and catching skills.

The physical therapist and/or adaptive physical education teacher have the major responsibility for planning and facilitating gross motor skills development. They are responsible for training and assisting the classroom teacher in organizing the classroom to encourage gross motor skills development. They should be pivotal members of the team that provides services to severely multihandicapped children functioning at the sensorimotor stage.

Case Study: Sally.

Sally's gross motor skills evaluation determined that she is currently functioning on a 0–1 month level with emerging head control (Table 41). Thus, her gross motor IEP objectives aim not only to improve head control, but also to encourage balance and righting reactions (Table 36).

Sally's IEP

Gross Motor Goal: Sally will improve head control and automatic reactions.

Objective A: Sally will be able to lift her head while kneeling in a prone stander on 12 out of 15 trials during a 20-minute period on 3 consecutive data days as implemented by teacher/assistant under physical therapist supervision.

Objective B: Sally will be able to turn her head to right/left side when supine and tilted on a Merry Molehill on 4 out of 5 trials on 3 consecutive data days as implemented by teacher/assistant under physical therapist supervision.

Objective C: Sally will be able to turn her head to right or left side when prone and tilted on a Merry Molehill on 4 out of 5 trials on 3 consecutive data days as implemented by teacher/assistant under physical therapist supervision.

Case Study: Bud. Bud's gross motor evaluation (Table 42) indicates functioning at the 11-month level. He moves freely among various positions (e.g., sitting, crawling, standing) and uses balancing and righting reactions. While he ambulates well behind a small pushcart, he experiences difficulty when walking with one hand held. He also experiences difficulty pulling up to stand independently. Thus, his gross motor goal is to improve mobility skills.

Bud's IEP

Gross Motor Goal: Bud will improve mobility skills.

Objective A: Bud will pull to stand beside furniture independently using the half-kneel position rather than total reliance on upper extremities and trunk on 4 out of 5 trials on 3 consecutive data days as implemented by teacher/assistant under physical therapists's supervision.

Objective B: Bud will walk forward 100 feet with one hand held on 4 out of 5 trials on 3 consecutive data days as implemented by teacher/assistant under physical therapist's guidance.

Objective C: Bud will walk up stairs with minimum support (e.g., one hand held and one hand on railing) on 4 out of 5 trials on 3 consecutive data days as implemented by teacher/assistant under physical therapist's supervision.

Fine Motor Skills Activities

Fine motor skills involve the development of the efficient and accurate use of the hands and fingers. Fine motor skills normally develop in a predictable sequence among non-handicapped children (Table 36). The main objectives of a fine motor development program include the following: (1) facilitating grasp acquisition and refinement, (2) eye-hand coordination, (3) developing specific arm movements while maintaining grasp on objects, (4) independent play, (5) persistence at tasks, (6) social skills such as turntaking, and (6) cognitive skills such as part-whole relationships, size, form, color relationships, and problem-solving (Bailey & Wolery, 1984).

Programming in the area of fine motor skills generally involves the child using numerous kinds of manipulatives. Toys and manipulatives need to be carefully evaluated to insure that they facilitate skill development in the desired areas. The primary fine motor skills to be developed during the sensorimotor stage include the following skills: (1) grasp and release, (2) finger control, (3) eye-hand coordination, and (4) arm movements while grasping, which can be facilitated by a wide variety of activities (Table 43).

Prior to any fine motor activity, each child must be positioned appropriately, which may include adapting equipment to provide the best learning situation. "Children with poor sitting balance need to have enough physical support so that they won't be concerned or distracted from the task" (Kieran et al., 1980, 94). Stabilizing the child at the hips will usually provide him/her with enough support so that s/he can use the trunk and arms without difficulty (Finnie, 1979).

Orthopedically handicapped children frequently require special assistance in order to be successful. Cerebral palsied children may become over-excited and stiff during activities, so the teacher should use a calm, encouraging voice rather than a loud, cheering, excited voice. If an arthritic child's hands are too stiff to enjoy manipulating play dough or clay, his/her hands may be soaked in warm water prior to the activity (Kieran et al., 1980).

Deaf-blind severely multihandicapped children may require numerous adaptations prior to activities. Each case must be considered individually regarding amount of residual vision and functional usage, amount of residual hearing and functional usage, communication mode, gross motor abilities including reflexes, and righting and balance reactions. Regardless, deaf-blind severely multihandicapped children will require individual adaptations and one-on-one direct teaching in order to be successful.

Direct teaching of fine motor skills involves a number of specialized techniques. It may involve using the adult's hand over the child's hand (hand-over-hand) during initial training as the adult manipulates the child's hand in completing the activity. Gradually, the adult's assistance is phased out. Direct teaching involves the teacher modeling the task, directing the practice, and supervising independent task performance. With deaf-blind severely multihandicapped children, the learning of a new task may involve co-active movement as the child and teacher move together, feeling the gross and fine motor movements involved in task completion. Deaf-blind children may need tactile cues in order to understand the expectations of the task.

Case Study: Sally. Sally's overall functioning is at the 0–1 month level. No fine motor goals were planned for her.

TABLE 43
FINE MOTOR SKILLS ACTIVITIES

Grasp and Release Activities	Finger Control Activities

• *Fill N' Dump Activities:*
    6–12 months use containers with large opening (milk carton, coffee can, oatmeal box) and small objects to place in containers and dump out (spools, measuring spoons, clothespins, corks, poker chips). *12–24 months* decrease size of container and opening (plastic milk bottle).
 	
• *Water Play:* Use warm water and many items—sponges and shampoo bottles for squeezing, spoons, bowls, containers with/without spouts, eggbeaters, cups, tubes, straws, funnels, water toys.
• *Sand Play:* Use many of the water toys plus shovels, spoons, buckets.
• *Animal Cage:* Put spring-type clothespins around the rim of a box to make cage.
• Squeeze nerf balls and squeeze toys.
• Pick up small items such as raisins and put in bowl.
	• *Play Dough:* Good for poking, pinching, grasping, squeezing, holding, pulling, rolling.
	
	• *Finger Paint:* With pudding (Chap. 4), with vaseline on waxed paper.
	
	• *Gadget Board:* manipulate locks, latches, plugs, zippers, levers, snaps, buttons.
	• Play "Itzy Bitzy" Spider.
	• *Easel Painting*
	• *Opens & Closes Containers:*
	    Opens & closes match boxes, crayon boxes, plastic refrigerator containers, bandaid boxes, unscrews lids.
	• *Presses Buttons with Thumb*
	• *Turns Knobs*
	• *Winds Up Toys & Music Boxes*
	• *Rings Small Bells*
	• *Finger Puppet Games*
	• *Unwraps small packages and wrapped candy*

Arm Movements While Maintaining Grasp Activities

Eye-Hand Coordination	
• Place objects in container. • Puts rings on stick. • Strings large beads. • Puts pegs in pegboard. • Scribbles with large crayon. • Pours from one container to another. • Build block, box tower (attach velcro to blocks/boxes to help stack). • Sand/water play. • Cut stiffened jello into squares with dull knife/spatula. • Make *collage* —activities (paste, tear, place, pat). Materials: paper, paper plates, foam meat trays, egg cartons, pictures, yarn, buttons, foam bits, wood pieces, beans, macaroni, etc. • Pop beads. • Build with magnetized marbles.	• Sand/water play • *Make Music:* Hit drum with sticks, play tambourine (pie tin with pop bottle caps), shake string of bells. • Tear paper/cloth. • Use cookie cutters to cut out play dough, finger jello, etc.). • Shake small marshmallows from a cubical tissue box. • Pour tinted water from plastic syrup bottle into large mixing bowl. • Stack empty boxes/empty cans.

REFERENCES: Kieran et al., 1980; Lerner et al., 1987; Fallen & Umansky, 1985; Bailey & Wolery, 1984; Pope, Undated.

Case Study: Bud. Bud's fine motor evaluation (Table 42) indicates functioning on the 10-month level with splinter skills to the 14-month level. His fine motor objectives aim not only to improve fine motor skills, but also to learn eating prerequisite skills that generalize to replacing his cup gently on the table.

Bud's IEP

Fine Motor Goal:	Bud will improve fine motor control.
Objective A:	Bud will place small objects (e.g., spools, corks, poker chips) into a wide-mouth container (e.g., coffee can) (after picking them up on cue) on 4 out of 5 trials on 3 consecutive data days as implemented by teacher/assistant under occupational therapist's supervision.
Objective B:	Bud will place objects (e.g., spoons, plastic cups, small plastic bottles) on the table without dropping after picking them up on cue on 4 out of 5 trials on 3 consecutive data days as implemented by teacher/assistant under occupational therapist's supervision.

Activities to Prevent Respiratory Problems

Infants and children with severe hypotonia may show evidence of stridor, a harsh respiratory sound caused by intrinsic or extrinsic blockage of the upper airway (Haynes, 1983). A high-pitched noise is likely to be the result of obstruction of the laryngeal level while a low-pitched noise is likely to be caused by tracheal problems (Haynes, 1983).

Frequent change of position in the severely handicapped child is probably the single most important measure for preventing respiratory problems. Periodic positioning on a wedge with the head toward the lower end facilitates postural drainage and respiratory health. Proper positioning will help to prevent rib cage deformity and pooling of secretions and will facilitate improved chest excursion (Lunnen, 1984).

Self-Help Skills Activities

The development of self-help skills are extremely important to handicapped children in promoting normalcy, acceptance, and socialization as well as enhancing their educational situation. The self-help skills of eating, dressing, toileting, and grooming normally develop in a sequential manner closely related to the child's development in oral-motor skills (Table 38) and fine and gross motor skills (Table 44). It should be noted that the acquisition of specific motor skills serves as prerequisites for various self-help skills. Thus, it is extremely important that the classroom teacher, occupational and physical therapists work very closely as a team in planning specific individual educational programs, specific task-analyzed sequences, specific modifications, and adaptive equipment for deaf-blind severely multihandicapped children.

Before significant progress in self-help skills can be made, strategies for inhibiting any abnormal reflex patterns should be identified and implemented (Fallen & Umansky, 1985). The child's specific area of concern including hypertonicity or hypotonicity, status of righting and balance reactions, joint range of motion, muscle strength and function, any respiratory or medical conditions must be considered in planning a specific self-help skills developmental program. Additionally, the programs of deaf-blind children will need to be planned around utilization of any residual vision and/or hearing abilities, input from the secondary senses, and the primary communication mode.

Feeding/Eating Programming. The major problems interfering with the acquisition of feeding/eating skills with severely handicapped children include low levels of cognition and consciousness, hyper- or hypo- sensitivity to stimulation, and poor head and trunk control (Blaskey, 1984). For children who are hypersensitive, desensitization may be necessary preceding each feeding session. Techniques of desensitization such as firm pressure on the lips, firm stroking of the gums, firm stroking and pressure with a tongue blade intraorally and on the tongue assist in inhibiting hypersensitivity that may result in tonic bite, reflexive gag, and problems with jaw opening (Blaskey, 1984).

A program designed to address feeding/eating problems of severely handicapped children frequently involves the use of proper positioning and handling of the children to minimize abnormal reflex patterns and to enhance and support the most normal patterns of movement (Fallen & Umansky, 1985). Positioning is especially important during feeding to prevent respiratory problems. For feeding, the child should be positioned with the trunk at a minimum of a 45° angle (seated at 90° is preferable) with the head balanced in a neutral position between flexion and extension (Lunnen, 1984). If the neck is allowed to extend in what has been

TABLE 44

INTERRELATED MOTOR AND SELF-HELP SKILLS DEVELOPMENT

	Age		
	3-6 mos.	*6-9 mos.*	*9-12 mos.*
MOTOR SKILLS:			
Gross	• Sits in highchair.	• Sits alone, arms free. • Stands holding furniture. • Pushes up on hands & knees.	• Pulls to stand by using furniture. • From sitting position, squats to play. • Pulls from sitting to standing. • Walks with help.
Fine	• Hand to mouth behavior. • Plays with hands at midline. • Purposeful reach & grasp.	• Transfers objects hand to hand. • Moves fingers with some control. • Scissors grasp.	• Pincer grasp. • Pokes & probes with index finger. • Reaches out both arms to catch ball. • Uses arms & hands to hold object.
	3-6 mos.	*6-9 mos.*	*9-12 mos.*
SELF-HELP SKILLS:			
Eating	• Holds bottle. • Begins to swallow from cup. • Sucks some solids from spoon. • Basic chewing begins.	• Brings bottle to mouth & holds alone. • Feeds self cookie. • Sucks food from spoon. • Uses scissor grasp to pick up food.	• Controls drooling. • More control over lips, tongue, jaw. • Feeds self finger foods.
Toileting			• Pays attention to acts of elimination.
Dressing			• Holds out arm for sleeve.
Grooming			
	12-18 mo.		*19-24 mos.*
MOTOR SKILLS:			
Gross	• Stands—arm free to play. • Walks alone. • Sits down, bending knees from free standing in one position. • From standing, squats to play. • Seats self in small chair.		• Throws ball overhand. • Squats to pick up object & re-erects. • Gets down from adult chair. • Runs stiffly. • Walks up & down stairs holding rail. • Walks pulling, pushing, or holding toy.

TABLE 44 (Continued)

Fine	• Uses stick to beat drum. • Places objects in container. • Places objects on table without dropping.	• Strings beads using both hands. • Plays with play dough (rolls, pounds, squeezes, pulls). • Puts pegs in pegboard. • Pours from 1 container to another. • Turns knobs. • Unscrews lids.

SELF–HELP SKILLS:

Eating	• Chews appropriately. • Grasps spoon & shows some use. • Holds cup by handle & lifts to mouth for sip.	• Sucks using straw. • Begins to chew food with mouth closed. • Uses spoon, spilling little. • Drinks from cup with 1 hand unassisted.
Toileting	• Indicates when elimination has occurred. • Dry following nap. • Begins to sit on potty.	• Daytime urination control (age 2). • Requires assistance with clothes & wiping. • Dry following nap.
Dressing	• Takes off shoes & socks. • Tries to put on shoes.	• Finds large armhole. • Shows preference for certain clothes. • Removes pants/sweater. • Unzips large zipper (jacket). • Attempts putting on some clothes independently. • Puts arms in sleeves when coat held.
Grooming		• Attempts to brush teeth, modeling adult.

REFERENCES: Caplan, 1971; Fallen & Umansky, 1985; Stillman, 1978; Lerner et al., 1987; Bailey & Wolery, 1984.

termed the "bird feeding" position, the glottis is not able to close effectively over the trachea, and there is essentially an open channel for the aspiration of food into the lungs (Lunnen, 1984, 308). Head and trunk control can be facilitated by positioning the child in his/her orthokinetic wheelchair for feeding.

Severely handicapped children frequently lack good jaw control necessary for sucking and swallowing. Teachers can assist children lacking good jaw control by using the thumb, index, and middle fingers to give the jaw support (Fallen & Umansky, 1985). Additional techniques to enhance sucking and swallowing include stimulating sucking by stroking downward gently on the child's cheek, using jaw control to keep the child's lips closed during swallowing, and holding the child's jaws closed while rubbing the outer gums to produce saliva which stimulates swallowing (Fallen & Umansky, 1985).

In feeding the severely handicapped child, food should be placed on the middle of the child's tongue because food placed on the front of the tongue may cause tongue thrusting, and food placed too far back on the tongue stimulates the gag reflex (Bailey & Wolery, 1984). Additionally, the caregiver should avoid scraping the teeth or roof of the mouth with the spoon because a bite reflex may be stimulated (Bailey & Wolery, 1984).

Severely handicapped children require direct teaching to learn self-feeding. Prior to planning a child's oral motor-feeding program, the teacher should carefully review the gross and fine motor skills prerequisites to eating (Table 44). The child cannot be expected to accomplish the self-help eating tasks without at least a moderate degree of attainment in the gross and fine motor-related skills. For example, a child cannot be expected to bring his/her bottle to mouth and hold it unless s/he demonstrates hand-to-mouth behavior, a purposeful reach and grasp, and some finger control. Many kinds of adapted equipment are currently available to assist children in self-feeding, such as spoons secured to the hand by means of a velcro strap.

The feeding/eating program of a handicapped child not only considers the child's specific sensory deficits, positioning and handling, remnant reflexes, stimulation of normal eating patterns, required individual modifications and adaptive equipment necessary, but also nutrition. The occupational and physical therapists aim not only to improve function, but also to assure that the student receives a well-balanced diet and ample amounts of liquid. Severely handicapped children may need to be programmed to eat a wider variety of foods of many textures and different temperatures. Malnutrition is a significant concern with many severely handicapped children. Low fluid intake can negatively affect the urological system, toileting training programs, and overall health of the child.

Case Study: Sally. Sally's evaluation report (Table 41) indicates overall functioning at the 0–1 month level. She has poor lip closure and problems coordinating sucking, swallowing, and breathing. She eats using a suckling pattern. Her oral motor development goal aims not only to help establish correct eating patterns, but also to develop those muscles necessary for speech production.

Sally's IEP

Oral Motor Goal:	Sally will improve oral motor functioning.
Objective A:	Sally will demonstrate lip control by bringing her lips together at the rim of a cup and drinking 3 consecutive sips with minimal spillage on 4 out of 5 trials on 3 consecutive data days as implemented by teacher/assistant under physical therapist's guidance.
Objective B:	Sally will demonstrate tongue lateralization when a food stimulus is placed between her teeth on 4 out of 5 trials on each side of her mouth on 3 consecutive data days as implemented by teacher/assistant under physical therapist's guidance.

To assist Sally in achieving Objective A, a cut-out cup is helpful during training so the caregiver can see Sally's mouth while drinking and assist her with jaw control so she will take small sips rather than elongated sucking.

Sally consumes food with a suckling pattern, so she experiences difficulty coordinating sucking and swallowing, as evidenced by gagging. Since she consumes food with a suckling pattern, she is fed a school lunch which has been ground in a food processor. To achieve tongue lateralization (Objective B), some of Sally's food such as green beans or a cheese sandwich are left unground and are broken into small pieces. These small pieces of food are held between her teeth to the side of her mouth so that she is unable to use the suckle pattern and must move her tongue to the sides of her mouth.

Training can be given at other times during the day using crackers or other food preferences. Crackers dissolve easily in the mouth and do not usually cause choking. An electric toothbrush and toothpaste are effective in stimulating tongue lateralization with some children. Vibration is contraindicated for anyone under the age of two years or who has a history of seizure problems.

A coated spoon and the assistance of jaw control during eating enables a child with poor motor control to eat more normally. The coated spoon enables food to slide into the mouth easier than a conventional spoon. Jaw control stabilizes the jaw to allow Sally to improve lip closure, although not complete. Without jaw control, Sally's oral motor skills are not developed enough to enable her to exercise the jaw control she needs in order to eat without spillage. Tongue lateralization is much more difficult without jaw control.

Case Study: Bud. Bud's evaluation report (Table 42) indicates eating skills functioning within the one-year range with higher splinter skills. He self-feeds bite-sized finger foods, brings his spoon to his mouth independently, and picks up his cup and drinks independently. However, he does not always bite off an appropriate-sized bite from a sandwich; he requires assistance scooping food into his spoon; and he does not return his partially full cup to the table, but releases it in midair. Bud's eating objectives are to improve skills in these specific areas.

Bud's IEP

Eating Goal:	Bud will improve self-feeding skills.
Objective A:	Bud will be able with tactile cue to scoop bites of food using spoon and adapted scooping bowl on 8 out of 10 trials on 3 consecutive data days as implemented by the teacher/assistant under supervision of the physical therapist.
Objective B:	Bud will be able with tactile cue to return his cup to the table without spilling after drinking 4 out of 5 times on 3 consecutive data days as implemented by teacher/assistant under guidance of physical therapist.

Toileting Programming. Normally, toilet training begins between 12 and 18 months of age (Table 44), by which time gross motor skills are developed to the point that the child could walk to the potty chair and sit down, after receiving assistance with his/her clothes. Toilet training has been extensively task-analyzed and the process found to be of enormous assistance with severely handicapped children who are not orthopedically handicapped. As with the feeding skills, the programming for the deaf-blind severely multihandicapped child may not easily follow a normal developmental sequence, due to the numerous interacting handicapping conditions. Thus, it is extremely important that the teacher and physical therapist work closely in determining the child's specific functioning level, strengths and weaknesses in order to plan an appropriate functional skills program.

The success of a toileting program with severely handicapped children depends on a number of factors or prerequisite skills. Prior to initiating training, the child should possess the gross and fine motor skills necessary to accomplish the tasks (Table 44). The program for orthopedically handicapped children who are not ambulatory or who possess atypical movement patterns may require significant modification not only of the process, but also of the specific procedures. The orthopedically handicapped and/or severely multihandicapped child may require adaptive equipment to assist in learning toileting skills. Although toileting skills are not expected to be mastered by the end of the sensorimotor stage, they certainly should be initiated and be in training process.

Toilet training requires that the child possess the basic cognitive abilities to understand cause and effect, to understand urination and defecation, to understand voluntary control, and to understand the process/procedures expected of him in order to accomplish this task. The child needs to be under instructional control—able and willing to follow the teacher's directions. The child should have no medical problems which preclude bladder or bowel control, no urological disorders, and should possess sphincter control. The child should be on a fairly consistent schedule with bodily functions. Additionally, the child's family needs to be willing to continue toilet training at home.

A majority of severely retarded children are not developmentally mature enough to begin toilet training before five years of age. Many severely handicapped children need special equipment such as urine alarm systems to facilitate the child's understanding of elimination and to alert caretakers to his/her need for assistance (Fallen & Umansky, 1985).

Bailey & Wolery (1984) have provided some general suggestions regarding the toilet training process including the following: (1) train daytime toileting first, (2) train bladder control before bowel, (3) train both boys and girls initially to sit on the toilet to urinate, (4) train, during later stages, to indicate a need for elimination, and (5) night-time training is facilitated by using a urine alarm system or other adaptive equipment. The teacher should not begin a toilet training program in a hasty manner. Prior to implementation of a training program, the teacher should establish extensive systematic observation and data collection (2–4 weeks) to determine the student's own schedule of wet and dry. When a stable pattern is established, the teacher should initiate training by taking the child to the bathroom a few minutes prior to his/her consistently wet baseline, and the child should be reinforced for urination in the toilet/potty. Gradually the child will gain the cognitive understanding of the task expected of him/her.

Toilet training should not be implemented with deaf-blind severely multihandicapped children without a physical therapy evaluation to determine any specific abnormal/atypical sensorimotor functioning. The physical therapist and classroom teacher will design a specific sequential program for each child as needed, considering the child's residual vision and hearing, gross and fine motor skills, cognition, communication mode/level, and dressing skills. Orthopedically handicapped children may require significant process modification and transfer training from wheelchair to toilet.

Case Study: Sally. Sally is functioning at the 0–1 month developmental level in all areas, so toilet training is inappropriate for her.

Case Study: Bud. Bud's evaluation report (Table 42) indicates that he has begun toilet training. He urinates in the toilet almost every time he is placed on it and frequently defecates in the toilet as well. He does not indicate a need to go to the toilet and wets his pants if not placed on the toilet 50–70 minutes since the last toileting period. Currently, Bud does not yet appear to understand the cause-effect relationships involved in toileting and does not understand when elimination is about to occur. By having him on a closely monitored toileting schedule to match his biological clock, Bud should eventually understand the relationship between elimination and sitting on the toilet.

Bud possesses the gross motor skills to be successful in the toilet training program. He can walk and move freely among various positions and can seat himself on the potty chair.

Bud's IEP

Toileting Goal:	Bud will improve toileting skills.
Objective A:	Bud will, with tactile cue, sign "toilet" as he sits on the potty during 4 out of 5 toileting incidents on 3 consecutive data days as implemented by the teacher/assistant.
Objective B:	Bud will, with tactile cue, assist with pushing his pants and underwear down prior to sitting on the potty 4 out of 5 times on 3 consecutive data days as implemented by teacher/assistant.

Dressing Programming. Nonhandicapped children generally begin to show an interest in dressing between 9–12 months of age (Table 44) when they begin to actively participate in dressing by holding out arms for sleeves and legs for pants. By 12–18 months of age, the nonhandicapped child frequently takes off socks and shoes unaided. The process of mastering dressing skills occurs over a period of years with kindergarteners and many 1st graders needing assistance with rain boots, zipping and buttoning coats, tying hoods, and tucking in shirts.

The severely handicapped child with or without orthopedic impairments utilizes the same sequence of skill development (Table 44), but at a much slower rate, and requires direct teaching in all phases. Since the severely handicapped child progresses at a rate of 40% or less than that of a non-handicapped child, s/he may be five years old or older before possessing cognitive, fine, and gross motor skills necessary to be successful in beginning undressing/dressing training.

Prior to the initiation of a program in dressing training, the physical therapist needs to carefully evaluate the child to determine if there are remnant reflexes; the status of muscle tone, strength, and function; and range of motion. Bailey & Wolery (1984) indicate additional evaluation areas, including the accuracy of volutional arm movements and ability to move both arms at the same time, the abilities in static balance and automatic reactions, and the presence of a palmar grasp. Through determination of motor functioning abilities, the physical therapist not only determines level of initiation of skills programming, but also the positioning needs of children to accomplish dressing/undressing tasks. Since the child's positioning in all dressing tasks is critical because each posture determines the muscles s/he uses, the severely multihandicapped child may need help in finding the proper position to make the task easier (Fallen & Umansky, 1985).

Orthopedically handicapped children should have developed some basic gross and fine motor skills prior to attempting dressing skills, including the ability to position hips, roll from side to side, sit up from a lying position, sit stabilized with at least one arm free, and shift weight using push-up or pull-up maneuvers (Bridgford, 1984). Children also need to possess a strong palmar grasp to use in pushing off garments by placing the thumb between the body and the clothing and pushing with the arms while maintaining the thumb inside the garment (Bailey & Wolery, 1984).

It is easier for orthopedically handicapped children to sit while dressing and undressing because that position provides the best balance. For children with cerebral palsy, a seated, well-balanced position minimizes the stiff and/or uncontrolled muscle movements (Kieran et al., 1980).

Undressing/dressing training is usually taught by one of two methods: forward chaining or backward chaining of the task-analyzed sequence of steps. **Forward chaining** is the process that begins training with the first step in the sequence. For example, in putting on a T-shirt, the child learns first to push his/her head through the neck opening, and the teacher helps with the rest of the dressing. Gradually, the child learns each step and is able to put the shirt on independently. **Backward chaining** begins the training sequence with the last step in the process. For example, the teacher assists the child in pulling the T-shirt over the head and pushing the arms through the sleeves, stopping the process just before the shirt tail is pulled over the trunk. The child is then taught, hand-over-hand, to pull the shirt over the trunk. Both forward and backward chaining have been used successfully in teaching severely handicapped children dressing skills. Snell (1987) suggests there is some new research to indicate forward chaining—teaching each step to be performed in its natural sequence—may lead to quicker mastery than backward chaining. Regardless which procedure is selected, the process should always be the same (Kieran et al., 1980).

Some generally accepted guidelines for teaching severely multihandicapped children include the following: (1) prior to initiating self-dressing, encourage active cooperative participation by the child (Snell, 1987); (2) teach dressing/undressing at natural times (e.g., arriving and leaving school, prior to and after toileting); (3) train in accordance with the sequences of difficulty (e.g., undressing is easier than dressing); (4) train to maximize acquisition and generalization (Bailey & Wolery, 1984); (5) assist parents in selecting and adapting clothing to promote independent functioning (Bailey & Wolery, 1984).

Orthopedically handicapped children may need additional modifications and assistance during dressing/undressing training, including the following: (1) put clothes on the more affected limb first; (2) allow the child to use the more affected hand for support rather than forcing its use; (3) gently straighten a stiff arm/leg before trying to put something on it; and (4) relax the ankle/foot by bending the leg before trying to put on a sock or shoe (Kiernan et al., 1980).

Success is more attainable with the beginning dresser if modified clothing is used during training sessions. Knitted pullover shirts two sizes larger than normal with loose raglan sleeves are easier to learn to put on than shirts with buttons or zippers. Initially, use large pants with elastic waist bands rather than jeans with zippers and snaps. Large buttons with large buttonholes are easier than small buttons, and velcro fasteners are easier than buttons for initial training. Tubular socks with no heels and tennis shoes with velcro strips facilitate putting on socks and shoes. Iron-on appliques help to distinguish the front of the garment from the back (Fallen & Umansky, 1985).

In preparation for dressing practice, some **play activities** can assist with the process. The child can be encouraged to place rings made of various articles and sizes on and off the arms/legs/head such as hula hoops; rings made from belts, knotted scarves, embroidery hoops, loops of stretchable material (Bridgford, 1984). Dressing up in mother's or father's clothing is fun for most young children and uses the same motor patterns as self-dressing.

Regarding learning to button, snap, and zip, Snell (1987, 379) cautions, "While button, snap, and zipper boards or dolls with clothing seem to be useful, skill generalization may be a problem for the learner with severe handicaps." Children should practice buttoning and snapping clothes on their own bodies because buttoning clothes you aren't wearing requires movements that are opposite from those needed to button your own clothing (Kieran et al., 1980). Additionally, buttoning and snapping clothes you are wearing requires you to look down to perform the task, which is a very different perspective than that required to button a doll's clothing.

By the cognitive functioning age of 18–24 months, children are not expected to have mastered undressing and dressing skills. These abilities will continue to develop for a number of years. As previously stated, it is crucial that the physical therapist have a major role in evaluating and designing the dressing training program of severely multihandicapped children. For children who are also deaf-blind, substantial modifications, to include tactile cues (Table 58) must also be considered.

Case Study: Sally. Since Sally's overall functioning level in all developmental areas is at the 0–1 month level, she lacks the cognitive and motor skills to begin a functional dressing training program.

Case Study: Bud. Bud's evaluation report (Table 42) indicates that he independently removes his shirt, jacket, or coat on tactile cue and assists while being dressed and diapered by pushing his arms through sleeve openings and raising his body. His major dressing objectives will continue the independent undressing process and begin the dressing process.

Bud's IEP

Dressing Goal:	Bud will improve independent dressing skills.
Objective A:	Bud will be able, with tactile cue, to push down elastic waist pants to the knee using palmar grasp on 4 out of 5 trials on 3 consecutive data days as implemented by teacher/teacher assistant under guidance of physical therapist.
Objective B:	Bud will begin, with tactile cue, to put on a knit T-shirt by pulling it over his head to his neck using a palmar grasp to hold the neck open on 4 out of 5 trials on 3 consecutive data days as implemented by teacher/assistant under physical therapist's guidance.

Grooming Programming. During the sensorimotor stage, there are no independent grooming tasks expected of the child. The child functioning cognitively at the two-year level may show interest in hair brushing, hand-washing, and teeth brushing. An adult should begin cleaning the handicapped child's teeth as soon as they appear, especially if there are any feeding problems such as tongue thrust, drooling, high palate, or gum hypertrophy due to seizure medication (Fallen & Umansky, 1985). A soft toothbrush and water or soft cloth dipped in water may be rubbed over the gums and teeth to clean them. Handwashing is facilitated by using liquid soap dispenser, hand brushes, and sponges that attach to the sink. Combs and hairbrushes with long handles may assist with hair brushing.

IEP Monitoring. IEP monitoring of sensorimotor and self-help skills is an extremely important part of the assessment process. Developmental progress can be monitored periodically using tables/lists of norm skills such as Normal Sensorimotor Development (Table 36), Reflexes and Automatic Reactions (Table 37), Activities of Daily Living (Table 40). Frequent (daily/weekly) data on programming skills (e.g., general norm skills task-analyzed) can be efficiently collected by indicating task analyses on a grid. (See Chapter Two, "IEP Monitoring.)

SUMMARY

Motor development in nonhandicapped children follows a sequential pattern, a cephlocaudal and a proximal-to-distal direction, and is related to maturation. The motor patterns of a newborn infant consist of innate reflexes and automatic reactions. The reflexive movement is gradually replaced by purposeful movement. Reflexes and automatic reactions, the basis for posture and movement, also provide an indication of CNS development and brain maturity. Brainstem level reflexes (e.g., ATNR, STNR, TLR, neck righting) which indicate the pull of gravity on the immature system should be inhibited by about 6 months of age. Automatic reactions of righting and balance begin emerging about 6 months of age to make the postural adjustments that maintain balance during movement, maintain the body in alignment with itself, and assist in breaking or preventing falls.

Reflex development, postural development, locomotion, fine motor skills, body image, spatial-temporal relations, and motor planning develop interactively. Thus, in a span of two years, the normal child has progressed from a reflexive infant with no postural control and no locomotion skills to a child with good postural control who walks and runs with relative ease. The two-year-old child has developed fine motor skills to use the pincer grasp, use fingers individually, open and close simple containers, and marks with a crayon. The development of normal oral motor patterns is also influenced by reflexes, muscle tone, positioning, sensory integration, and behavior.

Atypical/abnormal sensorimotor development hampers progress in all developmental areas (e.g., motor skills, cognition, communication, self-help skills) because early learning has a motor basis. Sensorimotor dysfunction occurs as a result of primitive reflexes, poorly developed automatic reactions, tactile deficits, defective motor planning, and/or poor development of postural control, body image, and spatial relationships. Motor dysfunctions (e.g., cerebral palsy) may be due to deficits in **muscle tone** (e.g., hypertonic or hypotonic), **muscle control** (e.g., involuntary muscle vibrations), and/or **muscle strength** (e.g., paresis or plegia).

Therapeutic evaluations involve determination by the physical therapist of the child's functioning abilities in motor development, reflex development, muscle tone, muscle strength and function, joint range of motion and muscle length, posture, sensory integration and processing, gait, respiratory status, and activities of daily living. The evaluation seeks to determine the child's progress toward normal developmental milestones and degree of developmental motor delay. The physical therapist uses systematic observation of active and passive movement, of postural control, of the child during daily activities, of spontaneous movement in various positions and ambulation, and formal/informal checklists.

The evaluation provides information to be used in planning the individual educational program including proper handling and positioning to remediate specific deficits; the adaptive equipment and activities to promote independence in daily functioning. Deaf-blind severely multihandicapped children may require considerable modification in programming, depending on residual vision and hearing abilities. Self-help activities are an extremely important part of the programming of deaf-blind severely multihandicapped children in promoting normalcy, acceptance, and socialization.

Chapter Six

COGNITION: EVALUATION AND PROGRAMMING

The ability of the child to receive and integrate input from the world about him will govern, to a large extent, his level of cognitive functioning and his ability to establish and elaborate on meaningful concepts (McInnes & Treffry, 1982, 153).

- Cognition
  Information Processing
  Cognitive Capacities
  Cognitive Products
  Information Processing Problems
- Sensorimotor Stage Cognitive Development
- Sensorimotor Stage Cognitive Evaluation
- Sensorimotor Stage Cognitive Programming
- Summary

The process of thinking or cognition is involved in skill acquisition in every area of developmental learning: sensory development, fine and gross motor skills, receptive and expressive language, self-help skills, and social-emotional development. Thus, it is extremely difficult to isolate cognition as a construct for discussion separate from these developmental functioning areas.

COGNITION

Cognition is a hypothetical construct which exists only as an inference; therefore, it cannot be observed in the physical sense (Mann & Sabatino, 1985). Hypothetically, cognition can be considered from three major perspectives: as a process, as a capacity, and as a product (Mann & Sabatino, 1985). The cognitive process, frequently referred to as information processing, is concerned with receiving, interpreting, and managing information. Cognitive capacities include structures, skills, and abilities that make cognitive processing possible, while cognitive products include the cognitive perceptions, images, concepts, decisions that may be expressed behaviorally in oral or written language or drawing (Mann & Sabatino, 1985). These three hypothetical perspectives of cognition — process, capacity, product — are interwoven and interdependent concepts.

Information Processing

Information processing is a global concept involving various levels or processes of cognition. It is the process by which the brain receives information from sensory perceptions, interprets and mediates the information using thinking and memory strategies, and acts upon the information by means of a verbal (vocal), fine motor, or gross motor response. No one knows precisely how cognition occurs; however, it is known that all cognitive functioning relies on neurological functioning and occurs in the brain during neurological functioning.

A hypothetical information processing construct (Table 45) was developed to facilitate the conceptualization of information processing through three major stages or mechanism systems including transmission of information, central processing of information, and behavioral responses to information. Within these three systems, information processing can be viewed as involving separate components including the following: (1) Sensory Register, (2) Sensory Perceptions, (3) Sensory Integration, (4) Short-term Memory, (5) Working Memory, (6) Long-term Memory, and (7) Responses (Table 45). It should be understood, however, that it is not possible to represent the complex activity of the human brain in terms of a unidimensional model or schematic drawing, and that each component is not totally separate and discrete, but has numerous interconnections among the various sensory motor and memory systems. It should also be understood that time lapse between attention to stimuli and a behavioral response may take place in a matter of seconds or milliseconds.

Sensory Register

During the initial stage of information processing, transmission of information, the focus is on transforming raw stimulation into a form that ultimately can be used in the Central Processing of Information Stage (Table 45). The sensory systems are continually being bombarded with raw stimuli from all aspects of daily life. This raw stimulation from all sensory systems (auditory, visual, tactile, kinesthetic, vestibular,

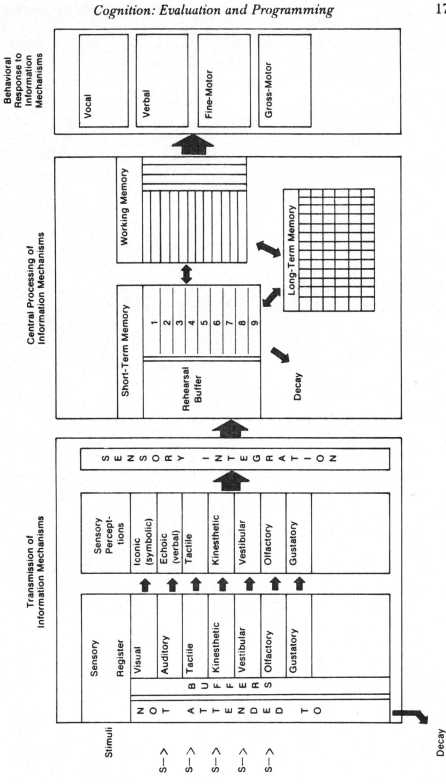

Table 45 INFORMATION PROCESSING: A HYPOTHETICAL CONSTRUCT

References: Mayer, 1981; Llorens & Burris, 1981; Wyne & O'Connor, 1979; Kirk & Gallagher, 1979; Atkinson & Shiffron, 1968.

olfactory, gustatory) is channeled to the Sensory Register, which can be likened to a computer screen or monitor. The raw data on the monitor cannot be processed without action to cause recoding. Likewise, the raw sensory stimuli by itself does not create information or cognition (Mann & Sabatino, 1985).

One of the major control processes in the **Sensory Register** is attention. As the raw sensory stimuli pass through the Sensory Register, the **Control Process: Attention** targets some sensory stimuli for attention. Stimuli not attended to passes out of the system (e.g., off the monitor) and is lost as decay. Raw stimuli selected for attention passes through the sensory buffers or filters that code the raw stimuli into specific sensory stimuli. The Sensory Register, then, receives raw stimuli, temporarily holds, organizes, and codes it to prepare for transmission to Sensory Perceptions.

For example, a girl is walking down the street on a lovely spring day when suddenly a snarling dog jumps out of the bushes at her. The raw stimuli concerning the warmth of the sun, the light floral scent in the air, and sounds of a distant freeway cease being attended to and pass from the Sensory Register as decay. However, raw stimuli regarding the incident is attended to—snarling dog (auditory), dog jumping out of the bushes at her (visual), cold sweat from fear (tactile), kicking at the dog (motor, kinesthetic, vestibular)—and passes into the buffers of the Sensory Register to be organized and coded as sensory stimuli.

Visual information appears to use iconic (symbolic) codes and processes information simultaneously, while auditory information uses echoic (verbal) codes and processes information sequentially (Mann & Sabatino, 1985). It is felt that visual and auditory buffers, under normal circumstances, code the raw stimuli into sensory information more effectively than the buffers of the secondary senses (Mann & Sabatino, 1985). "Most of our thinking, however, proceeds in the form of cognitive codes that are not readily identifiable or understandable by our conscious minds. Ultimately, they are physical and electrochemical in nature" (Mann & Sabatino, 1985, 167).

Sensory Perceptions

Sensory stimuli are transferred from the Sensory Register to the Sensory Perceptions component of the Transmission of Information Mechanism (Table 45). Sensory perception is sensation with meaning, or the cognitive interpretation of what the child has seen or heard, etc.

Sensory perception normally begins to develop within the first days or weeks of life. At this stage, meaning is attached to incoming stimuli from the visual, auditory, tactile, vestibular, kinesthetic, gustatory, and olfactory channels. The meaning attached to the sensory stimuli is primarily at the recognition and discrimination stage of labeling or naming. Cognitive abilities typically associated with Sensory Perception include discrimination (e.g., visual, auditory, tactile, etc.), recognition (e.g., visual, auditory, etc.), figure-ground perception (e.g., auditory, visual, etc.) (Table 46).

For example, as little Johnny walks into the house, home from school, he smells a delicious odor. Attention to the raw stimuli passes through the Sensory Register buffers which organize and code the information as olfactory stimuli and transfer the information to Sensory Perceptions. The information is compared to previous similar stimuli; the child utilizes olfactory figure-ground to clarify the characteristics of "pure" scent, olfactory discrimination to separate the odor from other similar odors, and olfactory recognition to finally determine the odor came from the kitchen and fresh chocolate chip cookies baking.

Sensory Integration

Sensory Integration is the most complicated of the Transmission of Information Mechanisms and is one of the most difficult components, even for handicapped children who possess normal organic sensory systems (Table 45). Sensory integration is the stage in which individual sensory perceptions are integrated and utilized together. "Each sensory stimulus needs to be organized and integrated with information from other concurrent sensory activity and from stored information in the cortex in order to complete the process of perception" (Morrison et al., 1978, 78).

At the Sensorimotor Stage of development, sensory integration is primarily concerned with the integration of distance (near and far) perceptions (e.g., visual, auditory, tactile) with movement and motion perceptions (e.g., kinesthetic, vestibular). Sensory integration, then, is a complex process of cross-modal association and multiple stimulus integration (Morrison et al., 1978). Cognitive processing abilities that foster sensory integration include perceptual-motor integration, perceptual memory-motor integration (e.g., visual memory with a motor response), perceptual speed, perceptual memory, perceptual association (e.g., auditory-visual association), spatial orientation (Table 46). Even a simple perceptual-motor task requires the integration of sensory perceptual information from several sensory modalities (Anwar, 1986).

Table 46 Cognitive Capacities

To Facilitate Transmission of Information

Sensory Perceptual Skills

Discrimination:
Visual
Auditory
Tactile
Kinesthetic
Vestibular
Olfactory
Gustatory

Recognition:
Visual
Auditory
Tactile
Kinesthetic
Vestibular
Olfactory
Gustatory

Figure-Ground:
Visual
Auditory
Tactile
Olfactory
Gustatory

Closure:
Visual
Auditory
Tactile

Perceptual Information Skills

Auditory-Visual Assoc.
Auditory-Visual Assoc.
Visual Percept. Speed

Perceptual-Motor:
Visual-Motor
Auditory-Motor
Tactile-Motor

Olfactory-Gustatory
Visual-Gustatory
Visual-Olfactory
Tactile-Gustatory
Auditory-Tactile
Visual-Tactile
Visual-Vestibular
Visual-Spatial Orientation
Eye-Hand Coordin.
Eye-Foot Coordin.
etc.

To Facilitate Central Processing of Information

Memory Integration

Memory:
Auditory
Visual
Tactile
Kinesthetic
Vestibular
Olfactory
Gustatory
Auditory Sequential
Visual Sequential
Visual Imagery
etc.

Cognitive Strategies
—Cognitive Behavior Modification
—Cognitive Task Analysis
—Metacognition
—Metacomprehension
—Metalistening
—Meta attention
—Metalinguistics
—Learning Strategies

Control Processes

Organization
Chunking
Clustering
Charting
Categorizing

Coding
Mediation
Rehearsal
Imagery
Metacognition
Meta Memory

Cognitive Control Styles
Field Inde-pendence-Dependence
Leveling-Sharpening
Scanning-Focusing
Reflective-Impulsive
Constricted-Flexible

Cognitive Skills

Micro-Thinking Skills:
Recall
Translation
Interpretation
Application
Mneumonics
Synthesis
Evaluation
Reasoning:
Inductive
Deductive
Analogical
Inferences
Cause-Effect
Critical Thinking Skills

Thinking Strategies
Problem Solving
Decision Making
Conceptualizing

Sensorimotor
Object Concept
Imitation
Anticipation
Object Permanence
Causality
Object Constancy
Means-Ends classification

To Facilitate Behavioral Responses

Vocal
—Oral-Motor
Planning
—Intonation
Code
—Receptive Language
Analysis

—Verbal
—Linguistic Rules
Speech-
Articulation
Code
—Receptive Language

Motor
—Motor Skills-Fine & Gross
—Motor Planning
—Body Image
—Spatial-Temporal Relations
—Reflexes or Automatic Reactions

References: Morrison et al., 1978; Mann & Sabatino, 1985; Mercer, 1987; Beyer, 1987.

During the sensorimotor stage of development, a strong relationship exists between cognitive development and motor development. In order to learn new motor skills, the child depends on the integration of visual and kinesthetic information. The child must encode information from these two sources and store it in a format suitable for subsequent movement planning, execution, and evaluation (Anwar, 1986, 1972).

Short-Term Memory

The Central Processing of Information Mechanisms are concerned with all of the possible manipulations of information involving memory including coding and storage, retrieval, recall and remembering, problem solving, imagination, reasoning, visualization, conceptualization, daydreaming, decision-making. The short-term memory is conceptualized as the active part of our memory—our conscious mind (Mann & Sabatino, 1985). The short-term memory functions in the immediate present—the here and now.

The rehearsal buffer of the short-term memory (Table 45) gives it some voluntary control over the information it selects for manipulation (Atkinson & Shiffron, 1968). Not all sensory information is retained by the short-term memory for consideration, only that information attended to or rehearsed in some way. Unlike the sensory register, which appears to have unlimited capacities for acquiring information, the short-term memory has a limited capacity of 4–9 symbols or coded items of information (Mann & Sabatino, 1985). The short-term memory appears to store items sequentially or serially into the nine memory slots (Table 45). Several major tests have a digit span subtest requiring children to repeat given digits backwards to gain an estimate of the size of the student's short-term memory capacity. The capacity of STM is developmental in nature with the average preschool child able to use three STM slots or remember three short simple directions, while the average adult capacity is seven plus or minus two bits of information. Information does not remain in the short-term memory long, as evidenced by how long one can remember a string of individual digits. Without rehearsal of some kind, much information placed in short-term memory decays.

The efficiency, effectiveness, and capacity of the short-term memory can be enhanced by the conscious use of STM control processes. Control processes are the links, associations, organization plans, coding techniques, etc. used by students in an effort to remember information. Short-term memory control processes include chunking, coding, organization, and rehearsal (Table 46). Chunking is a STM control process to allow more information to remain in STM at one time. For example, if a student were given seven individual digits (e.g., 9, 5, 7, 3, 8, 2, 6), they would be placed sequentially into the first seven STM slots and be at capacity for the amount of STM information to handle. However, if the student chunked the digits into groups of three digits each (e.g., 9-5-7, 3-8-2, 6 - -), the student would only have information in three STM slots, which is much easier to remember than if using single digits in single slots. Chunking has proved to be an efficient method for students to use in improving their short-term memory capabilities.

Coding and organization are conscious short-term memory control processes that enable the students to categorize and classify information, organize it by conceptual strategies, or group according to topics. These processes not only increase the capacity of the STM, but also assist in encoding the information for long-term memory storage. Rehearsal not only serves as a buffer initially for incoming information, but also assists in retaining information in STM longer. Rehearsal can be reproductive (e.g., an exact representation of the input verbally spoken over and over) or reconstructive such as reorganized in some way to synthesize information or restructured into a diagram.

The short-term memory is a very active central processing mechanism, sending recoded information to long-term storage (LTM) or bringing information from LTM into conscious consideration in STM. According to some theories, there is a separate Working Memory which retains information needed shortly by STM (Table 45). There appears to be a continuous flow of information between STM and the Working Memory.

Working Memory

There are a number of different theories regarding the Working Memory (WM). In this hypothetical construct, the Working Memory is depicted separate from STM but closely interacting. Bower (1975) suggests that the working memory manages the information currently being learned, which is neither the focus of the active STM nor in the distant edges of LTM. For example, at the beginning of the school day, the teacher may write all of the assignments on the chalkboard and remind the students that the assignments are due before going home. Each assignment as it is being completed will remain in active STM while the completed assignments (e.g., location of paper and reminder of time due) and uncompleted assignments remain in WM. Thus, a continuous flow of information between the conscious STM and the Working Memory is evidenced. Working Memory may place the assignment data, once completed, into long-term storage, if needed for future reference, or return it to the STM for decay.

Long-Term Memory

The long-term memory (LTM) store is assumed to be a permanent library of all information that we possess but are not immediately using. LTM stores our perceptual-motor skills, spatial models of all sorts, verbal concepts, math formulas, laws and properties, personal beliefs, etc. (Mann & Sabatino, 1985). Control processes which facilitate the storage of information into long-term memory include various organizational schemes (e.g., chunking, clustering, mneumonics, coding), mediation, rehearsal, metacognition, and metamemory (Table 46). Long-term memory storage can be likened to a computer's auxiliary direct access storage facility which has a vast network of interconnections among the classified, categorized, and cross-indexed information stored within it.

"A major distinction in LTM information storage is made between semantic and episodic memory. Semantic memory involves organized retrieval of meaningful information. Episodic memory involves memory of specific events in one's life" (Mann & Sabatino, 1985, 176). Semantic memory tends to be systematically organized and stored, both categorically and associatively, while episodic memory is affective and not well organized and tends to be stored only associatively (Mann & Sabatino, 1985). Some theorists hypothesize that LTM stores information by using two separate systems of order: (1) semantically in language codes, and (2) analogically in image codes, while others propose LTM uses one all-purpose code for storage.

Mann and Sabatino (1985) indicate that all humans have the same types of information processing systems. However, these systems may differ in size and quality of structures, efficiency of architectural arrangements, effectiveness of control mechanisms and processes that govern the speed and accuracy of information flow, coding, and retrieval, and the power of the executive processes that operate the entire information processing system (Mann & Sabatino, 1985, 184).

Behavioral Responses

The information processing cycle is not complete until the child makes some sort of behavioral response to indicate a flow of information has indeed occurred. The major Behavioral Response to Information Mechanisms include vocal responses, verbal responses, fine-motor responses, and gross motor responses (Table 45). During the early months of sensorimotor development, the average child uses differentiated vocal sounds (e.g., crying, yelling, cooing, chuckling) to indicate wants, needs, and responses to the environment. During the second year of life (i.e., 18 months), although the child cannot yet communicate verbally, the vocal sounds s/he makes carry the intonation patterns of adult speech so s/he is able to communicate using vocal sounds and gestures. At the late sensorimotor stage (18 months–2 years), verbal responses are limited primarily to one-word statements or utterances. Verbal responses eventually develop into sophisticated rule-governed communication systems: speech, the oral articulatory code, and written language.

Early motor responses to stimulation are whole body responses. As the neurological system of the child develops, responses become more differentiated and less obvious. During the first months of life, a sudden loud noise will cause the whole body to react, while later, the same noise may elicit eye blinking or shoulder movement. Cause and effect learning begins rapid development with reach and grasp skill development. Gross motor responses include a myriad of behavioral actions (Table 36), including body language. The gross motor response will depend on the instructions given through the information processing procedures. Fine motor behavioral responses also include numerous developmental behaviors (Table 36) and self-help skills (Table 40). School-aged children rely heavily on fine-motor and perceptual-fine motor integration to complete assigned tasks requiring manual dexterity (e.g., puzzles), handwriting assignments, creative writing, and activities of daily living. As with gross motor responses, the choice of fine motor response will depend upon the information processed.

Cognitive Capacities

Transmission of Information

Cognition can be studied in terms of the "cognitive capacities, structures, aptitudes, skills, etc. that create or otherwise make cognitive processes possible" (Mann & Sabatino, 1985, 2). Cognitive capacities which facilitate the transmission of information to Central Processing include Perceptual Skills and Sensory Integration Skills (Table 46). The skills listed and many others assist in the labeling and classification of sensory stimuli and the integration of sensory perceptions from multiple sources. The majority of children develop these skills almost automatically and are able to apply them to acquisition of preacademic and academic skills. Handicapped children frequently experience difficulty in acquiring the perceptual and perceptual integration skills that are prerequisites to learning to read.

For most children, the auditory and visual perceptual and perceptual-integration skills are the most relevant for academic learning. Auditory and visual discrimination are essential for the development of the concept of objects, as well as being important in learning sound/symbol associations (prerequisites to reading). Visual discrimination is required for labeling letters and numerals. Auditory and visual recognition are necessary in labeling and naming items, determining object concepts, and abstracting characteristics of items and objects. Visual figure-ground discrimination is essential for a child to focus on one word or item on a page of words or items. Auditory figure-ground, the ability to focus on a particular auditory stimulus in a world of noise, is required for a child to process language receptively.

For most deaf-blind children, the tactile and kinesthetic systems will provide their major learning modes rather than auditory and visual channels. With reduced access to clear visual and auditory perceptions, it is much more difficult to develop the concepts of objects and object permanence, primary sensorimotor stage cognitive skills. The amount of residual vision and hearing a child possesses and can be trained and encouraged to use will significantly affect sensory integration skills in quality and quantity.

Central Processing Information

Numerous capacities, structures, aptitudes, and skills facilitate the central processing of information from reception in Short-Term Memory to Working Memory to Long-Term Memory and in reverse as information is recalled for utilization. Some of the capacities that facilitate memory development include perceptual-memory integration, cognitive strategies, control processes, cognitive control styles, and cognitive skills (Table 46). Discussing these areas may be an exercise in semantics because numerous groupings and labels exist. **Perceptual-memory integration** skills (e.g., visual memory, auditory memory, tactile memory, etc.) are important prerequisite skills to comprehension and understanding (Table 46). Auditory memory, the ability to retell what was heard, is a prerequisite to listening comprehension, which requires not only memory of information heard, but also demonstration that the information was understood.

Control Processes are processes to assist the memory stores to work more effectively and efficiently (Table 46). Organizing information (e.g., chunking, clustering, charting, categorizing, mneumonics, coding, etc.) assists the memory process by keeping information in the short-term memory longer and by building associations which facilitate long-term storage. The reorganization of information helps to synthesize it into major component parts and facilitates understanding. Charting and mneumonics provide visual as well as auditory storage cues. Organizing information also assists in the retrieval of information. The more interconnections between items stored, the greater the access to information. Mediation is a control process that keeps information in STM longer by pondering the situation, its characteristics, and/or ramifications. The Rehearsal Control Process serves several functions: it helps to screen information prior to placement in short-term memory store, and assists in keeping information in STM longer either by reproducing an exact copy of the input or reorganizing the information for continued input. Imagery is very useful in remembering data that is visual, real, or pictorial. When paired with verbal (e.g., linguistic) information, the learner places the information in storage in two forms—symbolic and semantic, thus increasing the child's chances for long-term storage and efficient retrieval. Metacognition and metamemory require a certain degree of maturity of the child to allow the child to mentally "step back" and observe his/her own mental functioning and devise means to facilitate memory by knowing his/her own strengths and weaknesses.

Cognitive Strategies are specific procedures used in education to assist students in increasing memory storage and retrieval and thereby improving academic learning (Table 46). Some of the more popular new cognitive strategies in education include cognitive behavior modification, cognitive task analysis, metacognition, metacomprehension, meta-attention, meta-listening, and other "meta" skills. **Cognitive behavior modification (CBM)** combines behavior modification techniques with self-treatment methods (e.g., self-monitoring instruction, self-evaluation, and self-verbalization)" (Mercer, 1987, 235). CBM generally involves a number of steps in a training sequence including: (1) cognitive modeling (e.g., adult performs required task, talking through the thinking process), (2) external guidance (e.g., child performs same type of task using adult's cognitive modeling as a guide), (3) covert self-guidance (e.g., child performs the task verbally, directing himself), (4) fading overt self-guidance (e.g., child whispers instructions to himself while performing the task), and (5) covert self-instruction (e.g., child performs task using inaudible speech to give self-direction) (Meichenbaum, 1980). CBM strives to assist the child to remain on task and to develop inner speech to help the child during problem-solving situations.

Task analysis is a familiar process to special educators, conducted in preparation to teaching a new skill to a student. The process generally involves three stages of activities: (1) the skill is subdivided into smaller subskills/components, (2) each subskill specifies in behavioral terms the conditions and criteria for mastery (IEP objectives), and (3) teacher determines methods and materials to teach each subskill, specific to a particular student. The teacher has just completed a cognitive task analysis. Others have referred to Bloom's taxonomy of cognitive objectives as a cognitive task analysis for the cognitive domain (Mann & Sabatino, 1985). The author proposes that exercises such as construction of Tables 45 and 46 are exercises in cognitive task analysis.

"Metacognition refers to an individual's knowledge about his cognitions and his ability to control them" (Mercer, 1987, 235). Metacognition as a process involves self-planning, self-monitoring, self-checking, self-correction, and self-direction (Mann & Sabatino, 1985). The other "meta" strategies, including metacomprehension, metalistening, meta-attention, metalinguistics, involve the same processes but are area or skill specific. The primary goals of the "meta" strategies are to teach the student to become an active learner and independent in completing assignments and handling problem-solving situations.

Cognitive Control Styles are concerned with students' primary orientations to learning. Cognitive styles that do not facilitate learning are often changed or managed by using cognitive behavior modification. Cognitive or learning styles currently considered important to special educators include field independence-field dependence, leveling-sharpening, scanning-focusing, constricted-flexible, and reflective-impulsive (Table 46). **Field independence** represents the ability to resist inaccurate perceptions and is a characteristic of intrinsically motivated students while field-dependent students learn best under conditions of external reinforcements (Mann & Sabatino, 1985). **Levelers** are significantly influenced by past learning experiences, while sharpeners are able to view new learning situations and problems more objectively by resisting effects of previous learning. **Scanners-Focusers** refer to the amount of attention students direct toward the task; scanners quickly skim assignments while focusers are able to deliberate and think through assignments. **Reflective-Impulsive** are terms used to describe conceptual tempo, or the degree to which the student ponders a problem or task before responding. **Constricted-Flexible** are terms which refer to the student's control in the learning situation and ability to respond correctly in spite of distractors (Mann & Sabatino, 1985).

Handicapped children tend to be field-dependent, levelers, scanners, impulsive, and constricted in their cognitive control styles. This information suggests some primary implications for teaching. Levelers may need direct teaching instruction involving one method to reach the correct answer. Providing several solution methods for choice or providing choices of both correct and incorrect answers may be confusing. Field-dependent students learn best when rewarded or controlled using token systems or other reinforcement systems. They experience difficulty with motivation and behavior control. Scanners and impulsive students may need cognitive strategies (Table 46) to help direct their attention and organize themselves to complete assignments. Students approaching learning from a constricted view may experience considerable difficulty with generalization and need specific training in each setting where a task is to be performed. Levelers, additionally, may require specific transitions between concepts so the memory traces from previous tasks don't interfere with current tasks. For example, levelers may have significant difficulty learning to "borrow" in subtraction if taught immediately after "carrying" in addition.

> Cognitive skills are a collection of mental abilities related to thinking activities. They include knowing, recognizing, developing concepts, organizing ideas, remembering, problem-solving, labeling, relating cause and effect, drawing inferences, and developing rules and generalizations (Lerner et al., 1987, 240).

Cognitive skills have been organized in numerous ways. Micro-thinking skills primarily refer to skills that involve one or two processes in order to answer the question or complete the task assigned. They include such skills as recalling answers, interpreting something read, applying a skill in a new situation, analyzing information, synthesizing information to write a summary, evaluating the appropriateness of a character's behavior, etc. (Table 46). Critical thinking skills involve more abstract thinking and several micro-thinking skills in such tasks as detecting bias, identifying logical fallacies and inconsistencies in reasoning, distinguishing relevant from irrelevant information, etc. (Beyer, 1987). Thinking strategies (e.g., problem solving, decision-making, conceptualization) not only require the use of one or more micro-thinking skills and critical thinking skills, but also a specific procedure to direct thinking. For example, the problem-solving strategy includes the following five steps: "(1) recognize the problem, (2) represent the problem, (3) devise/choose solution or plan, (4) execute the plan, and (5) evaluate the solution" (Beyer, 1987, 44).

Specific sensorimotor stage cognitive skills have been indicated, including object concept, imitation, anticipation, object permanence, causality, object constancy, means-ends, classification (Table 46). These skills are discussed later in this chapter.

Intelligence as a cognitive capacity is of major concern to the special educator in terms of evaluation, labeling, and programming. Intelligence is viewed as the capacity of the child to learn, at least as a measure or estimate of the child's capacity to be successful in the regular public school curriculum. Scores on intelligence tests are major determiners of the level of services (e.g., resource room, self-contained) handicapped children will receive and the type of educational programming (e.g., regular curriculum, minimum competencies, prevocational, self-help). Intelligence is generally viewed as an all-encompassing construct including information processing (Table 45) and numerous cognitive capacities (Table 46).

Behavioral Responses to Information

The behavioral responses of a child at the conclusion of an information processing incident will generally be vocal, verbal, fine or gross motor behaviors (Table 45). Each of these types of behavioral responses to information processing, however, are facilitated by specific cognitive capacities. Vocal responses tend to be a major response mode of children functioning at the sensorimotor stage of development. Vocal responses become pre-verbal responses to the environment. Meaningful, though non-linguistic, vocal responses are predicated upon an adequate oral musculature (Table 51), oral-motor planning, and the child's knowledge of the adult intonation code. Vocal utterances using the appropriate intonations paired with simple gestures are very effective in communicating the preverbal child's wants, needs, and emotions.

Verbal responses follow a developmental sequence (Table 53) predicated upon expressive language prerequisites (Table 51). Nonhandicapped children by four years of age are fluent communicators, using all of the major sentence forms. Prerequisites to fluent verbal responses include vocal skills and prerequisites (Table 46), understanding of the linguistic rules of our language, adequate articulation, and good receptive language skills.

Appropriate behavioral motor responses require various prerequisites, depending on developmental level of the child. The higher functioning sensorimotor stage child's motor responses depend on adequate reflexes and automatic reactions, age-appropriate fine and gross motor skills, motor planning abilities, body image, and spatial-temporal relationships. Appropriate motor skill development also depends on such skills as laterality, directionality, eye-hand and eye-foot coordination. Spatial-temporal relationships also include acquiring form consistency and position in space.

Cognitive Products

Cognitive products are the end result of cognitive processing (Table 45) and utilization of the cognitive capacities (Table 46). Cognitive products "may be entirely cognitive in nature, e.g., perceptions, images, concepts, decisions; they may also be expressed behaviorally, e.g., in oral language, written composition, or drawing" (Mann & Sabatino, 1985, 2). Cognitive products include all of the physical "things" that discriminate our lives from that of our cave-dwelling ancestors and the concepts, images, and decisions upon which their production was predicated.

In schools, the cognitive products include the concepts and ideas upon which the completion of academic assignments are based. Cognitive products include the knowledge of music and the songs played by the band or sung by the chorus; the knowledge of the rules and procedures of various sports and the execution during basketball games; the creative image and the sketch or oil painting; the creative ideas and the poem or short story.

With sensorimotor stage children, the cognitive products may include the concept of toilet and independent toileting; the concept of scooping food into a spoon and the execution; the concept of motor planning and toddling around the table to get a toy; the concept of pleasure and laughing or smiling.

Information Processing Problems

All cognitive functioning relies on neurological functioning; thus substances and experiences that improve the efficiency of neurological functioning also improve or impair cognition (Mann & Sabatino, 1985). "Damage to the nervous system's nuclei and ganglia is likely to have devastating effects on specific cognitive functions, e.g., visual, auditory, and memory ones" (Mann & Sabatino, 1985, 35). Genetic defects, birth trauma, accidents and injuries that damage specific parts of the nervous system usually cause specific types of cognitive deficits.

Information processing or cognitive processing problems may occur due to an interruption in (1) attention to stimuli, (2) reception of stimuli, (3) storage and processing of information, and (4) expression of cognitive abilities (Fallen & Umansky, 1985). A neurological or sensory impairment may interfere with the child's ability to attend to a stimulus long enough to process it into short-term or long-term memory storage. Acquisition of information first requires attention to the relevant stimulus; however, some severely handicapped children may be unaware of their surroundings and be unable to benefit from the stimulation that appears spontaneously in the environment (Fallen & Umansky, 1985).

Children with visual and/or hearing impairments may be unable to receive stimuli appropriately or may receive distorted or garbled information. Problems may occur at the Sensory Integration (Table 45) stage. The child who is unable to use vision to integrate auditory and tactile cues learns much later how to maintain contact with his/her environment (Fallen & Umansky, 1985). "If vision is not available, simultaneity of spatial organization may be lost, and if hearing is lost, an appreciation of order or succession may be disturbed" (O'Connor & Hermelin, 1986, 187).

A moderate-to-severe brain damage may disrupt the storage and processing of information and result in various levels of mental retardation. A minimal brain damage may disrupt some storage and information processing skills resulting in learning disabilities. A general problem of severely mentally handicapped children is that they seem deficient in cognitive strategies and information acquisition strategies (Brown, 1974). Anwar (1986) indicates that inappropriate stimulus acquisition strategies in severely mentally handicapped students may reflect an overall structural deficit in general information organization and storage. Students who evidence deficits in control processes (Table 46) may have significantly less accessibility to the information already acquired because it was not organized and integrated well prior to storage. Since simultaneous comprehension of a large number of items can only be accomplished in vision, visually impaired children may experience a severe reduction in simultaneous comprehension abilities.

Sensorily deprived or deficit children may experience significant disabilities in encoding and transferring information. O'Connor and Hermelin (1986, 188) indicate "if the subject suffers from congenital deafness or severe linguistic disability, he may not automatically encode a presented input in a verbal form, but perhaps in terms of the code of some other modality." They go on to indicate that various modalities operate according to different procedural rules; thus, there may not be automatic transfer from one modality to another, so if verbal information was encoded as visual information, the consequent output may be significantly different than expected.

The expression of cognitive abilities may be significantly affected if the handicapped child has speech disorders and/or orthopedic impairments that result in poor oral motor control which interfere with articulation and speech production. Orthopedic impairments hinder progress in fine and gross motor development, thus inhibiting the early exploratory behaviors and underlying cognitive processes, as a result delaying acquisition of such cognitive skills as object permanence and causality. Anwar (1983) indicates that severely mentally handicapped adolescents experienced difficulty when visually derived and stored information had to be translated into motor movements. Additionally, retarded children experience difficulty in generalization, transferring the results of any training to a new situation.

In the case of deaf-blind severely multihandicapped children, cognitive processes may be interrupted due to all four causes: interruption to attention to stimuli, reception of stimuli, storage and processing of information, and behavioral responses or expression of cognitive abilities. Defective hearing and vision may interrupt and severely reduce the child's ability to attend to stimuli and receive clear and undistorted stimuli. Brain damage resulting in severe and profound mental retardation interferes with the ability to process and to store information. Many deaf-blind severely multihandicapped children have orthopedic handicaps and/or oral/motor control deficits impairing the child's communication skills as well as fine and gross motor skills, making the demonstration of any cognitive product very difficult.

SENSORIMOTOR STAGE: COGNITIVE DEVELOPMENT

The majority of deaf-blind severely multihandicapped children function within the sensorimotor stage of cognitive development. "Piaget's sensorimotor stage of development covers the first two years of life, the period from birth until the emergence of language" (Lerner et al., 1987, 163). It is during this stage that the child learns through sensory perception, movement and motor skills, and interactions with the environment.

Cognitive Development

"Sensorimotor skills are those behaviors acquired during infancy and thought to be precursors to basic thinking and conceptual development" (Bailey & Wolery, 1984, 162). The primary cognitive acquisitions of the sensorimotor stage include object concept, anticipation, imitation, object permanence, causality, object constancy, and intentional behavior (Table 47). "Each of these sensorimotor skills develops in a logical progression from motor movements to the concept to understanding that symbols (e.g., pictures) represent the object."

At birth, the infant's behavior is reflexive in nature. Gradually, as the child integrates sensory perceptual information (Table 47) with motor movement explorations, s/he begins to develop concepts and understand labels attached to these concepts. The child begins to anticipate events such as feeding from cues (e.g., bib put on, assembly of dishes). Increased fine and gross motor skills development allows the child to explore objects within easy reach and to use locomotion to explore objects out of reach.

The 8-to-12-month-old child begins to coordinate two schemata, or ways of interacting with objects and to use intentional behavior to encourage adults to continue interactions or to seek toys dropped or out of reach. The child begins to understand the use of symbols in the form of pictures or miniature representations (Table 47). One of the most significant acquisitions during this period is the development of object permanence — the knowledge that an object continues to exist even though s/he cannot hear, touch, or see the object (Ruff, 1982). For sighted children, the development of object permanence begins with visual fixation and tracking or following an object or person (Bailey & Wolery, 1984). Exploration

TABLE 47
SENSORIMOTOR STAGE COGNITIVE SKILL DEVELOPMENT

Age	Behavior
0–1 month	• Reflex activity only (e.g., sucking, crying, grasping). • No differentiation of stimuli.
1–4 months	• Hand-to-mouth coordination. • Differentiation via sucking reflex. • Beginning pre-causal understanding (e.g., sucks thumb). • Visual following, auditory orienting. • Beginning to anticipate events, show curiosity. • Sporadic imitation (verbal and gestural). • OBJECT CONCEPT ATTAINED.
4–8 months	• Eye-hand coordination beginning. • Imitative assimilation, verbal and gestural. • Repeats action to continue consequence. • Beginning notion of object permanence. • Searches for objects partially hidden. • ANTICIPATION ESTABLISHED.
8–12 months	• Consistently imitates invisible movements. • Imitates similar novel sounds. • Coordination of two schemata. • Examines 3-dimensional objects. • OBJECT PERMANENCE ATTAINED. • Onset of intentional behavior. • Secures objects seen hidden under/behind a barrier. • Touches adults' hands to continue game. • Beginning to use symbols.
12–18 mos.	• New means through experimentation. • Follows sequential displacements and gains hidden objects. • CAUSALITY ATTAINED. • Imitates new behaviors systematically and new sounds.
18–24 mos.	• REPRESENTATIVE IMITATION. • Capable of deferred imitation. • Internal representation—represents things and events in mind using images, symbols, and language. • New means through mental combinations. • INTENTIONAL BEHAVIOR (MEANS–ENDS) ESTABLISHED. • Uses trial and error to solve problems. • Capable of true thought. • OBJECT CONSTANCY ESTABLISHED. • Matching and classification.

REFERENCES: Wadsworth, 1984; Mann & Sabatino, 1985; Lerner et al., 1987; Bailey & Wolery, 1984.

and curiosity enhance the child's understanding of causality. "Causality refers to children's recognition of causes for interesting events, particularly the infant's realization that behavior can produce changes in objects. The social component of causality has to do with the infant's ability to realize that other people can cause important things to occur" (Bailey & Wolery, 1984, 165). The child discovers new means or methods of performing a specific activity through experimentation.

Imitation is developmental in nature, beginning in the average child from 1–4 months of age with sporadic imitation, generally vocal in nature, and progressing to clear representational imitation by 18–24 months of age (Bailey & Wolery, 1984). Learning to imitate involves the child acquiring the ability to match his/her behavior (e.g., verbal, vocal, motor movement) to that of the model. Most young children spend a considerable amount of time involved in the observation and imitation of siblings, peers, and caretakers. "Imitation not only facilitates the development of representation and symbolic thinking, but also opens up a world of potential learning opportunities" (Bailey & Wolery, 1984, 83).

By two years of age, the average nonhandicapped child realizes that s/he can affect his/her environment through intentional behavior. The acquisition of intentional behavior (means-ends) represents the beginning of true thought as the child has acquired concepts, images, symbols, and language to discuss ideas and consider objects and people not physically present. "Means-ends behavior involves purposeful problem-solving using both objects and people. It is the ability of the child to separate the procedures (means) for solving a problem from the goal (ends) of the solved problem" (Bailey & Wolery, 1984, 162). A major development during this period is understanding object constancy—that objects and people placed in different settings remain essentially the same. The normal two-year-old child has acquired preacademic skills in matching shapes, textures, and sizes, and classifying objects by form or shape and action or function.

Cognitive Developmental Delays

Handicapped children appear to develop sensorimotor skills in a similar sequence to that of nonhandicapped children (Table 47). However, the particular characteristics of the handicapping condition may cause significant delay or may severely retard the acquisition of the sensorimotor skills and, depending on the handicap, some of the developmental steps may be omitted.

Object concept appears from one to three years delayed in blind children due to failure to reach for objects and inability to use vision to integrate auditory and tactile cues to maintain contact with the environment (Fallen & Umansky, 1985). The blind baby experiences difficulty in learning object permanence because "vision provides perceptual information about the physical attributes, functions, and relationships of objects which are necessary for concept formation" (Sonksen, 1983, 93).

The congenitally blind child cannot imitate actions easily, making the learning of skills much harder (Hunt & Wills, 1983). Handicapped children must be trained to imitate, while nonhandicapped children generally learn verbal and gestural imitations in a social or game-like situation. Since vision is the major coordinating sense, deficits in vision will severely impact acquiring skills that require integration of various sensory perceptual skills as well as perceptual-motor integration.

The mentally retarded child by definition has cognitive deficits and/or cognitive delays. "Most evidence points to problems in memory and attention being responsible for the mentally retarded child's subnormal performance compared with her normal peers" (Fallen & Umansky, 1985, 271). Ellis (1970) proposed that mentally retarded children have memory problems due to a lack of rehearsal strategies. The Information Processing Construct (Table 45) suggests that difficulties anywhere in the information processing process will significantly impair or disturb the acquisition and storage of information and the ability to demonstrate such knowledge.

The physically impaired child who is unable to move freely may be unable to manipulate objects, to recognize his/her influence on the universe, and may not change position to view surroundings from different perspectives (Fallen & Umansky, 1985). The physically impaired child may be significantly delayed in accomplishment of the reach and grasp skills, which inhibits causality and object permanence.

The deaf-blind severely multihandicapped child, however, experiences not only the individual effects of hearing impairment, visual impairment, mental retardation, and, frequently, physical impairment and/or other health concerns, but the multiplicity effect of these handicapping conditions. Thus, the progress toward cognitive development in deaf-blind severely multihandicapped children is extremely slow as the child learns nothing spontaneously.

SENSORIMOTOR STAGE: COGNITIVE EVALUATION

Cognitive assessment is conducted for two primary purposes—diagnostic labeling (evaluation) and program planning. Diagnostic labeling frequently requires the use of norm-referenced tests which, at the developmental or preschool level, consist primarily of lists of skills (e.g., fine and gross motor, receptive and expressive language, self-help skills) which should be accomplished by average children at specific ages. The child is observed systematically and assessed through clinical teaching to determine his/her functioning level. Scores are reported in age ranges or age scores (e.g., 1–4 months range in expressive language or 4.2 years in fine motor skills). These norm-referenced instruments allow the examiner to determine how a child compares to same-aged peers on various tasks and to determine an intelligence quotient, cognitive functioning range or mental age. These scores are used in determining degree of mental retardation, and suggest types of services needed by the child (e.g., resource room, self-contained classroom). The majority of these norm-referenced diagnostic instruments are administered by the school psychologists and are not available to teachers.

The Callier-Azusa Scale, subscale Cognition, is useful in determining a developmental functioning level in cognition. Informal developmental assessments such as Sensorimotor Stage Cognitive Skill Development (Table 47) facilitate determining functioning levels for diagnostic labeling.

Assessment for planning students' short-term objectives, particularly those of severely multihandicapped children, requires very specific information including task analyses of specific skills. Cognitive Skills Hierarchies (Table 50) provide detailed information for program planning. It is not enough to know that the teacher needs to provide instruction in imitation. The teacher using the task analysis of the skills involved in the development of imitation can begin at the child's highest known level of achievement and successively provide higher cognitive-level imitation skills.

Numerous sources have task-analyzed most of the areas of concern of severely handicapped children. A useful guide is **A Manual for the Assessment of a Deaf-Blind Multiply Handicapped Child** (Randolph et al., Undated).

Case Study Evaluation Report: Sally

Sally's psychological report indicates the functioning profile of a deaf-blind severely multihandicapped child who is functioning at the newborn cognitive level (Table 48).

TABLE 48
SALLY'S PSYCHOLOGICAL REPORT

Current Evaluation:	The Callier-Azusa Scale CA 4 yrs, 8 mo.
	MA Newborn

(IQ range is Profound.)

Sally's cognitive development was assessed by a psychological examiner using *The Callier-Azusa Scale* and on a separate occasion by an educational examiner using *The Scale of Cognitive Development: Sensorimotor Stage.* The results indicated essentially the same functioning abilities.

Sally's level of cognition was assessed at the 0–1 month, newborn level. She responded to touch stimulation by smiling or vocalizing when her cheek was stroked. She made no definite response to noise and very inconsistent responses to colored light. She will cry when she feels discomfort, usually intestinal, or when she is placed in a position she doesn't tolerate. Sally is beginning to exhibit some hand-to-mouth behavior when placed on her back or side. She is generally unresponsive to her environment unless an adult intervenes with tactile input. After tactile contact, Sally will smile or vocalize, demonstrating the beginning of cause-effect understanding.

Case Study Evaluation Report: Bud

Bud's psychological report indicates that he is functioning within the profound range of intellectual abilities (Table 49). His current cognitive functioning is below the six-month level with splinter skills up to the one-year level.

COGNITIVE PROGRAMMING: SENSORIMOTOR STAGE

"The underlying premise of early childhood special education is the belief that programmatic intervention can enhance cognitive development for at-risk and handicapped children" (Lerner, 1987, 225). Schiffe and Foulke (1982) indicate that early experience is of particular importance in programming the central nervous system and developing learning sequences because after the preschool years, the nervous system is less pliable and responsive to tactile and auditory stimulation. Handicapped children may require a more structured program than nonhandicapped children because they are not as likely to explore their environment,

TABLE 49
BUD'S PSYCHOLOGICAL REPORT

Previous Evaluation:
(PSR) The Psychological Stimulus Response
Evaluation for Severely Multiply Handicapped
Children (Muller et al., 1977):

	CA	2 yrs., 3 mos.
	MA	3–4 mos.

Current Evaluation:
Callier-Azusa Scale (Cognition)   CA   8 yrs., 6 mos.
                                   MA   3–4 mos.

Bud was assessed through interviewing his teacher. He was observed at the lunch table in the classroom. During this period, he was observed to involve himself in frequent self-stimulation. The stimulatory repertoire reported and observed includes hitting his head with his fist, poking his head repetitively with his finger, poking his ear, rocking, vocalizing, thumb sucking with simultaneous eye poking, rubbing his eyes with his fist, batting his head with open palm, and chewing objects.

He has no usable vision and a severe hearing loss. However, he reacts to tactile and kinesthetic stimulation and is especially fond of moving equipment. He moves appropriately on a rocking horse, a rocking chair, and a swing. Interaction with objects is limited to banging them, especially banging them against his head.

Object permanence for familiar objects around the room (table, swing) seems to be developed. Bud may bump into other objects in his path. Cause-effect also seems emerging as he knows how to manipulate the rocking horse, rocking chair, and swing. He pulls out large pegs from a pegboard and removes objects from a container one at a time.

Communication skills are very limited, but Bud can now sign "drink."

Bud is functioning within a profound mentally handicapped range of intelligence.

---

may not learn through simple manipulation, and may not independently engage in exploratory behaviors that facilitate long-term growth (Bailey & Wolery, 1984).

> The importance of exploration and the effects of inadequate exploratory skills becomes even more apparent when considering young children with sensory or motor impairments that can reduce such opportunities. This results in the secondary handicap of deficits in experiences (Bailey & Wolery, 1984, 100).

Handicapped children appear to progress developmentally through a similar sequence of sensorimotor skills as nonhandicapped. However, some handicapping conditions such as mental retardation change the rate of progress. Some handicapping conditions such as physical impairments deprive the child of experiences which encourage using motor skills to solve problems. Deaf-blind severely multihandicapped children may be severely delayed in progress due to deficits in all major information input systems, thereby causing no spontaneous learning.

Bailey & Wolery (1984) emphasize teaching handicapped children horizontally as well as vertically. Vertical instruction occurs when emphasis is placed on accelerating children's attainment of developmental milestones, including specific sequences of sensorimotor skills. Horizontal instruction aims to teach generalization of skills by having the child perform them in a variety of situations. Functional skills should be taught in functional settings: for example, toilet training should occur in the bathroom.

Cognitive programming involves facilitating the development of the following sensorimotor stage skills: (1) object concept, (2) imitation, (3) anticipation, (4) object permanence, (5) causality, (6) object constancy, (7) intentional behavior (means-ends), (8) matching (e.g., shapes, textures, sizes, colors), and (9) classification (e.g., function, color, shape, size). The Sensorimotor Cognitive Programming Skills Hierarchies (Table 50) was prepared to assist teachers in informally assessing students' functioning levels, but primarily to assist in writing specific behavioral objectives in the sensorimotor cognitive skills areas.

Object Concept

Object concept—the first major cognitive skill to be acquired—is attained by nonhandicapped by about 4 months of age (Table 47). This skill is acquired years later in severely multihandicapped children.

Activities to assist in developing object concept with deaf-blind severely multihandicapped will primarily utilize the tactile sense, encouraging manipulation and tactually exploring objects (Table 50). Some of the first object concepts will probably involve eating/feeding utensils and other items used in daily living. Tactile development is a prerequisite skill to cognitive development for the deaf-blind child.

Anticipation

The average four-month-old child begins to anticipate daily events such as eating and bathing, by eight months of age, clearly understands the concept of anticipation (Table 47). In nonhandicapped children, the development of this skill begins very early with whole body reactions to cues and progresses to anticipation based on individual sensory cues (e.g., visual, auditory, or tactile-kinesthetic). The child soon learns that preparations in the kitchen (e.g., getting little jars out of the cabinet, formula out of the refrigerator, etc.) are connected with his/her mealtime. Various cues assist the child in learning routines of the family.

For deaf-blind severely multihandicapped children, anticipation is not spontaneously learned by observing mother's routine and that of other family members. The deaf-blind severely multihandicapped child must have systematic teaching to develop anticipation. Skill development should begin almost as soon as the child is brought home from the hospital. Since vision and hearing do not provide primary cues, the caregiver should use tactile cues in teaching anticipation.

When picking up the deaf-blind infant, slip your hands under him/her and indicate the coming action with a false start, pause to allow the child to anticipate the coming action, then pick him/her up (McInnes & Treffry, 1982). Use cues to indicate specific events, always using the same cue. For example, prior to feeding, use a signal (e.g., stroke the cheek or touch finger to lip or touch nipple and later spoon to lip) to indicate the next activity. It may take some time for the deaf-blind severely multi-handicapped child to learn the "signal" system; therefore, the signals should be closely related to the activity and all caregivers should use the same signal to assist in generalization.

McInnes and Treffry (1982) suggest that each family member or caregiver have a special signal that identifies them. Always make initial contact using the special signal. Thus, the child will eventually anticipate inter-actions with various persons.

Imitation

By eight months of age, the average child understands and enjoys verbal and gestural imitation (Figure 47). "Many severely retarded children do not learn how to imitate and must be taught this skill. Research has clearly demonstrated that handicapped children do not learn as efficiently through observational learning as nonhandicapped" (Bailey & Wolery, 1984, 81). "Learning to imitate focuses on the infant acquiring the capacity to match his/her behavior to that of a model" (Bailey & Wolery, 1984, 82).

Verbal imitation is very important in developing oral motor skills and the speech muscles needed for sound/speech production. Imitation of gestures is crucial in learning manual signs/natural gestures (Table 50). Initially, "cognitive development requires that the infant/child engage

TABLE 50
SENSORIMOTOR COGNITIVE PROGRAMMING SKILLS HIERARCHIES

I. OBJECT CONCEPT
_____ Holds object briefly.
_____ Holds object and uses randomly.
_____ Explores object sensorily (i.e., visually, orally, tactually).
_____ Independently recognizes objects for their function.
_____ Uses object for purposeful action (i.e., rolls ball).

II. IMITATION
_____ Responds verbally to familiar vocal productions.
_____ Imitates familiar sound patterns (babbling).
_____ Imitates familiar gestures.
_____ Imitates unfamiliar sound patterns.
_____ Imitates complex familiar gestures.
_____ Imitates familiar words and new words.
_____ Imitates unfamiliar visible gestures.
_____ Engages in extensive imitation of words.
_____ Initiates a new behavior similar to those in repertoire.
_____ Uses common objects that indicate knowledge of function (i.e., sweeps with broom, wipes face with napkin).
_____ Uses gestures/manual signs to represent objects/activities.
_____ Imitates a new sequence of behaviors.
_____ Imitates an activity/behavior sequence after considerable elapsed time.
_____ Engages in imaginary play by using objects to represent other objects.
_____ Reproduces activities which normally occur in a different context.

III. ANTICIPATION
_____ Anticipates a familiar event from whole body cues.
_____ Responds to cues from another person by participating their movement activity.
_____ Recognizes familiar object or beginning of familiar activity.
_____ Anticipates a routine event from visual, auditory, and/or tactile-kinesthetic cues.

IV. OBJECT PERMANENCE
_____ Unaware of object after it disappears.
_____ Reacts to disappearing object.
_____ Searches momentarily for an object that has disappeared.
_____ Plays purposeful primitive hiding games (covering and finding, dropping and searching).
_____ Finds partially hidden object.
_____ Finds completely hidden object.
_____ Finds object under superimposed objects.
_____ Finds object after systematic search.
_____ Reacts to brokenness of objects.
_____ Recognizes that an object continues to exist after s/he can no longer see, touch, hear, or smell it.

V. CAUSALITY
_____ Repeats actions to produce interesting result (i.e., bats mobile, rocks rocking chair).
_____ Uses a gesture to indicate the activated object.
_____ Starts movements of objects.

Table 50 (Continued)

_____ Looks for ways to activate object.
_____ Recognizes that a person is causing the action.
_____ Recognizes the reason for the action.
_____ Searches for an independent cause.
_____ Tries to activate an object by any method.
_____ Tries to copy method of activation of object.

VI.   OBJECT CONSTANCY
_____ Briefly remembers location of object.
_____ Recognizes an object as same, whether viewing all or part of object.
_____ Examines objects by manipulating them.
_____ Associates several familiar objects with specific actions (i.e., rocking chair, rocking horse—rocking action).
_____ Demonstrates knowledge that a disappeared object may be found in different places.
_____ Locates objects in customary places.
_____ Understands that a picture represents real object.
_____ Knows which items are necessary to carry out familiar activity (i.e., eating—bowl, spoon, etc.).

VII. INTENTIONAL BEHAVIOR (Means-Ends)
_____ Development of mouthing objects.
_____ Uses one or more behaviors with objects.
_____ Makes a simple movement toward an object.
_____ Makes a complex movement toward an object.
_____ Development of "letting go."
_____ Achievement of visually directed grasp.
_____ Repetition of action for interesting result.
_____ Engages in several actions with objects.
_____ Overcomes obstacle to reach for object.
_____ Letting go of one object to get another object.
_____ Uses some form of locomotion to get object.
_____ Uses an object to get an object.
_____ Combines two behaviors to get an object.
_____ Puts small objects in and out of container.
_____ Demonstrates solutions to problems without engaging in trial and error behaviors (representation of means).

VIII. CLASSIFICATION
_____ Groups objects by function (relational classification).
_____ Groups objects by common attributes of size, color, shape (descriptive classification).
_____ Groups items by general categories (i.e., fruit, animals—generic classification).

IX.   MATCHING
_____ Matches two distinctly different shapes.
_____ Matches two distinctly different colors.
_____ Matches two distinctly different textures.
_____ Matches two distinctly different sizes.

REFERENCES: Lerner et al., 1987; Stillman, 1966; Dunst, 1980; Rudolph et al., Undated; Stevens, 1973.

in encounters with objects in the environment" (Wyne & O'Connor, 1979, 65). Sensorimotor intelligence has a motor basis; thus, as the child imitates various activities and engages in imaginary play, s/he is increasing in understanding of concepts.

Imitation training will initially involve considerable systematic observation to determine spontaneous sounds or actions the child engages in. These sound patterns and movement patterns will serve as initial imitation activities as the teacher imitates the child, encouraging the child to continue the responses (Table 50). Imitating the child may be reinforcing and assist in making accidental sounds and movements become purposeful.

Imitation is an extremely important skill for the severely multihandicapped child to acquire because it serves as a prerequisite to many of the other developmental skill areas. Coactive movement (e.g., manipulating the child to assist in activities) may be a very important way for the deaf-blind child to learn imitation.

Bailey & Wolery (1983, 8) provide a summary of procedures for teaching children to imitate, including the following: "(1) imitate the child; (2) provide models appropriate to the child's developmental level; (3) provide assistance (prompts, when necessary—e.g., mirrors, physical prompting); (4) make imitation activities enjoyable; and (5) reward the child's imitative responses."

Object Permanence

Nonhandicapped generally attain object permanence by 12 months of age (Table 47). The child recognizes that an object continues to exist even after s/he can no longer see, touch, hear, or smell it. The year-old child will systematically search for "lost" objects. The child learns that mother still exists, although in another room out of sight. His/her toys still exist even though dropped out of sight over the side of the crib or highchair. Severely multihandicapped children may take many years to acquire the concept of object permanence. Object permanence is a fairly high level of sensorimotor cognition, requiring many prerequisites of motor skill development and acquisition of other cognitive skills such as object concept, anticipation, and imitation.

Many of the Secondary Senses Activities (Table 34) are effective in teaching object permanence. Object permanence is not actually a teacher-taught concept, but a self-discovery process as a result of carefully organized and presented activities by the teacher. For severely multihandicapped children, acquisition of this concept may be a very gradual realization. The activities used in setting the environment to encourage object permanence should be presented in a game-like or enjoyable situation including activities such as searching for toys in a carpeted barrel or "feely" bag, sand and/or water play with cups and toys, digging for objects in buried sand, playing hide-and-seek games, "peek-a-boo," and making a game of the child's self-explorations of dropping things off the highchair or out of the crib.

Unlimited opportunities exist during daily activities to play hide-and-seek, including the following: (1) take off child's coat on arrival, move out of sight but near, "Where is your coat?" (2) move cup or spoon from usual place, "Where is your cup?" (3) during dressing practice, wad T-shirt up in your hand, "Where is your shirt?" Try to involve secondary senses, especially tactile and olfactory, in the exploratory behaviors. Hiding items with a scent initially assists in the location of objects (e.g., oranges or scented food, perfumed toy or scarf, "smelly" stickers on objects) and helps the child "get the idea" of the task.

Causality

Causality involving sensorimotor knowledge is usually attained by nonhandicapped children by about 18 months of age. The child realizes that s/he can make objects move with whole body motion such as rocking in a rocking chair or with specific movements such as moving toy cars with one hand. The child learns to explore a new toy by searching for ways to activate it. The child's later understandings of cause-effect relationships are based on his/her sensorimotor understandings of causality (actions caused by motor initiation). Handicapped children generally progress through a similar sequence of skills (Table 47) as they gain understanding of causality, but sensory modifications must be made for deaf-blind and physical modifications made for orthopedically handicapped. The social component of causality has to do with the child's ability to understand that other people can cause things to occur that affect him/her directly and that s/he can do things that cause others to act, eventually in predictable ways (Bailey & Wolery, 1984).

Initial learning about causality often occurs as the child performs a motor act for a pleasurable or interesting result (e.g., batting a mobile, moving in a rocking chair). Toys that vibrate, move, produce sound or light after the child pushes or hits them (e.g., roly-poly toy, toys secured by suction that can be hit, pound-a-round, music box toy) are useful in developing the notion of causality. The more active handicapped child may use rocking and bouncing toys, small toy pianos, record players designed for children that play after the lid is shut, toy typewriters that make noise when hit, inflated balloons, balls, glow-toys can be used in causality training. Vibrating pads and lighted mobiles attached to mercury switches are often used with the lower-functioning child to begin causality understanding.

Daily living training provides many opportunities to assist in causality development, particularly the "accidents." Failure to set the cup on the table results in spilled milk. Spoons and cups not secured or held appropriately may drop to the floor. Putting clothing on incorrectly can be used in cause-effect training. The whole process of "getting the idea" about toilet training involves understanding causality.

Object Constancy

The concept of object constancy is attained by nonhandicapped children near the end of the sensorimotor stage (e.g., about two years of age) and is predicated upon acquisition of object concept and object permanence understandings (Table 47). The child gradually learns that an object retains its characteristics regardless of the setting in which it is located. The child is able to generalize that a highchair is the same, whether in the kitchen, living room, family room, or local restaurant. Object constancy allows a child to develop visual closure in which his/her mind completes a picture based on viewing the picture with a piece gone. Gradually, the child learns that various items are customarily located in certain places and which items are necessary to carry out familiar tasks.

With handicapped children, the generalization of object constancy cannot be assumed; thus, skills are taught and practiced in numerous settings with a variety of materials and various caregivers or teachers. While feeding/eating may initially be conducted at the table in the classroom, it should also at some point occur in the lunchroom, and parents continue the generalization process at home in the kitchen and at restaurants. Other daily activities are perfect settings or situations to foster the concept of object constancy (e.g., the jacket worn to school is the same one worn home). The idea of ownership ("mine") contributes to acquisition of object constancy. Mother as room mother or school volunteer assists the child in understanding that people remain the same although they may have different roles and be in different places.

Intentional Behavior (Means-Ends)

"Means-Ends behavior involves purposeful problem-solving using both objects and people. It is the ability of the child to separate the procedures (means) for solving a problem from the goal (end) of the solved problem" (Bailey & Wolery, 1984, 162). The onset of understanding intentional behavior occurs at about 8–12 months of age (Table 47). The child gradually learns that s/he can have some effect on their environment. Locomotion skills allow the child to seek toys/objects out of reach and to move within the environment. The child learns to make purposive movements. The action-motor learning assists the child in the development of symbolic understandings as s/he learns to solve problems without trial/error behaviors.

The development of intentional behavior begins with early reach and grasp or reach and bat motions, and mouthing objects (Table 50). All of the activities which help develop imitation, object constancy, and causality contribute to the acquisition of the concept of means-ends. Secondary Senses Activities and Motor Development Activities are helpful in developing the concept of intentionality. Initially, the child makes things happen as s/he plays in water or sand, fingerpaints, builds with blocks or jello cubes, bangs on rhythm band instruments, makes "things" of play dough, makes "things" work. Gradually, the child learns that the adult can be used as a tool to get things the child cannot reach, to buy things at the store, to help put on boots, to show him/her how to do something s/he can't do or suggest ways to solve the problem.

Classification and Matching

Classification and matching are high-level sensorimotor stage skills which require the child to classify and match items by size, shape, color, and texture (Table 50). Again, there are numerous opportunities during daily activities in which matching and classification can occur (e.g., group eating utensils—spoons, plates; match pictures of clothing to clothing items; match chairs). Numerous toys are on the market that facilitate matching as well as items the creative teacher can collect. A box of matching and classification items might include some of the following:

crayons and tagboard colored squares, blocks of many sizes and colors, balls of several sizes and colors, matchbox trucks and cars of various colors, dollhouse furniture and pictures of furniture, pictures of fruit/vegetables and smelly stickers, measuring cups and spoons, various sizes/colors of beads, large buttons of various colors and designs, pictures of food and plastic representations, pictures of common domestic animals and small toy animals, paper dolls and clothes, textured items.

During various seasons of the year, the teacher can have children match real leaves to plastic leaves, pine cones of various sizes, flowers of various types and colors, rocks of various sizes, etc. The only limit on items for matching and classification is the teacher's imagination.

Cognitive Program Planning

Sensorimotor Cognitive Skills Hierarchies (Table 50) and Sensorimotor Stage Cognitive Developmental Levels (Table 47) are helpful in planning students' Individual Education Programs (IEPs); annual goals and short-term objectives. Developmental checklists assist teachers not only in preparing annual plans, but also in noting future target goals and providing direction to the planning. Hierarchies are especially helpful with planning objectives.

Case Study IEP: Sally

Sally is functioning primarily on a reflexive level, generally unresponsive to her environment unless an adult initiates contact tactilely. After tactile contact, she responds by smiling or vocalizing; thus, she appears to be demonstrating the beginning of causality understanding. Her IEP Goal is to improve cognitive abilities in cause-effect behavior. At this level, causality is learned through sensorimotor activities which allow or encourage her to repeat actions to produce a result (Table 50).

Sally's IEP

Cognitive Goal:	Sally will improve cognitive abilities in cause-effect behavior.
Objective A:	Sally will make any arm or leg movements to activate an auditory, visual, or tactile reinforcer using a mercury switch for 8 out of 10 movements of 20-

Objective B:
second duration each during a 15-minute period on 3 consecutive data days as implemented by teacher/ teacher assistant under physical therapist guidance. Sally will make batting or hitting movements to activate an auditory, visual, or tactile reinforcer attached to a mobile on 8 out of 10 trials on 3 consecutive data days as implemented by teacher/teacher assistant under physical therapist guidance.

The use of active stimulation programs have been successful with low-functioning children. The active stimulation equipment generally used with Sally includes an arm/leg mercury switch, a head mercury switch, a pressure pad switch, and a computerized control box. The arm/leg switch, when placed accurately on the child's arm or leg, will pick up any slight movement of these extremities made by the child. The movement moves the mercury, which in turn activates the reinforcer. The computerized control box allows variables to be programmed into it. For Sally, the control box has been programmed to activate the reinforcer for each movement of 20 seconds duration. As Sally's skills improve, the control box can be programmed to allow her to make two or more movements or maintain the movements for a predetermined amount of time before receiving reinforcement.

To work toward the objective of increasing cause-effect behavior through arm/leg movements, Sally will be positioned in a supine position. This positioning is comfortable and tolerated very well by Sally. It does not require her to have as much control or strength to move her extremities as when in a semireclined or upright position. Sally will have a mercury switch attached to her forearm or lower leg or shoe. The switch must be positioned on her arm/leg so that her slightest movement will be recorded. As Sally moves her arm/leg, the switch activates a reinforcer such as a visual reinforcer of colored lights or a rotating color wheel; an auditory reinforcer of environmental sounds or music; a tactile reinforcer such as a vibrating pad; and/or an olfactory reinforcer such as an aroma disc. To help Sally use all of her senses, a variety of reinforcers will be used during programming.

When Objective A has been achieved, the next phase of more purposeful cause-effect behavior will focus on getting Sally to hit a mobile placed within her reach. She will be positioned either in supine or side-lying with the mobile near her. The mercury switch will be attached to the mobile. Each batting/hitting movement will activate the reinforcers previously indicated. The reinforcer will be changed as progress is made to be certain that the cause-effect behavior is truly being established and Sally is beginning to exert some control on her environment.

Case Study IEP: Bud

Bud appears to be functioning within the 6-to-12-month range (Table 49). He appears to have acquired **object concept** for familiar objects (e.g., eating utensils and toys). He uses movement toys (e.g., rocking chair, horse, and swing) for **purposeful action** and independently recognizes these objects for their function. Bud has some **imitation** skills and has learned to sign "drink." He **anticipates** eating time when the spoon is placed in his hand. Lack of vision and hearing have considerably delayed acquisition of object permanence; however, he appears to have object permanence for his favorite motion toys and for some familiar objects within the classroom such as the table. Causality is limited to manipulating the rocking horse, rocking chair, and swing. Object constancy also is emerging as he knows the location of the motion toys and uses them appropriately. He examines objects by briefly manipulating them; then uses them to bang on the floor, table, or his head. Bud has some idea of intentional behavior as he feeds himself, locomotes about the classroom, uses motion toys, and puts small objects in a container.

Cognitive Skills Hierarchies (Table 50) are useful in determining specific levels for purposes of program planning. Object concept, causality, and intentional behavior require that students use objects for purposeful action and interact appropriately with other objects. The Sensory Stimulation Profile (Tables 14, 22, 26, 27) will be consulted to determine a menu of reinforcers for Bud to be used in developing his cognitive abilities.

Bud's IEP

Cognitive Goal:	Bud will improve cognitive abilities in intentional behavior.
Objective A:	Bud will interact with common objects appropriately (e.g., no head-banging) during such activities as stringing beads, building a 3-block tower, etc. on 4 out of 5 trials on 3 successive data days as implement-

	ed by teacher/teacher assistant.
Objective B:	Bud will search tactilely for objects presented for exploration and removed to within various reach distances during primitive purposeful hiding games on 8 out of 10 trials on 3 successive data days as implemented by teacher/teacher assistant.

IEP Monitoring

Deaf-blind severely multihandicapped children progress very slowly. Frequent collection of performance data on very specific objectives assists the teacher in determining if/when a change of behavior has occurred that may show new growth in an area or new problem areas. Data collection charts using Programming Skills are helpful in documenting performance toward the various cognitive skills. Since the sensorimotor cognitive skills are interrelated and students often work on several during the same period, it is helpful to have the skills task analyses on the same grid(s).

Teachers will want to periodically collect data regarding developmental progress. Checklists (Table 47) may be helpful in monitoring cognitive developmental skill progress.

SUMMARY

Cognition is frequently viewed from three major perspectives: as a process, as a capacity, and as a product. Information processing is the cognitive process by which the brain receives information from sensory perceptions, interprets and mediates the information using thinking and memory strategies, and acts upon the information by means of a verbal, fine motor, or gross motor response. No one knows precisely how cognition occurs, but a construct was proposed to facilitate conceptualization that involves three major stages or mechanism systems (e.g., transmission of information, central processing of information, and behavioral responses to information) and seven separate components (e.g., sensory register, sensory perceptions, sensory integration, short-term memory, working memory, long-term memory, responses). Cognitive capacities are the structures, aptitudes, and skills that create or otherwise make cognitive processes possible. Many of these perceptual and memory skills are under voluntary control and can be taught or trained. Some of the most popular "new" cognitive strategies include cognitive behavior modification and metacognition. Of primary concern to special education teachers are the cognitive control styles usually used by handicapped children.

Information processing problems can and do occur in handicapped children at every point in the process. These cognitive processing problems are primarily due to an interruption in: (1) attention to stimuli, (2) reception of stimuli, (3) storage and processing of information, and (4) expression of cognitive abilities. Deaf-blind severely multihandicapped children experience difficulties due to all four reasons because of sensory deficits, brain damage, and psychomotor delay.

The sensorimotor stage of cognitive development, birth to 18–24 months, is the stage in which the child learns through sensory perception, movement and motor skills, and interactions with the environment. The primary sensorimotor cognitive skills include object concept, anticipation, imitation, object permanence, causality, object constancy, and intentional behavior. Each of these skills develops in a logical progression from motor movements to concept attainment. The acquisition of intentional behavior represents the beginning of true representational thought and enables the child to engage in problem-solving behavior.

Severely multihandicapped individuals are frequently fixated within the sensorimotor stage of cognitive thinking for a lifetime. At best, it takes many years for them to gradually attain the sensorimotor stage cognitive skills. Vision impairments and physical handicaps delay/impede attainment of object concept, object constancy, causality, imitation, object permanence, and intentionality. Severely multihandicapped children do not learn spontaneously. Direct teaching of cognitive concepts involves providing the activities and materials and organizing the environment to encourage self-discovery. Cognitive skills programming is intertwined in the total programming for all of the developmental areas—sensory stimulation, motor skill development, communication skill development, and social skill development, and relies significantly on sensory and motor skill development.

Chapter Seven

RECEPTIVE/EXPRESSIVE LANGUAGE: EVALUATION AND PROGRAMMING

Without adequate means of communication, the child is unable to progress through the stages of cognitive development appropriate to his age (McInnes & Treffry, 1982, 8).

- Language Development
  Language Development Prerequisites
  Nonintentional and Intentional Prelanguage
- Language Evaluation
- Expressive Language Prerequisites Programming
- Summary

CONSULTANTS:
Marion Howells, M.Ed.
Janet Sorth, M.A.

" A fundamental and pervasive problem in working with deaf-blind children is achieving adequate communication" (Sternberg, 1979, 36). The communication problems of deaf-blind severely multihandicapped are extremely severe. Deaf-blind severely multihandicapped children frequently continue to function communicatively at the prelinguistic stage due to auditory deficits that severely impact development in receptive and expressive language, to vision deficits that severely restrict exploration and concept development, to severe cognitive deficits that delay representational thought, to oral motor skill deficits that may preclude intelligible expressive language, to motor skill deficits that delay exploration, to fine and gross motor skill deficits that preclude natural gestures, and to social/emotional developmental deficits that reduce or eliminate the need for pragmatics or social language. "Visual impairment and hearing loss do not have an additive effect on the development and education of the child, but rather a multiplicative effect" (Meyer, 1979).

215

LANGUAGE DEVELOPMENT

The acquisition of a means of communication is crucial to the cognitive development of deaf-blind children, regardless of whether the communication involves conventional gestures, object boards, manual signs, language boards, fingerspelling, palmwriting, etc. and/or speech. The sensorimotor stage of communication development consists of the foundation skills upon which fluent expressive language is predicated, but ends at 18 to 24 months prior to the acquisition of linguistic fluency.

Language Development Prerequisites

Language is the symbolic means by which we organize our thoughts and share these thoughts with others. Expressive language allows us to not only communicate our basic needs, but also our ideas. Language provides the means through which a child learns about his/her world and how to function in socially appropriate ways. Speech is the verbal language code used in expressive communication. Children who are severely delayed in language acquisition, then, lack the means to organize and share thoughts and basic needs.

The process of acquiring language is extremely complex. A child must have normal functioning prerequisite systems in order to develop language at age appropriate times. Prerequisites to normal language development include normal hearing, vision, intelligence, memory, and attention abilities. The development of language is closely interwoven with the development of other sensorimotor skills such as oral motor skills of sucking, swallowing, chewing, and various tongue movements which serve as prerequisite skills to express language (Van Etten et al., 1980).

Hearing Prerequisites

Children with normal hearing must experience both environmental and verbal sounds for at least 4,000 hours before they utter their first word (Fallen & Umansky, 1985). Among the most important developmental accomplishments of the sensorimotor stage child are the acquisition of auditory inner language and auditory receptive language skills which begin long before the production of expressive language of any consequence (Cox & Lloyd, 1976). A hearing loss represents one of the most serious of all deterrents to language acquisition because hearing is the primary sensory avenue involved in language acquisition (Myklebust, 1963). Any disturbance in the peripheral or central auditory mechanism disrupts to some degree the acquisition and use of normal communication (Cox & Lloyd, 1976, 125). If the hearing impairment interferes with the acquisition of auditory inner language and auditory receptive language skills, expressive language may be significantly delayed or never acquired.

Vision Prerequisites

The role of vision in language development is obvious at the labeling stage and with the higher linguistic functions of reading and writing. Vision also plays an important role in early language development. One of the first significant developments in language is joint attending, which allows the caregiver to linguistically mark objects for the child (Fallen & Umansky, 1985). Thus, frequent parent/child interaction, paired with parents' verbal descriptions and discussions, not only assists the child in naming items, but also helps to develop a gestural system and the intonation structure of language.

Cognitive Prerequisites

Language acquisition and functioning ability increase as mental age increases. Mentally retarded children not only experience delayed receptive language acquisition, but also experience delays in expressive language skills such as articulation. Language and cognition interact reciprocally in their development. Language provides a coding system to organize cognitive structures.

Memory is a cognitive skill which plays a significant role in the acquisition of language. Various kinds of memory—auditory memory, visual memory, sequencing memory, short-term memory, working memory, long-term memory—are all important prerequisites to adequate language development. Language rehearsal is required for placing information into short-term memory. Obviously, sensory deficits hamper the development of auditory memory and visual memory which, in turn, negatively impacts language acquisition. Since language rehearsal is a primary means of gaining access to short-term memory, a severe language deficit may greatly reduce the abilities of a student to consistently use his/her short-term memory and thus reduce the amount of information placed in long-term memory storage.

Attention Prerequisites

Attention skills have a significant impact on language acquisition. In order to learn language, children must consciously attend to specific information while ignoring figure-ground interferences. Adequate attention is required for the child to place information into short-term memory storage. Inadequate attentional skills or attention deficit disorder will reduce the following: (1) the rate of the child's acquisition of concepts, (2) his/her ability to perceive nonlinguistic (affective cues) others send, (3) his/her understanding of pragmatics or social/communicative turn-taking, (4) the acquisition of prelinguistic skills of intonation and using a gestural system, and (5) the ability to use correct pronunciation of sounds/words.

Oral Motor Prerequisites

The development of oral motor feeding skills is intrinsically related to the development of muscles necessary for speech. Many deaf-blind severely multihandicapped children experience difficulties in learning to speak because of delayed oral motor development and/or lack of integration of primitive reflex patterns. A comparison of the development of oral motor skills and pre/early speech skills illustrates the reciprocal nature of these skill development areas (Table 51).

Thus, the child who continues to experience primitive reflexes does not have the conscious oral motor control required for production of sounds and words. Lip, tongue, and jaw control necessary for eating and drinking are also necessary for vocalization of syllables. Tongue lateralization and purposeful usage are essential in the production of "T, D, L, TH" sounds. As the child gains oral motor control during feeding, s/he is also developing the muscle control necessary for speech.

Interdependent Prerequisites

Language prerequisite abilities in hearing, vision, cognition and memory, attention, and oral motor skills do not develop in isolation, but are interdependent in nature. The interdependence of these developmental areas results in a multiplicity of deficits in deaf-blind severely multihandicapped children that significantly delay expressive language acquisition (Table 52).

Deficient perceptual systems (e.g., vision, hearing) not only impact negatively the rate of language acquisition, but also the linguistic compe-

TABLE 51
DEVELOPMENT OF ORAL MOTOR SKILLS

ORAL MOTOR SKILLS	*PRE & EARLY SPEECH SKILLS*
0–2 months	
Bite reflex	Reflexive cry develops into meaningful cry
Rooting reflex	Vocal sounds of pleasure, A, E
Suck-swallow reflex	
2–4 months	
Coordination of sucking, swallowing, and breathing	Coordination of breathing with production of speech
Mouth poises for nipple	Cooing, beginning of babbling
Rooting reflex gone	Sounds of P, B, M
4–5 months	
Tongue elevation enables child to move food off roof of mouth	Continuation of cooing and babbling Sounds, P, B, M
Can bring lips together at rim of cup	
Tongue projects after spoon or nipple is removed	
5–6 Months	
Tongue reversal after spoon removed	New mouth movements feel good to child. Therefore, he experiments with lips, tongue, and jaw movements.
Tongue thrust decreasing	
Pre-rotary chewing, moves mouth up and down	Will occasionally vocalize with different syllables.
Swallowing is completely voluntary	Utters vowel sounds (ee, ay,ah, ooh).
Smacking noises with lips	
Sucks liquid from cup	
Bite reflex gone	
Gag reflex diminished	
Good lip closure	
6–7 months	
Pulls food off spoon with lips	More frequent vocalizing with different syllables at one time
Keeps lips closed while chewing	May appear to be naming objects in own language
Good control with lips and tongue	Tries to imitate speech/inflection.
	Experiments with own sound.
7–9 months	
Feeds self cracker	Imitates sounds like a cough, click, and animal noises
Bites cracker	
Holds feeding bottle	
Enjoys chewing	

TABLE 51 (Continued)

ORAL MOTOR SKILLS	PRE & EARLY SPEECH SKILLS
9–10 months	
Tongue lateralization inside mouth begins	Early practice for later formulation of T, D,
Can protrude tongue purposely; licks food	L, TH
off spoon	Knows "mama" means mother and "dada"
Drooling ceases	means father
Lateral movement of jaw	
10–11 months	
Lateral motion of tongue inside or outside	Use of first words
mouth	Occasionally tries to imitate new words
Lifts food from lower lip	Uses all sounds
Tries to feed self	
11–13 months	
Chews well, aware of tongue	Longer vocal patterns
	Begins to use 3 or more words consistently,
	but may be hard to understand

REFERENCES: Copeland et al., 1976; Cohen & Gross, 1979; Gard et al., 1980; Fallen & Umansky, 1985.

TABLE 52
EXPRESSIVE LANGUAGE PREREQUISITES

Hearing:	*Vision:*
Receptive Language	Joint-Attending
Auditory Inner-Language	Gestural System
Intonation Structure of Language	
Linguistic Labeling	
Cognition:	*Oral Motor:*
Object Concept	Suck, Swallow, Breathing Coordination
Imitation	Lip, Tongue, Jaw Control
Intentionality (Symbolic Thinking)	Vocalizes Consonant and Vowel Sounds
Memory—short-term	
long-term	
language rehearsal	

Attention:
Communicative Turn-Taking
Nonlinguistic Cues

tence attainable. These deficits interfere with understanding the oral language of others or receptive language, and with developing self-talking and redundancy or inner language. Reduced vision and hearing affects the prelinguistic ability to derive meaning from the intonation system of language, interferes with imitation (cognition) and the ability to form a gestural system for communication. Inability to jointly-attend (vision) with caregivers reduces linguistic labeling of items and concepts, and thus interferes with development of cognition.

A cognitive prerequisite to the attainment of communication at the intentional prelanguage stage is the ability to imitate. Gross motor imitation, fine motor imitation, and oral motor imitation assist the child in understanding the process by which new skills are attained, and assist in learning from others. The child who cannot imitate cannot model behaviors after peers or adults, and cannot derive usable information from his/her environment.

An additional cognitive prerequisite to the attainment of speech is the acquisition of intentionality (means-ends), which is the ability to use symbolic or representational thought. Sensorimotor concepts of intentionality are acquired through the senses and motor movement during exploration and skill development. The child learns to use symbolic thinking through motor movement and imitation. Language acquisition is learning to function in another symbol system.

The absence of inner language interferes with memory development since it is necessary to rehearse, usually verbally, to put information into short-term memory. Information is stored in long-term memory semantically, usually verbally coded. Reduced inner language reduces the redundancy with which a child repeatedly echoes another's words or his own, reducing language experimentation. Reduced short-term memory interferes with remembering the speech code that is used to label items and concepts.

Severely deficit oral motor skills can prevent verbal communication altogether; however, a moderate deficit can interfere with the child's ability to correctly pronounce words and to be understood communicatively. Deficits in both hearing and oral motor skills can result in a child being unable to pronounce words accurately, both because s/he could not hear the sounds and because s/he could not control the oral muscles required to make the sounds. A deaf child cannot master the intonation system of language to convey meaning without words.

Many deaf-blind students are unable to focus their attention on acquiring language prerequisite skills because they are focused on numerous self-stimulation behaviors. Hearing, vision, and attention deficits interact to interfere with the child's understanding of communicative turn-taking and with his or her ability to "read" non-linguistic cues provided by the speaker.

Thus, the combined deficits in expressive language prerequisite skills

(Table 52) result in no automatic linguistic learning. Prerequisite skills in hearing, vision, cognition and memory, oral motor, and attention areas must be consciously, consistently taught and integrated before the child can become communicative. The language acquisition program for many deaf-blind children will strive to move them toward achieving functional language.

Nonintentional and Intentional Prelanguage

Nonintentional Prelanguage

The initial level of communication development involves nonintentional prelanguage behaviors. These behaviors include vocalizations and/or actions that are primarily reflexive in nature such as startling to a loud sound, reacting to a touch, or making reflexive, undifferentiated crying sounds, usually during the first month of life. By rewarding the reflexive nonintentional vocalizations, a causality understanding can be developed, thus allowing the child to begin the intentional use of prelanguage.

Intentional Prelanguage

Prior to the development of intentional prelanguage communication, the child needs to have a reason for communicating, a means of communication, and a social awareness of the effects of his/her communication (Stremel-Campbell, 1985). For example, an infant who is hungry, wet, or uncomfortable has a reason for communicating and may cry at various levels of intensity as a means of communication until someone relieves the discomfort, which is a social awareness of the effects of communication. Thus the child begins taking action on his/her environment. Around 9–12 months of age, normal babies develop a gestural system by which they communicate to adults (Fallen & Umansky, 1985).

Intentional communication includes three primary levels of skills including (1) intentional prelanguage, (2) emergent language, and (3) language (Stremel-Campbell, 1985). Intentional prelanguage is a communication system which uses nonlinguistic behaviors to convey meaning to another person. Intentional pre-language behaviors include touching a person or object to gain attention, manipulating a person, extending or manipulating an object to gain another's interest, showing-off, eye-gaze that is persistent and directed toward a specific person or thing, vocalizations or noises to attract attention, communicative pointing, making gestures to symbolize action desired, and showing objects with under-standing and communication implied (Stremel-Campbell, 1985).

Prelanguage communication provides three important functions for the child and caregiver. First, it provides the parent with a means to determine the intention of the utterance (Mahoney, 1975). Secondly, prelanguage communication provides the child with a means to detect meaning. Thirdly, it provides the parent with feedback regarding the child's receptive language development.

According to Stremel-Campbell (1985), the most probable types of prelanguage behaviors used by children with severe handicaps would include (1) touching an object, (2) manipulating a person, (3) extending an object, and (4) use of gestures (e.g., pointing). "The emergence of the pointing gesture indicates the onset of representational abilities" (Stillman & Battle, 1986, 324). The pointing gesture is an indication of the child's first use of symbolism (an action used to make reference to something) (Stillman & Battle, 1986).

The prelanguage behaviors exhibited by individual children will depend on numerous factors in addition to hearing, vision, and cognitive functioning levels including fine and gross motor skills and other complicating illnesses or conditions. The young deaf-blind severely multihandicapped child with cerebral palsy may not have the motor control to use gestures or signing and thus may be forced to rely on nonlinguistic vocalizations to communicate wants or needs.

Receptive Language Development

Receptive language development involves the child's ability to under-stand spoken, gestural, and intonation communication directed at him. Early receptive language skills parallel or duplicate auditory functional skill development as the child first gains an awareness to sound, localizes sound, discriminates sounds, recognizes and labels sounds (Table 21). Receptive language skills also include understanding intonation and the various forms and functions of spoken language. Children usually function at least a level higher in receptive than expressive language skills because understanding precedes skill execution. Adequate receptive language is the foundation of expressive language development.

Receptive language is developmental in nature and is interrelated with simultaneous development in cognition, perceptual skills, attention, and memory. Receptive language development at the sensorimotor level (Table 53) in nonhandicapped children during the first six months of life involves a localization of sound and responding to voice intonation. By 7–12 months, the child responds to communication with a gesture and demonstrates understanding the meaning of "No" by stopping on-going action. The average non-handicapped child understands 300 words and follows simple two-step directions by the age of two years (Table 53).

TABLE 53
RECEPTIVE LANGUAGE DEVELOPMENT: SENSORIMOTOR STAGE

Age (months)	Behavior
1–3	Responds to speech by looking at speaker. Perceives syllable unit.
4–6	Turns to source of sound. Looks for speaker. Understands own name. Responds differently to aspects of speaker's voice (i.e., friendly/unfriendly)
7–12	Responds with gesture to "hi," "bye-bye," "up" when paired with gesture. Stops ongoing action when told "no" (accompanied by appropriate gesture and tone)
12–24	Responds correctly when asked "where." Understands prepositions "on," "in," "under." Comprehends 300 words. Follows request to bring familiar object from another room. Understands simple phrases with key words (i.e., "Get the ball"). Follows a series of two simple but related directions.

REFERENCES: Gard et al., 1980; Stillman, 1978; Cohen et al., 1976; Lerner et al., 1987; Fallen & Umansky, 1985.

Emergent Language Development

Emergent language refers to the stage of language development when the child is learning to speak single meaningful words or use signs to communicate. This stage occurs about 18 months to two years developmental age in nonhandicapped children. Prelanguage skills serve as prerequisite skills to emergent language and supplement emergent language as the child attempts to communicate ideas for which s/he has not acquired linguistic labels. Spoken words or gestures are abstract symbols for actual objects, ideas, persons, actions, wants, needs. Functioning at the emergent language level provides clues to cognitive development that is occurring. Spoken language development at the sensorimotor level involves primarily prelanguage gestures and vocalizations, or one word paired with appropriate intonation (Table 54). The sensorimotor stage ends with the emergence of intentional language.

TABLE 54
SPOKEN LANGUAGE DEVELOPMENT: SENSORIMOTOR STAGE

Age (mo.)	Behavior
0–3 mo.	Makes crying and throaty sounds. Cooing one-syllable, vowel-like sounds. Whimpers, chortles, gurgles, squeals, chuckles. Vocalizes independently of environment. Vocal-social response to adult's smile and talk.
4–6 mo.	Begins babbling strings of syllable-like sounds. Vocalizes moods of pleasure up to 30 min. Laughs out loud. Imitates several sounds. Utters vowel sounds (ee, ay, ey, oh, ooh) and a few consonant-like sounds. Experiments with own sounds. Tries to imitate inflections. Vocalizes pleasure and displeasure. Babbles to female voices.
7–9 mo.	Uses "m, n, t, d, b, p, z" in babbling multiple syllables. May say "dada" and/or "mama." Intonation patterns become distinct. Signals emphasis and emotions by vocalizing. Imitates coughs, tongue clicks, hisses. Uses "mama" and "dada" as specific names.
10–12 mo.	Learns words and appropriate gestures (i.e., "no" and shakes head). Says two or more words besides "mama" and "dada." May repeat a word incessantly. Imitates inflections, speech rhythms, facial attitudes. Uses jargon, sentences of gibberish. Expresses thoughts with one word. Babbles short sentences. Uses all sounds (consonants and vowels).
1–2 years	Uses intonation and one word to express thoughts (Holophrastic Stage). Uses single word plus a gesture to ask for objects (pointing). Says successive single words to describe an event (Telegraphic Stage). Uses 50 recognizable words (i.e., people, objects, events, function words). Refers to Self by name. Uses "my" or "mine" to indicate possession.

REFERENCES: Gard et al., 1980; Stillman, 1978; Cohen et al., 1976; Lerner et al., 1987; Fallen & Umansky, 1985.

LANGUAGE EVALUATION

A communication evaluation at the sensorimotor stage focuses not only on receptive and expressive language, but also on oral-motor skill development. Developmental skills lists (e.g., oral-motor skills, Table 38; receptive language skills, Table 53; expressive language skills, Table 54) are helpful in informally determining a child's functioning abilities. Diagnostic tests such as the **Receptive-Expressive Emergent Language Scale** (Bzoch & League, 1972) and **The Callier-Azusa Scale**, subtests Expressive Language, Receptive Language, and Speech (Stillman, 1978) are useful in determining the developmental skill levels of deaf-blind severely multihandicapped children.

Systematic Observation

Frequent systematic observation and data collection are important in determining a baseline functioning level with deaf-blind severely multihandicapped children. The child should be observed to determine his/her functioning abilities in the Expressive Language Prerequisite Skills (Table 52) in hearing, vision, cognition and memory, oral motor, and attention skills to determine functional readiness to begin a language intervention program. The Systematic Observation Form: Expressive Language Prerequisites (Table 55) was designed to be utilized during the systematic observation to determine the functioning level (e.g., mastery, learning, emergent) of the child in the various skill areas. The intentional expressive language prerequisites observed include **hearing skills** (e.g., receptive language, intonation, linguistic labeling); **vision skills** (e.g., joint attending with caregiver, use of gestures); **cognitive skills** (e.g., object concept; imitation—vocal; intentionality—means-ends; memory abilities); **oral-motor skills** (e.g., suck-swallow-breathing coordination, lip-tongue-jaw control, vocalization of consonants and vowels); **attention skills** (e.g., communicative turn-taking, non-linguistic social cues). Additionally, the child should be observed to determine his/her prelanguage behaviors (e.g., touching, manipulating a person, pointing, gestures, intonation of vocalizations), and the communication function (e.g., request a want/need, protest, social interaction) of the child's interactions (Table 55). Determining prelanguage deficits will assist in program planning in weak areas to prepare the child for emergent language training, either verbal, signing, or gestural.

TABLE 55

SYSTEMATIC OBSERVATION FORM: EXPRESSIVE LANGUAGE PREREQUISITES

Item											Category	Section
Non-Intentional Language											*Hearing*	INTENTIONAL EXPRESSIVE LANGUAGE PREREQUISITES
Receptive Language												
Understands Intonation												
Understands Linguis. Label.												
Joint-Attending with Caregiver											*Vision*	
Gestural System												
Receptive Language											*Tac-tile*	
Object Concept												
Imitation: Vocal, Gross/Fine Motor											*Cognitive*	
Intentionality (Means-End)												
Memory-Short-term, Long-term, Visual Audit.												
Suck, Swallow, Breath. Coord.											*Oral Motor*	
Lip, Tongue, Jaw Control												
Vocalizes Consonant/ Vowel Sounds												
Communicative Turn-Taking											*Attention*	
Notices Nonling. Social Cues												
Touching/Showing Object/Person											*Prelanguage Behaviors*	
Manipulating Person												
Pointing												
Gestures												
Vocaliz. with Intonation												
Request Want/Need											*Communication Function*	
Protest												
Social Interaction												

KEY:
  ✔ Mastery (observed 80-90% of the time)
  L. Learning (observed 50-79% of the time)
  E. Emergent (observed less than 50% of the time)
  N Not observed at all

The child should be systematically observed within the various environmental settings in which s/he functions to determine what functional vocabulary would give the child more control of his/her environment. The Systematic Observational Form: Functional Language Needs (Table 56) was designed to assist the teacher in determining which functional language the child appears to need or to possess the most readiness for learning—either verbal, gestures, or signs. The sensorimotor stage young child functions primarily in the classroom and the home; however, the older child may be learning to eventually function in a sheltered workshop situation and thus may show a need for a different vocabulary. The teacher may wish to observe the child in various settings using a blank grid sheet without indicated possible vocabulary and determine the vocabulary needed from the observational setting.

Case Study Evaluation Report: Sally

Sally's communication evaluation report (Table 57) illustrates the functioning abilities of a deaf-blind severely multihandicapped child functioning at the 0–1 month developmental functioning level. Sally does not possess any of the Expressive Language Prerequisite Skills nor any of the Prelanguage Behaviors or Communicative Functions (Table 54).

Case Study Evaluation Report: Bud

Bud's communication evaluation report (Table 59) indicates the functioning of a deaf-blind severely multihandicapped child functioning communicatively at the 8–12 month level. His Systematic Observation report indicates functioning at a wide variety of levels ranging from mastery (80+%) to not observed at all.

EXPRESSIVE LANGUAGE PREREQUISITES PROGRAMMING

The sensorimotor stage of development ends with the emergence of fluent expressive language; therefore, programming at this level is concerned primarily with language prerequisites or prelanguage skills (Table 55). Since deaf-blind severely multihandicapped children do not learn spontaneously, initial prelanguage training is integrated into the training of all developmental skill areas (e.g., oral motor, fine motor, and gross motor skills; cognitive; and social development). A number of prelanguage programs have been proposed for use with low-functioning severely multihandicapped children.

TABLE 56
SYSTEMATIC OBSERVATION: FUNCTIONAL LANGUAGE NEEDS

Skills:		Class-room	Lunch Room	Bath-room	Leaving School	Arriving School	Home
SOCIAL COM.	Hi						
	Bye Bye						
DIRECTIONS	Sit/Stand						
	Up/Down						
	Off/On						
	Help						
	No/Yes						
	More						
EATING	Eat						
	Drink						
	Cup/Spoon/Bowl						
	Cookie/Cracker						
DRESSING	Shirt or Coat						
	Hat						
	Pants						
	Shoes or Socks						

Key: ✔ Shows   Readiness/Need
     N   Shows No Readiness/Need

McInnes and Treffry Program

McInnes and Treffry (1982) indicate that for the majority of low-functioning, hypo-active, introverted, self-stimulating deaf-blind severely multihandicapped children, instruction will begin at the signal level with simple body signals while, with hyperactive, inattentive children, instruction will need to begin with bonding and co-active movement in enjoyable activities. They suggest following a series of programming

TABLE 57
SALLY'S COMMUNICATION EVALUATION REPORT

Case Study: Sally
Age: 4 years, 8 months

Sally was administered *The Callier-Azusa Scale*, Receptive and Expressive Communication subtests. Her performance indicates functioning at the 0–1 month level in receptive and expressive language. Receptively, she attends to the caregiver's voice when paired with a tactile cue. Expressively, she makes some spontaneous vocalizations.

The oral motor evaluation indicates problems coordinating sucking and swallowing, which suggests she would experience difficulty coordinating breathing with production of speech.

steps including the following: (1) alert the child to your presence, (2) alert the child of coming activity, (3) introduce activity, (4) do it, and (5) review what you have done.

Activity should never be started without indicating to the child by your special signal that you are present; then, using tactile cues, indicate the coming activity. For example, if you intend to do a body massage or range of motion activity with the child, s/he will probably need to be moved to a mat. Indicate that you intend to lift and move the child by placing your hands under the body in a false lift; wait for a few moments for the child to process the information before the actual lift occurs. Introduce the activity by giving cues. For example, if you wished to begin training in taking off a T-shirt off, manipulate the child through a false procedure. Hold the child's hands, press down on the T-shirt for tactile input, say "Off." Then, actually remove the T-shirt, going through the whole process co-actively: press downward on the T-shirt, say "Off," grasp tail of T-shirt with child's hands manipulated by adult's, and pull over head. Review by going through the motions.

McInnes and Treffry (1982) suggest several types of communication modes which include signals, gestures, class cues, gross signs, and speech, depending upon the functioning level of the child. **Signals** are simple body signals, usually tactile. **Gestures** include natural responses (e.g., shake head back and forth for "No," wave "Bye") which eventually evolve into formal signs. **Class cues** teach anticipation of events (e.g., give child bath towel to feel to indicate bath time). Many deaf-blind severely multihandicapped children may be unable to produce formal signs due to visual and/or motor deficits, so learn the approximated sign or **gross sign** through manipulation. **Speech** may be very slow to emerge in deaf-blind severely multihandicapped children because they resist eye contact,

TABLE 58

BUD'S COMMUNICATION EVALUATION REPORT

Name: Bud

Systematic Observation Form: Expressive Language Prerequisites

Intentional Expressive Language Prerequisites																							
Hearing				Vision		Tac-tile	Cognitive				Oral-Motor			Attention		Prelang.		Behavior			Communication Function		
Noninentional Language	Receptive Language	Understands Intonation	Understands Linguis. Label	Joint Attending with Caregiver	Gestural System	Receptive Language	Object Concept	Imitation-Vocal, Gross/Fine Motor	Intentionality	Memory	Suck, Swallow, Breath. Coord.	Lip, Tongue, Jaw Control	Vocalizes conson. & Vowel Sounds	Communicative Turn-Taking	Non-Linguistic Social Cues	Touch/Show Object of Person	Manipulating Person	Pointing	Gestures	Vocalizations With Intonation	Request Want/Need	Protest	Social
L	L	E	N	N	N	L	✓	✓	✓	L	✓	✓	E	N	N	N	N	N	*	L	E	L	N

NOTE: ✓ mastery L learning E emergent N not observed * signs "drink"

Bud was administered *The Oregon Project Skills Inventory for Visually Impaired and Blind Preschool Children* and observed systematically using the Systematic Observation Form: Expressive Language Prerequisites. His performance on *The Oregon Project* language subtest indicated functioning on the 8-month level with splinter skills up to the 13-month level. Receptively, Bud alerts to auditory stimulation over 70 dB by quieting or changing body movement, turns his head toward noise, and will stop an activity at least momentarily when told "No." He responds to tactilely felt signs to "stand," "sit," "drink," and "no."

Expressively, Bud has separate cries for different discomforts, gurgles and coos, repeats his own sound, and repeats the same syllable two or three times. He combines two different syllables in vocal play and sometimes imitates the voice intonation patterns of others. He can sign "drink," the only word he uses appropriately as a one-word request sentence.

Bud has adequate oral motor skills for learning speech. He has good coordination of swallowing and breathing, and good control of lips, tongue, and jaw movements.

which delays bonding, social interactions and social aspects of language, and retards a need for communication. Regardless of the instructional level, McInnes and Treffry recommend that everyone who interacts with the child use the same gestures, signals, class cues, and signs.

Bricker and Dennison Program

Bricker and Dennison (1978) have described a six-stage imitation training program to serve as prerequisite training for teaching expressive languages. The stages are as follows: (1) increase vocalizations, (2) gross motor imitation (familiar), (3) gross motor imitation (unfamiliar), (4) sound imitation (self-initiated), (5) sound imitation (model-initiated), and (6) speech sound imitation. They suggest attempting to increase the frequency and number of the child's vocalizations by imitating the sounds the child makes and encouraging the child to imitate these sounds. To increase a child's understanding of imitation, s/he should be encouraged to imitate his own familiar actions in various settings, then imitate unfamiliar easy motor actions. Beginning with imitation of sound made by child, try to make a game of sound-chaining: child makes sound, teacher imitates, child repeats sound, etc. Once the child understands sound-chaining of a self-initiated sound, encourage sound-chaining of a sound initiated by someone else. Later, use the same sound-chaining imitation procedure in learning to imitate easily integrated speech sounds.

Van Dijk Program

Van Dijk (1986) outlines an educational curriculum for deaf-blind children that begins with attachment or bonding between teacher or caregiver and child. Attachment is described as a three-step process involving (1) coactive movement, (2) structuring the child's daily routine, and (3) characterization. Coactive movement refers to the teacher and child participating together in activities usually initiated and enjoyed by the child. The teacher assists during activities, using "hands-on" manipulation when needed. The child's daily activities are highly structured and the same sequence always followed so the child can learn to anticipate his daily activities.

Characterization is a method used to identify each separate person who works with the child. For children who live away from home, a memory box system is used, including one box for each day. Inside each box is an item representative of the special activity of the day (e.g., swimming trunks), and on Friday or the day the child goes home for the weekend, the child will find articles symbolic of his family. Obviously, for most low-functioning deaf-blind severely multihandicapped sensori-motor stage children, the activities will need to be modified, but the sequence of skills to develop attachment is the same.

Only after attachment or bonding with the child has been established does the actual process of communication development begin. The communication process involves three major stages of skills including (1) anticipation, (2) use of drawings or picture language, and (3) imitation. Anticipation is developed through the use of natural gestures or manual gestures (e.g., time to eat—touch spoon to lip, place child's hand on cup). Higher functioning students may initiate activities using their own signal.

The use of drawings or simple pictures can be used with higher functioning children who have use of residual vision. "Making a drawing of an activity for which the child already has a sign often helps the child to memorize the sign better" (Van Dijk, 1986, 378). Abbreviated or simple picture drawings contribute to the development of representational thought—a prerequisite of expressive communication. For example, Van Dijk suggests that a circle may be used to represent a plate and a triangle to represent a sandwich.

The third major step in the development of communication involves acquisition of imitation. The process of imitation development includes a sequential series of five skills as follows: (1) resonance phenomenon, (2) coactive movements, (3) mirroring, (4) parallel, and (5) independence. Resonance phenomenon involves the child unconsciously participating in movement activity which the teacher initiates (e.g., teacher taps on table, child taps on table). With lower-functioning children, the resonance may need to be developed through activities such as the teacher with child on lap rocking the child in the rocking chair and encouraging the child to also move his body in the forward-back rocking motion. Coactive movement is encouraged in most tasks with deaf-blind children to allow them to feel the movement as they are initially manipulated through an activity, especially daily living activities.

Gradually, as the child's competence improves, the teacher and child can mirror the activity by performing it face to face (e.g., teacher and child sit on opposite sides of a small table, teacher picks up cup and child imitates). The next level of imitation activities involves parallel performance (e.g., teacher sits next to child and strings one blue bead, child strings one blue bead, etc.). Eventually, the child is able to perform the activity independently with no motor cues. Body awareness and body language are built into the motor-based program using pictures and dolls to assist in demonstrating appropriate motor movement. Once imitation is established, the child is ready to begin to learn expressive language via signs or speech.

Kaiser et al.'s (1987) Functional Approach

The major goal of the functional approach is to enable the child to use communication functionally and socially during their daily activities. Thus the functional words taught are child-specific and situation-specific so the child can interact communicatively within his environment. Kaiser et al. (1987, 251) suggest beginning functional language training through a process of encouraging nonverbal interactional strategies including (1) **directed attention** to the conversational partner, (2) **joint attention** on the environmental topic of interest, and (3) **joint activity** focused on the environmental topic of interest. The joint activity phase of the process involves three major strategies including the following: (1) **responsiveness** during joint activity as demonstrated by nonverbal turn-taking, generalized nonverbal imitation, and generalized instruction, (2) **initiating** nonverbal interaction, and (3) topic maintenance through sustained joint attention and joint activity.

Following the achievement of nonverbal communicative interaction, Kaiser et al. (1987, 251) recommend beginning verbal instruction that focuses on conversation. The three primary conversational strategies include the following: (1) **verbal responsiveness** to initiations of the conversational partner as demonstrated by verbal turn-taking, generalized verbal imitation, acknowledgments, adding information, (2) **initiating conversation**, and (3) **maintaining conversation** through seeking clarification of ambiguous information, adding topic-relevant information, seeking new information, and building upon the topic.

Milieu teaching procedures or naturalistic teaching procedures are those in which the communication training procedures are carried out in the natural environment as opportunities for teaching naturally occur. "These techniques have been used to teach adjectives, requests, social initiations, labels, two- and three-word sentences, and compound sentences" (Kaiser et al., 1987, 251).

Receptive Language

Case Study IEP: Sally

Receptive language programming at the prelanguage level is essentially the same as auditory stimulation programming (See Chapter 3). Thus, Sally's receptive language programming is at the auditory stimulation level. A variety of musical stimuli including musical toys (e.g., bells, music boxes, horns, rhythm band instruments) and distinctive music such as "Star Wars" sound track often attract attention. Some other materials used to produce interesting tones include the following: rattling or crumpling paper, opening velcro strips, and banging empty coffee cans. It is important to change the stimulus often because Sally accommodates easily to new sounds and loses interest.

Case Study IEP: Bud

According to Bud's communication evaluation report (Table 58), his receptive language is at the learning level. He receptively alerts to auditory stimulation over 70dB by quieting or changing body movement, turns his head toward noise, and will stop an activity at least momentarily when told "No." He responds to tactilely felt signs for "stand," "sit," "drink," and "no."

At the sensorimotor stage, receptive language skills are the same as auditory functioning skills (Table 21). Bud is functioning at the awareness level on auditory functioning skills. Receptive language for deaf-blind children also includes other modes of information input such as tactile-kinesthetic-vestibular. Bud is functioning at the Recognition and Discrimination level of Tactile-Kinesthetic-Vestibular Sensory Programming Skills (Table 32) as he discriminates four tactile messages. Since Bud has shown greatest learning through tactile cues, his IEP will continue to emphasize this area.

Receptive Language IEP

Name: Bud

Receptive Language Goal: Bud will improve recognition and understanding of tactile cues.

Objective A: Bud will demonstrate recognition and understanding of six new tactile cues by following the directions of the

> tactile cues to perform related self-help skills on 4 out of 5 tries, each for 3 consecutive data days as implemented by teacher/aide.

Tactile Body Cues (Table 59) are used to assist Bud in developing the concepts as well as the self-help tasks. It is important for the deaf-blind student to be able to determine the intent of others. Specific tactile cues provide a consistency in indicating the initiation of an interaction, the maintenance of an interaction, and termination of interaction (Stremel-Campbell, 1985).

Expressive Language

Expressive language serves a communicative function either orally or nonorally. The major communication functions include greetings, requests for assistance, requests for objects, requests for information, pro-tests, and comments (Kaiser et al., 1987). Early developing expressive language functions with severely handicapped students include (1) requesting objects, (2) requesting actions, and (3) protesting (Stremel-Campbell, 1985).

The selection of a communication system for a student is a very important decision-making process which should be undertaken with consideration of numerous factors including the following: age, cognitive abilities, receptive/expressive communication level, motor skill development (e.g., oral motor, fine, gross), degree of sensory impairment, use of residual sensory abilities, age of onset of sensory impairment, social and environmental functioning level, and obvious preference of the child. The communicative system decisions to be made include the following: (1) oral versus nonoral system, (2) nonoral (augmentative communication) aided versus nonoral unaided, (3) which aided system (e.g., picture or word board, computerized aid, etc.), and (4) which unaided systems (e.g., sign language, natural gestures). The determination of an appropriate communication mode should be developmental and made as the need arises with individual considerations and experimentation or trials with each mode.

Expressive language programming at the intentional prelanguage (sensorimotor) stage consists primarily of learning imitation (e.g., verbal, gestural) skills (e.g., McInnes & Treffry Program, Bricker & Dennison Program, Van Dijk Program). The Callier-Azusa Scale (Stillman, 1978) subtest Expressive Language indicates the following hierarchy of sensorimotor skills (imitation):

1. Indicates wants by signaling to continue activity;
2. Expresses wants through gestures or vocalizations;
3. Copies movements or vocalizations of teacher;
4. Imitates simple known movements, vocalizations, gestures.
5. Imitates new movements, vocalizations, gestures; and
6. Asks for or identifies objects by using gestures (64–66).

TABLE 59
TACTILE BODY CUES

Use with verbal input and before moving

SIT DOWN		Tap child's bottom while saying "sit down," then place child in position
UP		Gently pull up under child's arms while giving verbal cue, then pick up.
LAY DOWN		Rub hand down child's back while giving verbal cue, then lay down.
EAT		Tap child's mouth while giving verbal cue. Use spoon or child's hand.
DRINK		Use sign for drink—take child's hand and tip it back (drinking motion) while giving verbal cue.
SHIRT	OFF	Take child's hands and rub down on shirt and pull up on edge; while giving verbal cue, remove.
	ON	Rub shirt on child's chest, put shirt on, manipulate child to pull shirt down.
PANTS	OFF	Take child's hands and rub down on pants leg, push down on waistband, remove.
	ON	Rub pants on child's legs, manipulate child to pull up on waistband.
SHOES	OFF	Tap bottom of child's shoe, manipulate child to rub shoe, remove shoe.
	ON	Tap bottom of child's shoe on bottom of foot, put shoe on.
SOCKS	OFF	Rub child's hand over sock, push down on sock, remove.
	ON	Rub sock on child's foot, put sock on, manipulate child to pull up on sock.
COAT	OFF	Rub child's hand down zipper/buttons, remove coat.
	ON	Rub coat on child's chest, put coat on, manipulate child to pull up on zipper/rub child's hand down buttons.
HAT	OFF	Rub child's hand over hat, manipulate to remove.
	ON	Rub hat on child's head, manipulate to pull hat on.
DIAPER	OFF	Tap child's hand on diaper, remove.
	ON	Tap diaper on child, put on.
UNDERPANTS	OFF	Tap child's hand on pants, push down on waistband. Remove/push down to knees.
	ON	Tap child's hand on pants. Pull up on waistband.

SOURCE: Used by classroom teachers in Deaf-Blind Program, Special School District of St. Louis County, Missouri, 1985.

Case Study IEP: Sally

Sally's communication evaluation report (Table 57) indicates that she is currently functioning at the 0–1 month level with most of her verbalizations being non-intentional in nature. Initial programming will aim toward moving her into the intentional prelanguage stage of development with the lowest level skill (e.g., the **Callier-Azusa Scale**, Expressive Language) as her programming objective.

Expressive Language IEP

Name: Sally

Expressive Language IEP Goal: Sally will improve expressive communication skills.

Objective A: Sally will signal by vocalizing to indicate her desire for continuation of a movement activity (e.g. rocked in rocking chair) on 4 out of 5 trials on 3 consecutive data days as implemented by teacher/aide.

The specific objective was determined by completing the Stimulation Profiles to determine her likes and dislikes in auditory, visual, olfactory, gustatory, tactile-vestibular stimulation. The results of the Stimulation Profile indicated that Sally enjoys movement, especially being rocked in the rocking chair while sitting on the teacher's lap. Thus movement is used to reinforce Sally's attempts toward meeting the objective of vocally indicating continuation of an activity.

The teaching strategy will begin with the teacher providing a vocal signal using varied intonation as she rocks Sally. The teacher stops rocking and vocalizing, waits for a response from Sally, encourages a response by vocalizing the sound, pauses for a response, then repeats the sound and rocking. This sequence of events continues until Sally understands the cause-effect relationship between her vocalization and rocking.

Case Study IEP: Bud

Bud's current evaluation (Table 58) suggest functioning within the Intentional Prelanguage stage. He can sign "drink" and use the word appropriately. Thus he demonstrates emergence of the requesting function of language. He demonstrates understanding and use of the protesting function of language both verbally (e.g., yelling, crying) and nonverbally (e.g., becoming rigid and refusing to move, becoming limp and dropping to the floor, self-stimulating).

Although Bud is 8 years old and functioning communicatively at the

8–13 month level, a formal method of expressive language has not yet been selected for him. He has mastered some of the expressive language prerequisite skills (Table 58) including imitation and possesses adequate oral motor skills for speech. However, he still does not understand the social communicative aspect of language, does not engage in most prelanguage behaviors, and does not consistently demonstrate understanding of the communication function. Since he appears to have more ability currently to use signs (i.e., understands 4 tactile cues and uses 1 sign) than verbal language, his objective will focus on increasing utilization of signs. The words for signing will come from his receptive knowledge of signs (e.g., stand, sit, drink, no) and from words used in daily activities and self-help skills (Table 59). Bud's expressive and receptive language and self-help skills training will be paired for greater exposure, utility, and generalization.

Expressive Language IEP

Name: Bud

Expressive Language IEP Goal: Bud will improve nonoral expressive language communication skills (e.g., signing).

Objective A: Bud will demonstrate an increase in expressive language by signing the 4 self-help skills words he understands receptively at appropriate times on 4 out of 5 tries each for 3 consecutive data days as implemented by teacher/ aide.

IEP Monitoring requires periodic evaluation using norm lists such as receptive and expressive communication developmental lists (e.g., Tables 53 and 54) to provide the teacher with age-based functioning comparisons which are important during re-evaluation. Additionally, monitoring of objectives requires frequent data collection of functioning on curriculum-based or task-analyzed skill sequences. The Systematic Observation Form: Expressive Language Prerequisites (Table 55) provides an efficient format for continued, frequent progress monitoring.

SUMMARY

Deaf-blind severely multihandicapped children frequently continue to function communicatively at the prelinguistic stage due to auditory deficits, vision deficits, cognitive deficits, oral-motor deficits, fine and gross motor deficits, and social/emotional deficits. The interactive effect of such significant deficits prevents spontaneous language learning and usage. Since language acquisition and increased cognition are interdependent in development, it is crucial to assist the deaf-blind child in acquiring language, a representational symbol system.

Since the sensorimotor stage ends with the emergence of fluent language, the primary focus of the sensorimotor stage is the Intentional Expressive Language Prerequisites, or the prelanguage skills. The primary intentional expressive language prerequisite skills include the following: **hearing skills** (receptive language, intonation system, linguistic labeling); **vision skills** (joint attending, gestural system); **tactile skills** (receptive cues); **cognitive skills** (object concept, imitation, intentionality, memory); **oral-motor skills** (suck, swallow, and breathing coordination, lip-tongue-jaw control, vocalizing consonant and vowel sounds); **attention skills** (communicative turn-taking, nonlinguistic social cues); **prelanguage behaviors** (touching or showing, manipulating a person, pointing, using gestures, vocalizing with intonation); and understanding **communication functions** (request, protest, social interactions).

Early receptive language skill development parallels or duplicates auditory functional skill development as the child first gains an awareness to sound, localizes sound, discriminates sounds, and recognizes and labels sounds. Adequate receptive language is the foundation of expressive language development. Expressive language at the sensorimotor level involves primarily prelanguage gestures and vocalizations, or one recognizable word paired with appropriate intonation.

Evaluation of communication skills at the sensorimotor level requires considerable systematic observation of the child while executing the expressive language prerequisite skills. Programming generally involves teaching the deficits in prelanguage prerequisites. Most of the more formal programs involve teaching the child the skill of imitation (e.g., verbal, vocal, and fine and gross motor). Imitation appears to be a major foundation skill without which the child cannot be taught expressive language using words or signs.

Chapter Eight

SOCIAL/EMOTIONAL DEVELOPMENT: EVALUATION AND PROGRAMMING

No child is born social or anti-social. The nature of the child's attitude will depend on the learning experience of his formative years (McInnes & Treffry, 1982, 39).

- Normal Social and Emotional Development
- Normal Sensorimotor Stage Development
    Bonding
    Interactions with Adults
    Interactions with Other Children
    Interactions with the Environment
    Awareness of Self
    Play Skill Development
- Development in Handicapped Children
- Social and Emotional Evaluation
- Social and Emotional Programming
- Summary

The social and emotional growth and development of a child does not occur in isolation. Previous chapters have attempted to separate aspects of a child's growth and development into developmental components (e.g., vision, hearing, secondary senses, cognition, motor skills, communication) for individual analysis and programming. In reality, however, we cannot separate a child into individual components. Social and emotional growth and development are closely linked with all aspects of child development into a synergistic relationship.

Every normal child has the capacity for concurrent maturation of physical, emotional, and intellectual processes. He functions and grows as a whole unit with every part contributing to the effectiveness of the whole and with every part having an effect upon every other part (Robbins, 1964).

241

NORMAL SOCIAL AND EMOTIONAL DEVELOPMENT

Physical, mental, social, and emotional developmental behaviors are interdependent behaviors whose composite is the personality, or overall behavior pattern at any stage of development (Crow & Crow, 1953). Although children are not born social or antisocial, studies of infants show that behavioral differences or temperament (Thomas & Chess, 1977) or personality traits (Fallen & Umansky, 1985) become obvious shortly after birth. These behavioral differences or distinctive personalities are affected by the child's overall health condition, amount and kinds of activity, muscle tone, degree of coordination, muscular energy, responsiveness to sensory stimulation (e.g., vision, hearing, tactile, vestibular), tolerance of physical discomfort, overall mood (e.g., readiness to smile or cry), regularity of sleeping and feeding patterns (Crow & Crow, 1953; Lerner et al., 1987; Fallen & Umansky, 1985; Thomas & Chess, 1977).

NORMAL SENSORIMOTOR STAGE DEVELOPMENT

Newborns have few ways of expressing their feelings or emotions and show limited discrimination of people and situations or social behavior (Fallen & Umansky, 1985). The infant's social and emotional behavior depends to a great extent on whether his/her physiological needs are met. By the age of three months, the infant has begun to be a social individual, smiling in response to mother's or caregiver's face, voice, and/or smile. S/he responds to person-to-person contact with adults and other children. The three-month-old infant has begun to develop an emotional repertoire, including the ability to express joy and delight; distress, frustration or pain; surprise and interest (Table 60).

After the age of three months, the child's smiling and crying begin to take on social meaning. The child realizes that both crying and smiling can produce desired results in adults—attention. The four-to-nine-month-old child enjoys being near people and responds gaily to attention and play. The child continues to be very self-centered and uses many means to attract attention to himself, including those considered positive by adults (e.g., cooing, laughing, smiling) and those considered negative by adults (e.g., crying and shouting). The child soon learns that both negative and positive behaviors gain him/her the desired attention.

By about eight months of age, the child begins to display stranger

TABLE 60
SOCIAL/EMOTIONAL DEVELOPMENTAL SKILLS: SENSORIMOTOR STAGE

Age	Behaviors
0–3 mos.	Infant communicates by crying. Smiles spontaneously to mother's face, voice, smile. Responds to person-to-person contact with adults and children. *Emotions:* joy (delight), distress (frustration or pain), surprise, interest
4–9 mos.	Enjoys being near people and played with and responds gaily. Cries, smiles, kicks, coos, laughs to attract social attention. Plays a "game" with adult assistance. Responds differently to strangers than to familiar people, displaying timidity and shyness—stranger anxiety (8 months). Shouts for attention (8 months). Rejects confinement. Fights for disputed toy (9 months). Cries if other child cries. *Emotions:* enjoyment, protest, fear, anger, humor, teases, shyness.
10–12 mos.	Pays attention to his own name. Copies simple actions of others. Recognizes different tones of voice and responds. Recognizes himself as an individual apart from mother. Learning to cooperate. Participates in social activities. Actively seeks to maintain interactions with adult. Attempts to play with another child. Able to interpret the emotional expression of familiar adults. Tries to alter mother's plans through persuasion or protest. Displays separation anxiety when apart from mother. Shows guilt at wrongdoing. Developing a sense of humor. Teases and tests parental limits. Fears strange people and places. Can demonstrate affection. Periodic negativism increases. *Emotions:* anxiety, fear, affection, persuasion, protest, guilt, negativism.
1–2 years	Developing trust and confidence in the environment. Recognizes self in mirror or picture, and refers to self by name. Beginning to become independent. Imitates adult behaviors in play. Plays by self, imitating own play. Cooperates by helping to put things away. May become angry if activities are interrupted. Responds to simple commands by adult. Begins to realize that he can't have everything his own way. Social relationships with other children are awkward. Begins to play with other children, but is likely to hit, bite, or fight over a toy. Engages in social laughter. Shows anger through explosive expression of aggressive behavior. Child's mother is all-important. *Emotions:* Almost complete store of emotional expressions.

SOURCE: Crow & Crow, 1953; Caplan, 1973; Fallen & Umansky, 1985; Lerner et al., 1987.

anxiety, responding differently to strangers than to familiar people, displaying timidity and shyness with strangers. The eight-to-nine-month-old child begins exhibiting more influence over his/her environment by shouting for attention, loudly (vocally) rejecting confinement in the playpen or confined area, and even fighting for a disputed toy (Table 60). The nine-month-old child is beginning to learn empathy and may cry if another child cries. His/her emotional repertoire is becoming more sophisticated to include enjoyment, protest, fear, anger, humor, teasing, and shyness (Table 60).

By the time the average child is one-year old, s/he has made enormous strides in growth and development. The year-old child cognitively understands imitation, a prerequisite to language acquisition and other refined developmental skills; understands anticipation and object permanence, major sensorimotor stage accomplishments. The twelve-month-old child has developed the pincer grasp and uses it to remove objects from a container, can feed himself finger foods, and pick up his cup. Gross motor skills of the year-old child include crawling, pulling up to stand, and walking with help. Communicatively, the year-old child has mastered the adult intonation system which, paired with gestures and one understandable word or gibberish, convey his/her primary thoughts and wants/needs.

It is within this increasing ability to affect his/her environment that the year-old child continues to develop socially and emotionally. The year-old child is learning to cooperate and responds to different tones of voice. S/he recognizes herself/himself as an individual apart from mother, although mother continues to be very special and the year-old child may suffer separation anxiety when mother is gone. The child may even use protest or persuasion to attempt to alter mother's plans to leave. The year-old child is beginning to participate in social activities, actively seeking to maintain interactions with an adult, and attempting to play with another child (Table 60). The one-year-old is able to interpret the emotional expression of familiar adults, and s/he feels guilty at wrongdoing. The year-old child is also developing a sense of humor, and teases and tests parental limits. S/he fears strangers and new places. The year-old enjoys demonstrating affection, but also periodically reveals increasing negativism. Emotionally, the year-old's repertoire of emotions is very wide ranged, from delight, joy, affection, and humor to anxiety, fear, protest, guilt, and negativism (Table 60).

Imitation plays an important role in the development of a child's emotional behavior (Crow & Crow, 1953). Gradually, the child's emotional behavior develops from generalized expressions of emotionalism to focusing emotions on the person or object responsible for causing the emotional response. A child learns to respond to adult attitudes toward his emotional behaviors. The child of emotionally well-balanced parents usually learns early to control his/her emotions (Crow & Crow, 1953). The developing child soon learns that temper tantrums are not tolerated by adults or children.

The year-old child has gradually developed feelings of affection for his/her parents and/or those who care for him/her and play with him. The receiving of affectionate attention by others is very important to emotional growth as the child learns to transfer some of the affection from his/her family to other children and adults outside the home (Crow & Crow, 1953).

By the time a child is two years old, s/he has an almost complete store of emotional expressions. The one-to-two-year-old child is developing socially and in individual personality characteristics. The two-year-old recognizes himself/herself in a mirror or picture, and refers to himself by name (Table 60). S/he is developing trust and confidence in the environment and is beginning to be more independent. The two-year-old can play by independently imitating his/her own play and imitating adult behaviors in play. S/he will respond to simple commands by adults, but may become quite angry if their activities are interrupted. However, the two-year-old is beginning to realize that he cannot always have his/her way. The social relationships of the two-year-old with other children are still quite awkward and may degenerate into fighting or other aggressive behavior. The child's mother continues to be the most important single person in his life. Generally, the development of social and emotional behavioral patterns follow a similar sequence for most children.

Bonding

Emotional attachment or bonding is a very special affectionate reciprocal relationship which initially develops between mother or primary caregiver and the young child. Maternal love, however, is not an instinct that comes about automatically with the birth of a baby (Papalia & Olds, 1975). The bonding process begins at birth and develops gradually between mother and child over the first six months or so of life when a firm attachment bond is formed (Bailey & Worley, 1984).

Bonding between mother and child is actively nurtured by both parties. Mothers provide nourishment; a close, warm, secure environment; a friendly voice and a smiling face; and attend to physical needs. Physical contact (e.g., touching, caressing) is important for beginning emotional bonding (McInnes & Treffry, 1982). The infant actively attempts to bond with the primary caregiver, usually mother, by making eye contact and visually tracking her, by vocalizing more to mother, smiling more affectionately to mother, getting overall excited at seeing mother.

Kirk & Gallagher (1979) indicate the role of vision in human attachment as follows:

> Vision plays a critical role in the establishment of human bonds. The response smile to the human face, the discrimination of mother and stranger—the entire sequence of recognitory experience leads to mental representation and evocative memory. Eye-to-eye contact is the matrix of the signal system that evolves between mother and child (27).

Ainsworth (1964) indicates that during this attachment stage, the six-to-seven-month-old baby can also form affectionate secondary emotional bonds with one or more familiar figures, usually father and siblings. These early emotional bonds continue to be nurtured reciprocally throughout the child's life and serve as patterns for social and friendly relationships as s/he matures.

Attachment is critical to the child's growth and development in emotional and social skills, in cognitive and communicative abilities, in sensory development, and in the development of a self-identity or self-concept. Attachment provides the child his or her first social relationships (Lerner et al., 1987). Bonding appears to be a critical component in the rate of cognitive development and in the acquisition of perceptual-conceptual skills. Through the attachment process, mother encourages **visual development** (e.g., fixation, following, spatial relationship), **auditory development** (e.g., localization—mother's voice, discrimination—mother's voice from others), **tactile development** (e.g., touching, caressing, bathing, drying, smoothing on lotion/powder), **vestibular development** (e.g., carries baby upright, rocks baby in rocking chair).

Bonding is also very important to the development of communication as the child learns intonation, body language, joint-attending and linguistic labeling, and patterning of communication exchanges as mother talks to and cares for the child. Mother provides a secure base from which to explore as the child crawls out, toddles out, or darts out to explore and investigate the environment, running back for safety if startled or fearful. Attachment assists the child in developing a clear concept of self-identity (Fallen & Umansky, 1985). It provides the security to grow and develop in an accepting environment.

Interaction with Adults

A child's initial social and emotional growth is facilitated through his/her interactions and attachments to parents and other familiar adults. These early attachments form the basis of bonding with other primary adults throughout the child's lifetime. The young child's personality characteristics or behavioral patterns affect how mother, and later other adults, react to and interact with him/her. Caregivers respond differently to children of different temperaments, and these responses may lead to different social developmental outcomes (Lerner et al., 1987). Therefore, an important factor in the development of the child's social and affective behaviors with adults is the child's contribution to the relationship via his/her temperament.

Adult interactions, then, provide the basis for the infant's future learning. Interactions with adults determine the rate of growth and development of the child, not only in communication, cognitive, perceptual, social, and emotional skills, but also stimulate curiosity and exploration which, in turn, enable the infant to gain some control over body movements and to refine actions (Barraga, 1983).

The interactions developed with adults during the sensorimotor stage serve as patterns to establish relationships with other primary adults throughout life. The early interactions children have with adults are primarily responsive in nature (Table 61). The child smiles responsively and cooperates passively. Gradually, the child is able to discriminate familiar adults visually, auditorily, and tactilely and to react differently to strangers than to familiar people. S/he stops an activity in response to "No" paired with intonation, and responds to two sequential adult interactions (Table 61).

As the child matures, s/he begins to initiate interactions with adults by attracting their attention (e.g., kicking, cooing, or laughing) (Table 61). The sensorimotor stage child begins to participate in adult manipulation

TABLE 61
SENSORIMOTOR STAGE SOCIAL DEVELOPMENT SKILLS CHECKLIST

Interaction with Adults
    Responsive:
_____ Behavior reveals no awareness to adult stimulation.
_____ Smiles spontaneously at familiar adult.
_____ Attends to adult visually, auditorially, or tactilely.
_____ Cooperates passively with adult.
_____ Responds to adult's attempt to interact (e.g., smiles, vocalizes, accepts toy).
_____ Smiles spontaneously to pleasurable activity with adult.
_____ Responds differently to mother than to other caregivers.
_____ Responds differently to strangers than to familiar people.
_____ Responds by attending to his/her name.
_____ Responds to two sequential adult interactions.
_____ Stops activity in response to "No" paired with intonation.
    Initiative:
_____ Attracts adult's attention by kicking, cooing, or laughing.
_____ Identifies familiar adults using tactile, visual, and/or auditory cue.
_____ Participates in adult manipulation through action songs.
_____ Imitates simple actions of adults.
_____ Plays games with adult (e.g., "Pat-a-Cake").
_____ Attempts to maintain contact with familiar adults when start to leave.
_____ Actively seeks to sustain interactions with familiar adults.
_____ Shows interest in several adults other than mother.
_____ Shows preference for one or more adults.
_____ Actively seeks adult attention (e.g., cues and uses "pick-me-up" gesture.
_____ Leads adult through sequence of activities.
_____ Seeks adult's help.
_____ Initiates social dialogue with familiar adults.
_____ Seeks adult for play in an activity chosen by adult.
_____ Seeks adult for play in an activity chosen by child.
_____ Shows preference among adults that are non-family members.

Interactions with Other Children:
    Responsive:
_____ Ignores or is unaware of other children.
_____ Responds to other child's presence by smiling, staring.
_____ Responds to familiar children by smiling, vocalizing, teaching.
_____ Responds by attending when confronted by other child.
_____ Responds to other child's attempts to play.
_____ Shows signs of sympathy, affection, pity, guilt.
    Initiative:
_____ Vocalizes to other child's face or voice.
_____ Explores other child tactilely.
_____ Shows interest in same object as other child (e.g., tries to take it away).
_____ Attempts to play with other child (e.g., offers or shows toy).
_____ Plays game with other child (e.g., Peek-a-Boo, rolls ball, Pat-a-Cake).
_____ Shows specific preference for other child.
_____ Reverses role with other child (e.g., runner becomes chaser).
_____ Seeks another child to help.

TABLE 61 (Continued)

Interactions with the Environment:

Responsive:

_____ Shows awareness to presence of light, sound, tactile stimulation.

_____ Shows eating pattern or preferred feeding schedule.

_____ Responds to being touched, warmly wrapped, warm bath.

_____ Shows awareness to body movements (e.g., sucks fingers).

_____ Differentiates familiar and unfamiliar environments (e.g., quiets, clings to adult in unfamiliar place).

_____ Responds to noticeable changes in familiar environment (e.g., stares, cries, avoids changes).

_____ Responds to frustrating situations by self-stimulating or withdrawal, or temper tantrums.

_____ Anticipates familiar events from cues and responds accordingly (.e.g., adults putting on coat means "go," child gets his/her coat).

Initiative:

_____ Attempts to move or change positions.

_____ Engages in self-stimulation without objects.

_____ Vocalizes to show discomfort when hungry, wet, etc.

_____ Makes different vocalizations for different emotions.

_____ Expresses preferences for particular foods.

_____ Shows interest in objects (e.g., stares, smiles).

_____ Reaches out to explore immediate environment with hand, arm, foot, or leg.

_____ Shows curiosity and explores environment (e.g., hits mobiles, manipulates new toys).

_____ Shows interest in objects, but does not use appropriately.

_____ Shows preference for specific object.

_____ Seeks a particular object for comfort when stressed or tired.

_____ Uses objects for their specific function (e.g., pushes toy car, drinks from cup).

_____ Locates objects in room (e.g., table, rocking horse).

_____ Teases adults by treatening unacceptable behaviors (e.g., approaches light socket).

_____ Plays on object (e.g., swing, indoor slide) independently.

_____ Indicates to adult need to go to the toilet.

_____ Demonstrates social knowledge not to throw or play with food (at least while adult is looking).

_____ Demonstrates social knowledge not to bite, hit, or scratch people (e.g., before hitting, looks to see if adult is watching).

_____ Identifies objects as "own."

REFERENCES: Stillman, 1978; Rudolph, Bjorling, & Collins, Undated; McInnes & Treffry, 1982.

through action songs, to imitate simple actions of adults, and to play games with adults. The child becomes more dependent upon social interactions with adults and actively seeks to maintain interactions as the adult prepares to leave.

Interactions with Other Children

A child expresses social and emotional skills at play and in interactions with other children (Fallen & Umansky, 1985). The socialization skills of the sensorimotor stage child are at the initial stage of development as the child continues to be egocentric and focused on his/her own rapid growth and development. Initial interactions with other children are reactive in nature (Table 61). The infant's first interactions with other children are generally with siblings or children of significant adults. Gradually, the infant responds to familiar children by smiling and vocalizing, and later responds to another child's attempts to play.

As the young child grows and develops, especially in motor and communication skills, s/he begins taking the initiative in social situations by vocalizing to face or touch, and by showing interest in the same object as another child, even attempting to take it away (Table 61). The sensorimotor stage child may attempt to play with another child by offering or showing a toy, by playing games with another child such as rolling a ball, and by showing preference for another child. At a more sophisticated level, the sensorimotor stage child may seek the help of another child and may reverse play roles with another child (Table 61).

By kindergarten, some three or four years hence, the child will be expected to be a friendly socialized child, demonstrating his/her awareness of other people as separate persons (Fallen & Umansky, 1985). However:

> Until a child is able to view a situation from another's perspective, it is impossible for her to exhibit the qualities that comprise prosocial behavior. Sharing, cooperation, turn-taking, empathy, and helpfulness require an understanding of another person's needs and feelings (Fallen & Umansky, 1985, 336).

Interactions with the Environment

During the sensorimotor stage of development, the young child's social and emotional behavior is extremely variable, depending upon environmental and situational conditions, including the regularity of the child's schedule, presence of familiar persons or strangers, the location of the interaction (e.g., familiar or unfamiliar place, quiet place or shopping mall), and the number of persons present. The young child is easily over-stimulated by changes in schedule and activities, changes in diet, changes in location, changes in the number of people present, and the amount of activity within the environment. In secure, familiar settings with familiar persons, the young child's behavioral responses may begin to establish a fairly predictable pattern.

Initially, the infant's interactions with his/her environment are responsive in nature. The infant shows awareness to presence of light, sound, tactile stimulation; shows an eating pattern or preferred feeding schedule; responds to different temperatures (e.g., warm bath); shows awareness to body movements (e.g., sucks fingers) (Table 61). Gradually, the child learns to differentiate familiar and unfamiliar environments, and responds to noticeable changes in his/her familiar environment. The child may respond to frustrating situations in a number of ways (e.g., withdrawal, temper tantrums, self-stimulation). The young sensorimotor stage child learns to anticipate familiar events from environmental cues (Table 61).

The infant begins to interact with the environment soon after birth. As the child's abilities in gross and fine motor skills and communication skills begin to be more proficient, s/he has more skills with which to interact with the environment. The infant's initial interactions with the environment may involve attempts to move or change positions, engaging in self-stimulation (e.g., thumb sucking), vocalizing to show discomfort (Table 61). Gradually, the child learns to differentiate emotions and sources of discomfort and makes different vocalizations for different situations and circumstances.

The child exerts some control over the environment as s/he expresses preferences for particular foods. Developing fine motor skills allows the child to explore the environment by reaching out to touch toys, mobiles, and later to manipulate new toys. Development of gross motor skills allows the child to use locomotion to explore the environment and locate objects in the room (Table 61). Toward the end of the sensorimotor stage, the child may tease adults by threatening unacceptable behavior, but demonstrates social knowledge about table manners and not being aggressive to others (Table 61).

The two-year-old at the end of the sensorimotor stage has some control over his/her environment in using objects for their specific function, in ability to indicate wants and needs, in ability to move within the environment to gain items, and has some degree of skill in self-help areas (e.g., self-feeding). The child's view of the environment and of his place in that environment determines his reactions and behaviors (Yamamoto, 1963).

Awareness of Self

Research is consistent in reporting a strong relationship between self-concept and achievement, whether it be academic or social (Yamamoto, 1972). Research with mildly handicapped children (educable mentally retarded, emotionally disturbed, learning disabled, speech/language impaired) indicated that handicapped children experience significantly more negative self-concepts than non-handicapped children, accompanied by significantly greater amounts of anxiety (Jones, 1985). Although little if any research has been conducted concerning the self-concepts of severely/profoundly handicapped children, teacher observation notes a high degree of anxiety as exhibited in self-stimulation and the positive effects of praise and encouragement on task accomplishment. It appears that a positive self-awareness is important even to severely multihandicapped students who, in the past, were believed to have no self-concept.

The development of the self-concept begins in infancy and continues throughout one's lifetime, constantly undergoing modification in response to the environment (Lerner & Shea, 1982). By the time the child is six months old, he has begun to give evidence of having formed some more or less definite concepts about himself (Crow & Crow, 1953). These self-concepts or awareness of self-characteristics are predicated upon the interactions of numerous factors including the following: (1) Body Awareness, (2) Recognition of Attention, (3) Body Image, and (4) Concept of Child's Own Capabilities (Table 62).

The process of developing an accurate body image begins with body awareness which initially is manifested as total body responses to sensory stimulation and movement. Gradually, the child becomes aware of his/her body through visual exploration of self; sensory exploration with hands and mouth (e.g., sucking fingers, playing with toes); and studying himself/herself in the mirror (Table 62). The concept of body image develops concurrently with cognitive and fine and gross motor skills. The child develops an understanding of object concept and is able to discriminate himself/herself from objects and others. Their body image continues to develop as the child uses locomotion (e.g., crawling, walking) to move through space and become aware of directionality (Table 62). The recognition of body parts through matching with a doll to touch localization contributes to the development of body image.

TABLE 62
SELF–AWARENESS CHARACTERISTICS CHECKLIST: SENSORIMOTOR STAGE

Body Awareness:

_____ Responds to sensory stimulation and movement with total body movement (e.g., tactile, temperature changes).

_____ Shows awareness of own body (e.g., sucks fingers, plays with toes).

_____ Visual exploration of other body parts (e.g., observes hands).

_____ Engages in sensory exploration with hands, mouth, and eyes.

_____ Observes and studies self in mirror.

Recognition of Attention:

_____ Recognizes that adults/children are paying attention (e.g., talking, tickling, handling) to him.

_____ Responds to adult/child's attempts to play.

_____ Stops actions when told "No" paired with intonation.

_____ Recognizes own name when spoken by others.

_____ Differentiates positive/negative attention (e.g., cries to scolding, smiles to praise).

Body Image:

_____ Holds objects placed in hands.

_____ Differentiates self from objects and others.

_____ Concept of size of self in relation to objects and others.

_____ Knowledge and sense of self in space (e.g., balance during locomotion.

_____ Understands directionality related to self.

_____ Recognizes body parts on doll by matching to self or naming.

_____ Touches body part on cue (body awareness localization).

_____ Beginning to be aware of sex roles or sex typing characteristics (e.g., girls play with dolls, boys-trucks).

_____ Identification with same sex parent (e.g., pretends to be same sex parent in play).

Concept of Own Capabilities (Self-Concept Factors):
(Not of significant importance during sensorimotor stage)

_____ Athletic Skill.

_____ Personal Physical Attractiveness.

_____ Social Attractiveness (e.g., even-tempered and pleasant)

_____ Special Aptitudes (e.g., art, music, drama)

_____ Intelligence

_____ Academic Performance

_____ Peer Acceptance

_____ Moral Code

_____ Leadership Qualities

REFERENCES: McInnes & Treffry, 1982; Helms & Turner, 1976; Crow & Crow, 1953; Biehler & Hudson, 1986; Scholl, 1986.

The preschool child is just beginning to become aware of sex roles and is not concerned or self-conscious about behaving in sex-appropriate ways or of participating in activities with members of the opposite sex (Biehler & Hudson, 1986). Body image and concepts of maleness and femaleness begin to develop as the young child identifies with the same sex parent and imitates them and their sex role during play activities.

Related to the development of negative or positive concepts of self is the child's initial recognition of attention to him/her by others. The baby is an egocentric being and thrives on attention by adults and other children, not only to satisfying physical needs, but also for social attention (e.g., tickling, playing simple games, tummy kissing). As the sensorimotor stage child learns to interpret emotions through the intonation system, s/he begins to understand, attend to, and obey "No" when paired with appropriate intonation (Table 62). The young child learns to differentiate positive and negative attention and may cry when scolded and laugh when praised. Since preschoolers are quite egocentric in their thinking, they are partially insulated from subtle negative responses from others (Helms & Turner, 1976). The negative or positive attention from others is not always interpreted by young children, so these responses do not have the significant effect upon him/her that may occur with the older child.

A number of factors are involved in the development of the child's concept of his/her own capabilities, including the following: athletic skill, leadership qualities, moral code, temperament, peer acceptance, academic success, physical attractiveness, intelligence, and special aptitudes (Table 62). These factors are not of significant importance to the sensorimotor stage child, but are crucial to the self-concepts of elementary school-aged children and adolescents. The athletic skill differences in play among preschoolers is not significant as they generally are involved in free play or noncompetitive activities of short duration (Biehler & Hudson, 1986). Among young children, leadership qualities are not of tremendous concern as children rapidly switch or reverse roles (e.g., runner becomes chaser). Biehler and Hudson (1986) indicate that preschool children develop only a rudimentary understanding of moral codes, and if they break the rules or behave in immoral ways, their behavior is excused due to immaturity. Temperament, generally reflected as social attractiveness, begins to be important during preschool years, as adults and children alike prefer to interact with a pleasant, easygoing child. Young children are seldom involved in peer selection for play as adults are involved and present during activities, encouraging participation by all. Academic success, physical attractiveness, intelligence, and special aptitudes are not relevant to self-conception at the sensorimotor stage. These qualities, however, take on importance relevant to the importance prescribed them by significant others, especially parents.

Play Skill Development

Play is the work of a child. It is a natural activity that serves an essential role in the young child's development (Lerner et al., 1987). "The spontaneous and creative activities of play make invaluable contributions toward the child's learning of cognitive, language, motor, and social skills" (Lerner et al., 1987, 252). "Through play, the child gives expression to his impulses and to behavior that is social in nature. He displays his kind and degree of imagination, his ability to cooperate, and his sense of fair play" (Crow & Crow, 1953, 149).

Numerous theories exist regarding the functions, stages, purposes, and developmental sequences of play. Biehler and Hudson (1986) indicate the major functions of play as follows:

1. Play permits children to explore and experiment without risk.
2. Play permits children to practice roles.
3. Play permits practice without pressure to accomplish some specific task.
4. Play fosters imaginative and creative abilities.
5. Play permits release of emotional tension (333–334).

Fallen and Umansky (1985) discuss Piaget's three levels of play complexity: (1) practice play, (2) symbolic play, and (3) games with rules. Practice play emerges in the normal child between birth and four months of age as the infant plays by repeating satisfying bodily activities (Biehler & Hudson, 1986) and simple repetitive movements with an object such as shaking a rattle (Table 63). The infant engages in exploratory play (e.g., self and environment) and manipulates objects. The seven-to-nine-month-old child learns that actions affect objects as s/he makes mobiles swing, bangs toys, shakes toys to make different sounds, grasps dangling objects, and uncovers hidden toys (Table 63).

The 10-to-12-month-old child begins to apply learned movements to new situations and is concerned with the pleasure of the activity rather than the end result (Fallen & Umansky, 1985). S/he engages in numerous fine motor activities such as squeezing a doll to make it squeak, holding a crayon and imitating scribbling, stacking rings on a peg, putting small objects in and out of a container with intention; and gross motor activities such as learning to roll balls (Table 63). The play of the 13-to-18-month-old child is characterized by experimentation and ritualized play in activities such as dropping objects from his/her highchair and throwing objects from the play pen (Fallen & Umansky, 1985). S/he engages in solitary or on-looker play, initiates their own play, scribbles spontaneously

TABLE 63
PLAY SKILL DEVELOPMENT: SENSORIMOTOR STAGE

Age	Behaviors
	PRACTICE/PLAY
0–6 mos.	*Concepts:* Learns object concept, is beginning to anticipate. Initial exploration of self and environment.
	Behaviors:
	• Sensory exploration of own body.
	• Repeats satisfying bodily actions (e.g., movement and/or vocalizations
	• Manipulates objects (e.g., rattle, blanket).
	• Pulls at dangling toys within reach.
7–9 mos.	*Concepts:* Learns that actions affect objects.
	Behaviors:
	• Shakes toys to make different sounds.
	• Makes mobiles swing.
	• Bangs toys/spoon on table.
	• Grasps dangling objects.
	• Uncovers hidden toy.
10–12 mos.	*Concepts:* Applies learned movements in new situations, achieves object permanence, concerned with the pleasure of the activity.
	Behaviors:
	• Squeezes doll to make it squeak.
	• Holds crayon—initiates scribbling.
	• Stacks rings on a peg.
	• Dumps small objects out of container.
	• Rolls ball in imitation of adult.
13–18 mos.	*Concepts:* Engages in experimentation and ritualized play, achieves causality.
	Behaviors:
	• Solitary or on-looker play.
	• Initiates own play.
	• Scribbles spontaneously with crayon.
	• Puts small objects in and out of container.
	• Pulls toys while walking.
	• Carries or hugs doll or soft toy.
	• Puts pegs in pegboard.
	• Throws objects from playpen.
	• Deliberately drops toys and watches them fall.
	• Crawls pushing small car.
	EMERGENCE OF SYMBOLIC PLAY
19–24 mos.	*Concepts:* Uses familiar actions with new objects. Uses concrete objects to substitute for objects not there. Achieves imitation and intentionality.

TABLE 63 (Continued)

Age	Behaviors
	Behaviors:
	• Throws a small ball.
	• Paints with a large brush.
	• Puts different-sized rings on a peg.
	• Builds a block tower.
	• Plays with clay.
	• Transports blocks in a wagon.
	• Strings beads.
	• Moves (dances) to music.
	• Pretends (e.g., to sleep).
	• Rides a broom for a horse.
	• Plays house—imitates adult behavior.

REFERENCES: Helms & Turner, 1976; Fallen & Umansky, 1985; Lerner et al., 1987; Biehler & Hudson, 1986; Crow & Crow, 1956.

with a crayon, uses pull toys, carries or hugs a doll, puts pegs in a pegboard (Table 63).

"The emergence of symbolic play is evident in the last stage of the sensorimotor period (stage 6, 18-to-24 months). In this stage, the child uses familiar actions with new objects" (Fallen & Umansky, 1985, 410). Symbolic play at this level is usually solitary in nature and is the child's attempt to understand reality in ways that are meaningful. The 18-to-24-month-old child uses concrete objects to substitute for objects not there (e.g., rides broom for horse) as s/he begins to pretend. The child becomes more adept at fine and gross motor skills and plays refining those skills. The 18-to-24-month-old child moves to music, throws a small ball overhand, imitates adult behaviors in play, transports blocks or other toys in a wagon; strings beads, plays with clay or playdough, builds a block tower, puts rings on a stick, paints with a large brush (Table 63). Throughout the remaining preschool years, the child continues to refine symbolic skills; about three years of age, s/he begins social, interactive pretense play (Biehler & Hudson, 1986); and by about seven years begins Piaget's third stage of play—games with rules.

SOCIAL DEVELOPMENT IN HANDICAPPED CHILDREN

A severe handicapping condition significantly impacts a child's social, emotional, and play skill development, resulting in deficits or delays in interactions with adults, with other children, with the environment, and with the development of self-awareness.

Visual Impairment

A severe vision impairment will interfere with the child's social development by reducing the child's responsiveness to caregiver's signals by reducing the likelihood of spontaneous smiling, by interfering with visual attending to adults, by delaying discrimination of familiar and unfamiliar people, and by delaying bonding, which appears to be linked to eye contact (Table 60). Severe visual impairment interferes with the child's social development by reducing the child's interactions with adults in the following ways: reduces the child's curiosity and motivation to interact, delays bonding and recognition of family members, interferes with imitation of simple actions of adults, makes adult manipulations through action songs confusing, retards bonding with secondary adults, and delays initiation of activities with an adult (Table 61).

A severe visual impairment delays interactions with other children by reducing responsiveness to other children in the following ways: delays spontaneous smiling to other children, delays recognition and response to familiar children, delays responsiveness to another child's attempts to play, and delays acquisition of understanding the body language associated with guilt, pity, affection, sympathy (Table 61). A severe visual impairment reduces the child's abilities to interact with other children by delaying interest in another child's toy, by delaying initiation of play with another child by showing or offering a toy, by making games such as peek-a-boo very confusing, and by delaying the ability to reverse roles with another child.

Play skill development is interrupted or delayed in a child with a severe visual impairment in a number of ways. The practice stage of play may be retarded as the visually impaired child does not see the repetitive reactions of toys as s/he interacts with them. A severe visual deficit reduces the child's curiosity, exploration, and manipulation of toys. The delay in acquisition of reach and grasp skills delays learning that actions affect objects, and delays understanding of causality. A severe visual impairment in a child of normal intelligence will delay acquisition of sensorimotor skills such as object concept, object permanence, anticipation, and imitation. Delayed fine motor skills interfere with the acquisition of all visually directed activities such as putting pegs in a pegboard or rings on a stick. A severe visual impairment delays the acquisition of symbolic play.

A severe visual impairment will reduce or delay the child's responsiveness to the environment by delaying acquisition of the understanding of time relationships and eating/sleeping schedules, by delaying awareness and discrimination of sensory stimulation, by delaying differentiation of familiar and unfamiliar environments and changes in the environment, and by delaying child's ability to anticipate familiar events from cues and respond accordingly (Table 61). Interaction with the environment is delayed in severely visually impaired children in the following areas: showing interest in objects, exploratory behaviors, use of objects for their specific function, ambulation and the location of permanent objects in the room, playing on large outdoor toys, and acquisition of socially appropriate behavior.

Hearing Impairment

Hearing-impaired children tend to experience more social and emotional adjustment problems than vision-impaired children. They are frequently more impulsive, throw more temper tantrums, and use a physical expression of feelings due, in part, to a lack of a functional way to express feelings and emotions, and partly due to social imperceptions from misunderstanding a situation or circumstance. However, once the child has an alternate communication mode, these behaviors are reduced in frequency.

Hearing-impaired persons have a greatly reduced amount of information due to inability to hear and utilize the intonation system of pragmatics. The greatest handicap to hearing-impaired children is the lack of a verbal communication system. Hearing-impaired children will be delayed in the understanding of receptive language, even if paired with the intonation system. Interactions with adults may be confusing if the adult plays action song games with the child. The hearing-impaired child has fewer means at his/her disposal to initiate interactions, maintain interactions, and sustain interactions with adults.

Responsiveness of hearing-impaired children to other children during the sensorimotor stage probably is not significantly delayed because neither the handicapped nor nonhandicapped child relies on verbal language, but communicates through natural gestures. The sensorimotor stage hearing-impaired child may not have significant difficulties in free play. Activities requiring vocal songs such as "Pat-a-Cake" may be confusing due to receptive deficits.

The sensorimotor stage play skills of a deaf child with no other handicapping conditions may be similar to that of a normal child progressing through the same sequences of skills. Research suggests that hearing-impaired children may, however, spend more time in the solitary play stage and less time in the cooperative play stage.

Mentally Retarded

By virtue of the label, the mentally handicapped child experiences deficits in cognitive behaviors and progresses more slowly through the developmental skills. "The mentally retarded child often has difficulty giving the cues to the caregiver that elicit nurturance and reinforce the attachment process" (Fallen & Umansky, 1985, 343). Interactions with adults may be delayed if the child does not react motorically, visually, vocally, or affectively to adult interactions. It may take considerable time for the severely mentally handicapped child to be responsive to adults, children, and/or the environment. The severely retarded child rarely explores spontaneously, has poor attention skills and, as a result, learns slowly and does not spontaneously learn to imitate. Due to the short attention span, the severely retarded child has little interest or motivation to sustain activity of any kind and demonstrates no spontaneous play. The severely handicapped child must be taught to play with a toy because initial toy play will involve banging the toy repeatedly on the floor or on the child's head.

Since severely mentally handicapped children progress at a delayed rate in all areas (e.g., fine and gross motor, communication, cognition), they remain socially immature, which frequently makes their behavior socially inappropriate. They spontaneously engage in little social interaction which, in turn, delays social conversation abilities. Characteristic of severely mentally retarded children is limited cooperative play.

Physically Impaired

The physically impaired child, by virtue of his/her handicapping condition, experiences fine and gross motor skills delays or abnormalities. Their limited abilities in movement and/or poor control of voluntary motor acts interfere not only with the acquisition of play skills, but also with the acquisition of all developmental skills.

The physically handicapped child may experience problems responding to adults in the following ways: attempts to respond by smiling may look like a grimace, attempts to respond motorically may result in totally different responses than intended. Interactions with adults may be particularly unrewarding in situations where the adult attempts to manipulate the child through action songs and simple games if the muscles of the cerebral palsied child react the opposite of expectations. Imitation of simple adult activities may be particularly difficult for the physically handicapped child. The gross motor disabilities will interfere with the child's ability to seek an adult for play. Additionally, involuntary muscle responses may severely reduce the enjoyment experienced by the adult and child during cooperative play activities.

A physical handicap significantly interferes with the child's ability to play with other sensorimotor stage children who may not understand his/her disabilities and who are very egocentric. Attempts to offer a toy may result in hitting the other child with the toy. Attempts to reach and grasp may result in inability to grasp or, once grasped, may result in inability to voluntarily release the toy. The physically handicapped child may experience reduced opportunities for exploratory and practice play. His/her experiences in attempting to apply learned movements to new situations may fail because muscular movements are unpredictable. Games and activities requiring squeezing and other fine motor activities may be painful. The physically handicapped child may be very frustrated and upset at attempts to play.

Interactions with the environment for a physically handicapped child will be similar to those experiences with play skills. The child may experience extreme difficulties in exploration of the environment. The physically impaired child may be able to anticipate familiar events from cues, but be unable to respond appropriately. The cerebral palsy may also affect oral motor control, limiting the child's ability to express accurately wants and needs and to make different vocalizations for different emotions.

Deaf-Blind Severely Multihandicapped

The deaf-blind severely multihandicapped child is concurrently visually impaired, hearing impaired, severely mentally retarded, and frequently also physically impaired. Thus, the previous discussions regarding the results of the individual handicapping conditions all apply to the deaf-blind severely multihandicapped child. Social and emotional development, therefore, is very slow in developing, as are play skills. McInnes and Treffry (1982) indicate that due to physical deficits and tactile defensiveness, the deaf-blind child may be unable to form an emotional bond with parents. Since the deaf-blind child progresses so slowly, his/her behavior is frequently less acceptable to others because of the contrast between his/her present physical size and current developmental age (McInnes & Treffry, 1982). S/he has little chance of influencing the environment and of learning spontaneously from it.

Due to severe sensory deprivation, the deaf-blind child learns many things through motor activities and physical contact. Emotional bonding with deaf-blind students depends on physical contact (McInnes & Treffry, 1982).

> Many deaf-blind persons are extremely self-centered, even selfish, because they are most conscious of their own immediate wants and needs. Unless such individuals are directly exposed to the environment and the interplay of social activities, they tend to concentrate on their most urgent needs (Smithdas, 1981, 39).

Awareness of self and self-concept development is an area of significant delay for severely handicapped children. Body awareness develops very gradually in the absence of visual exploration and observation. The development of body awareness and body image must occur through tactile stimulation and exploration. Concepts of size in relation to others, knowledge and sense of self in space, directionality must be learned during locomotion activities. Recognizing body parts on a doll and matching to self must occur tactilely. It is difficult for the deaf-blind child to recognize when others are paying attention to him/her, and to discriminate whether the attention is negative or positive.

SOCIAL AND EMOTIONAL EVALUATION

Social and Emotional Development Evaluation

Social and emotional development are difficult areas to evaluate in terms of normal behavior because there is such a wide variance in normal behavior. Additionally, children functioning within the sensorimotor stage of development are extremely variable in their behaviors. Several types of data are sought during the evaluation process including developmental data which can be compared to norms to determine the child's functioning abilities in relation to normal same-aged peers. These data are valuable in determining the level of the child's adaptive behavior—a crucial concern of any diagnosis, especially in a diagnosis of mental retardation. The Callier-Azusa Scale, subscale Social Development (Stillman, 1978) is very useful in determining a developmental level in the child's interactions with adults, other children, and the environment. An additional resource to assess social and emotional behavior at the sensorimotor stage is Social and Emotional Developmental Skills (Table 60).

Another type of data sought during an evaluation is specific strengths and weaknesses in various skill areas to be used during the child's programming. This information is generally criterion-referenced or informal task-analyzed skills. Numerous instances of systematic observation in various settings (e.g., classroom, playground), at different times during the day, in different sized activity groupings (e.g., individual, small group), or in structured and unstructured activities may provide much information regarding the child's responsiveness and initiation of interactions. Systematic observation requires a means to organize data derived from numerous observations of the child in his/her interactions with adults, other children, and the environment.

A systematic observation form to collect data regarding the child's social development can be created by using the skills in Social Development Skills Checklist: Sensorimotor Stage (Table 61) and transferring them to a grid. (See Figure 7, "IEP Monitoring Folder," Chapter 2.) The same technique can be used to create systematic observation forms for other areas. Using a systematic observation form, it can be quickly ascertained if the child's interactions are primarily responsive or self-initiated; and if the interactions occur mainly with adults, other children, or the environment.

Home Adaptive Behavior Evaluation

Severely handicapped children may behave differently at home than at school. With older, higher functioning children, parents can be interviewed regarding playing with neighborhood children, associations in community activities and clubs, home chores, following family rules. These activities are beyond the capabilities of deaf-blind severely multihandicapped children functioning within the sensorimotor stage of development.

Many adaptive behavior scales begin at age two or three years, so the behaviors indicated are above the capabilities of the child functioning within the sensorimotor stage. Home adaptive behavior can be assessed by having parents check or respond to Social Development Skills (Tables 60, 61, 62, 63) or by using the systematic observation forms created with the same skills or by using the same skills in a "yes-no" questionnaire format. The home adaptive behavior information serves several purposes including providing a "biased, nonobjective" assessment of the child's functioning at home which can be compared to school functioning. The questionnaire also allows parents to be involved in the evaluation process and to understand the difficulty in assessing severely multihandicapped children. It provides parents some insights into the amount of consideration by many professionals that are involved in the evaluation/ re-evaluation of their child.

Case Study: Sally

Sally's mother used the Social Development Skills (Tables 61, 62, 63) and evaluated Sally's functioning at home. Sally's mother reports her child functioning at a higher level than noted at school—a very common occurrence (Table 64). Although Sally's mother knows that Sally is "deaf and blind," she does not perceive that some of the visual-like behavior engaged in by Sally may be Sally's accommodating to being held, to feeling vibrations and turning toward them. On the other hand, mother's observations may not be totally biased by her hopes that Sally can see; there may be more use of residual vision than measured in a clinical or school setting. Thus, the home assessments assist the teacher by providing the parents' observations and alerting the teacher to potential in areas not previously noted.

Case Study: Bud

Bud's home social behavior as assessed by mother appears to be at the 10-to-16-month level (Table 65). Bud's parents interact with him on a totally one-to-one basis and have learned over the years ways to interact with him. This information can be especially helpful to a teacher who is new to Bud. At home, Bud has the opportunity to interact with his nonhandicapped brother who initiates activity with him. In Bud's classroom at school, all of the children are deaf-blind severely multihandicapped functioning within the sensorimotor stage; therefore, there is little interaction among the children.

TABLE 64
SOCIAL/EMOTIONAL EVALUATION REPORT: HOME ADAPTIVE BEHAVIOR

Name: Sally
Respondent: Mother

Sally's home adaptive behavior was evaluated using the social development questionnaire and skills lists. Her overall home adaptive behavior appears to be at the 4–6 months level, as indicated by mother's responses.

Interactions with Adults. Sally shows awareness of the presence of an adult by visually following them as they walk across her field of vision. She responds to adults by smiling and making eye contact with them. Sally responds to her mother's voice, but not to the babysitter's unless paired with a tactile cue.

Interactions with the Environment. Sally shows an awareness of the presence of absence of light, sound, tactile stimulation. She has a preferred eating position and pattern, and has preferences in foods. She will cry when hungry. Sally is beginning to show awareness of body parts and movements, as she sucks on her fingers.

Interactions with Other Children. Sally was not seen to interact with other children. She shows no awareness of the presence of other children, not does she respond to other children's attempts to interact.

Generally, Sally demonstrates severely deficit responsiveness to her environment and the people in it.

Using a systematic observation form, Bud's teacher can indicate mother's responses regarding Bud's behavior at home. The teacher should indicate those responses labeled home on the same sheet used for several systematic observations of school behavior for comparison and analysis. In Bud's case, the analysis would probably reveal that the majority of social interactions were responsive reactions on his part rather than initiative interactions. This suggests that Bud needs to learn how to interact with adults, peers, and the environment by initiating interactions and thereby gaining more control of his environment.

Self-Awareness Evaluation

Evaluation of the self-awareness or the self-concept of young or sensorimotor stage functioning children is difficult. Self-awareness is generally evaluated by objective and/or subjective means. The objective means involve self-reporting or answering questions. Since the sensorimotor stage occurs prior to the acquisition of fluent speech, traditional questionnaires may not be used. Subjective means of evaluating self-perception generally involve projective techniques such as drawing pictures, using the imagination, describing ink blots. Subjective means of evaluation,

TABLE 65

SOCIAL/EMOTIONAL EVALUATION REPORT: HOME ADAPTIVE BEHAVIOR

Name: Bud

Respondent: Mother

Bud's home adaptive behavior was evaluated using the Home Adaptive Behavior: Social Development Skills lists. His overall home adaptive behavior appears to be at the 10–16 month level, as indicated by mother's responses.

Interactions with Adults. Bud's interactions with adults appear to be at the *10–12 months level.* He shows awareness of the presence of an adult from adult contact. He responds to person-to-person contact, studies or attends to an adult tactilely, and may attend to an adult's voice if the voice is extremely loud. Bud responds to an adult's attempt to interact by vocalizing. He differentiates familiar and unfamiliar adults. He is able to engage in interactions of at least two sequential exchanges and is able to play a game with an adult if the adult paces the game. Bud attempts to maintain contact with familiar adults and may respond to some signs.

Interactions with the Environment. Bud's interactions with the environment appear to be at the *10–12 month level.* He shows awareness to tactile stimulation and to light. He shows a preferred feeding schedule and preference for certain foods. Bud moves and changes position. He exhibits self-stimulating behaviors and vocalizes to show discomfort. He responds to tactile stimulation and warm baths. Bud exhibits different vocalizations and shows awareness of body movements and body parts (e.g., sucks thumb). Bud differentiates familiar and unfamiliar environments. He reacts to frustrating situations by tantrums and self-stimulation. He anticipates a familiar event in the presence of several cues, and seeks a particular object for comfort in a stressful situation or when tired.

Interactions with Other Children. Bud's interactions with other children appear to be at the *12–16 month level.* He shows awareness of the presence of another child by contact. He responds to other children's presence by smiling and touching, if other children make contact first. Bud smiles or vocalizes to another child's voice or contact. He will explore another child as an object. He attempts to initiate interactions with other children by reaching out and touching. He will accept a toy or food from another child. Bud is able to play simple games, such as a tickle game. He shows specific preference for another child—his brother.

---

then, are prohibited by lack of speech and by inabilities to draw a person.

The self-awareness of a sensorimotor stage child primarily involves body awareness, recognition of attention by others, and body image (Table 62). Areas usually considered in a self-concept evaluation, including athletic skill, leadership qualities, moral code, social attractiveness, intelligence, special aptitudes (Table 62), are not applicable to the young or sensorimotor stage child.

The most accurate assessment of self-awareness at the sensorimotor stage involves systematic observation on numerous occasions and in varied locations to begin to determine a pattern of behavior. Using the Self-Awareness Characteristics Checklist (Table 62), a systematic observation form can be prepared by adding skills to a grid. The teacher should observe the child over a several-week period at various times during the day in various settings to get an accurate baseline of self-awareness abilities.

Play Skills Evaluation

"For young handicapped children with mild and moderate delays, one of the most effective ways to assess the level of play development is through observational assessment" (Fallen & Umansky, 1985, 431). Systematic observation is also one of the most effective means of evaluating severely handicapped children.

Evaluation of play skills should result in determination of a developmental skills level and in specific strengths and weaknesses to be used in programming. A developmental functioning level can be determined by administering a developmental play skills checklist such as the Play Skill Development: Sensorimotor Stage (Table 63). The results of this instrument will provide a developmental level age range or age equivalent which can be compared to the child's other developmental functioning abilities.

The determination of specific strengths and weaknesses requires a criterion-referenced instrument or task analyses of various play skills. Few, if any, instruments specifically assess play skills as a separate area; usually play skills are included in other developmental areas such as socialization and motor skills. Specific strengths and weaknesses in play skill development can be determined utilizing systematic observation in various settings, different times during the day, over a several-week period to gain a pattern of behavior. For best success with observation, the observational areas should be carefully delineated. Thus, the programming play skills sequence in Play Skills Checklist: Sensorimotor Stage (Table 66) can be used in current form or transferred to a data collection grid.

Analysis of a systematic observation form will quickly indicate within which level of practice play or emerging symbolic play the child is functioning. The child's program can then be easily planned, based on the hierarchy of play skills.

SOCIAL AND EMOTIONAL DEVELOPMENT PROGRAMMING

While most children acquire appropriate social skills through daily interactions with adults and children, many young children have social imperception problems resulting in insensitivity to the subtle social cues

TABLE 66

PLAY SKILLS CHECKLIST: SENSORIMOTOR STAGE

Practice Play
  Exploratory Play
——————— Engages in sensory exploration of own body.
——————— Repeats satisfying bodily actions (e.g., movement, vocalizations).
——————— Explores objects using senses (e.g., visual, tactile).
——————— Manipulates objects (e.g., rattle, blanket).
——————— Pulls at dangling toys (e.g., mobiles) within reach.
  Action/Object Play
——————— Shakes toy repetitively to make different sounds.
——————— Makes mobiles swing.
——————— Bangs or pounds toys or spoon on table.
——————— Grasps dangling objects.
——————— Uncovers a hidden toy (searching behavior).
  Learned Movements/New Situations
——————— Squeezes doll to make it squeak.
——————— Rolls ball in imitation of adult.
——————— Holds crayon—imitates scribbling.
——————— Stacks rings on a peg.
——————— Dumps small objects out of container.
——————— Scoops with spoon or shovel in sand, etc.
  Experimentation and Ritualized Play
——————— Engages in solitary or on-looker play.
——————— Initiates play.
——————— Scribbles spontaneously with crayon.
——————— Puts small objects in and out of container.
——————— Pulls wheeled toys while walking.
——————— Carries or hugs doll or soft toy.
——————— Puts pegs in pegboard.
——————— Throws objects from playpen, etc.
——————— Deliberately drops toys and watches them fall.
——————— Crawls, pushing a toy car.
  Familiar Actions/New Objects
——————— Throws a small ball.
——————— Paints with a large brush.
——————— Puts different-sized rings on a peg in sequence.
——————— Builds a block tower.
——————— Plays with clay.
——————— Transports blocks in a wagon.
——————— Strings beads.
——————— Pounds pegs in a pegboard.
——————— Pulls string or turns handle to activate toy.
——————— Rocks a rocking horse.
——————— Swings in a swing (once started).
——————— Takes objects apart.

Table 66 (Continued)

Emerging Symbolic Play
   Uses Concrete Objects to Pretend
_____ Rides a broom for a horse.
_____ Plays "house" (imitating adult behavior).
_____ Moves (dances) to music.

REFERENCES: Crow & Crow 1953; Biehler & Hudson, 1986; Fallen & Umansky, 1985; Helms & Turner, 1976; Lerner et al., 1987.

given by others and to the appropriate behaviors required in various social situations (Lerner et al., 1987). Since the educational process for deaf-blind severely multihandicapped children requires consistent, one-to-one teaching, these children may continue to be very self-centered for a considerable time, exhibiting inappropriate social behaviors. The vision deficit reduces the signal information gained from body language and facial expressions. The deficit in auditory reception reduces the emotional cues from voice intonation. Cognitive deficits may preclude understanding and interpreting the social and emotional cues perceived.

Teaching the deaf-blind severely multihandicapped child social skills will be very difficult because the child cannot be taught social skills directly through imitation, trial and error, or by patterning, due to vision and hearing deficits. Any educational sequence for deaf-blind children initially requires the development of a bond between the child and the caregiver so the child has a trusted "communicator between him and his environment" (McInnes & Treffry, 1982, 40).

Since deaf-blind severely multihandicapped children do not learn spontaneously, an organized program must be provided. The social development program should include the following goals: (1) develop self-perception and body image, (2) develop sensitivity to the feelings of others, and (3) learn appropriate ways of acting in social situations (Lerner et al., 1987). These goals can be achieved through programming for interactions with adults and children, interactions with the environment, self-awareness skills, and play skills.

Interactions with Adults and Children

Programming objectives will be determined from the results of the systematic observations conducted during the evaluation of the child.

The initial interactions with adults and children will be reactive or responsive in nature (Table 61). Deaf-blind severely multihandicapped children generally experience difficulty in initiating interactions with adults and children.

"Three of the factors that appear to be the most crucial to the early development and learning of visually handicapped children are body manipulation, sound stimulation, and stable relationships with the environment" (Barraga, 1983, 31). Body manipulation and body play help the deaf-blind severely multihandicapped child to begin gaining an awareness of self as s/he develops a bond with mother (caregiver). As previously discussed, the caregiver should develop a signal language with the child, using body language to enable the child to anticipate and predict the intentional behavior about to occur and to discriminate among adults and children. Social development cannot occur unless the child enjoys the interactions and desires more interactions with adults and children.

The emotional bond between the deaf-blind severely multihandicapped child and the caregiver(s) will usually be established through routine activities which s/he enjoys (McInnes & Treffry, 1982). Caregivers (teachers) will need to spend considerable time bonding prior to any educational programming. Manipulating a passive child through activities in a routine sequence without prior bonding may achieve few positive results, will not contribute to developing cognitive skills of anticipation and prediction, and may frighten the child. Emotional bonding should provide emotional security and lessened anxiety as the child develops trust in his/her caregivers. Barraga (1983) indicates that body play and manipulation help the child learn new movement patterns, contributing to emotional security and reduced anxiety and thus reducing the need for self-stimulation and bizarre behaviors.

Since social skills for the sensorimotor stage child develop with the development of cognition, motor skills, and communication skills, every interaction with the child should be geared toward increasing abilities in all of these areas. Specific educational kits do not exist solely for the purpose of developing social skills in deaf-blind severely multihandicapped sensorimotor stage children. Activities to develop secondary senses and motor skills provide enjoyable situations within which to begin development of social skills.

Case Study: Sally

Sally's home adaptive behavior evaluation indicates an awareness of the presence of adults and responses to an adult's attempt to interact tactilely. Thus her interactions with adults are all responsive in nature. Sally's objectives in cognition and expressive language were designed to encourage her to initiate interactions with adults and her environment; therefore, additional social development objectives are not necessary at this time.

Case Study: Bud

Bud's social evaluation report (Table 65) indicates that he is both responsive to adults and children and initiates interactions with adults and children (i.e., brother). Bud appears to be very responsive to adults in all of the sensorimotor areas except those requiring hearing. He apparently does not know his name. He responds inconsistently to "No" spoken loudly, paired with intonation. Bud interacts with adults; usually the adult interacts first. Bud can sign "drink" and will indicate that desire. He engages in no social dialogue with adults. His expressive language objective is to learn four more self-help words (signs). Attainment of this objective will give Bud more ways to interact with adults.

Bud is unaware of the presence of other children unless contact is made. At school, he has no interactions with other children. At home, he both responds to and shows initiative interactions with his brother. At present, Bud's other IEP objectives meet his socialization needs. As he acquires more sign language and play skills and consistently uses objects appropriately (e.g., no head banging), opportunities should be provided at school to interact with higher functioning children for 10–20 minutes daily.

Interactions with the Environment

"The goal of any successful program must be to provide an environment which allows each child to develop the necessary social skills and emotional stability through planned interaction within an ever-widening circle of adults and peers" (McInnes & Treffry, 1982, 36). Since the deaf-blind severely multihandicapped child suffers from deficit distance senses, little means of communication, and evolving gross and fine motor skills, exploration of the environment is not spontaneous as with nonhandicapped children. Since his/her environment is bounded by his random reach, motivation to explore is minimal (McInnes & Treffry, 1982).

Initial environmental exploration training involves auditory, visual and tactile sensory stimulation activities to stimulate interest and motivation in exploring and concepts to assist the child in identifying or understanding what they may find during exploration. Interactions with the environment are encouraged in all programming areas: sensory skills, fine and gross motor skills, cognitive skills, receptive and expressive language skills. Since the deaf-blind severely multihandicapped child functioning within the sensorimotor stage learns primarily through motor and movement activities, the environment must provide opportunities to explore and learn motorically. The child needs to learn to not only to respond to the environment, but also to initiate interactions within the environment. The child's programming will be determined by the results of the systematic observation and administration of adaptive behavior checklists.

Case Study: Sally

Sally's evaluation report (Table 64) indicates responsive interactions with the environment, including awareness to the presence of light, sound, tactile stimulation. Initiative interactions include indicating (1) a preferred eating position and schedule, (2) food preferences, (3) beginning awareness of body parts and movements (e.g., sucks her fingers). The next responsive objective which Sally needs to acquire is responding to being warmly wrapped, warm bath (Table 61). This skill is included in Sally's tactile stimulation objective. Sally's next initiative objectives are to show interest in objects and reach out to touch objects in the environment (Table 61). These skills are included in Sally's tactile stimulation objectives (Objective B) and in her Cognitive Objectives. Thus Sally needs no additional IEP objectives in the area of interactions with the environment.

Case Study: Bud

Bud's evaluation report (Table 65) indicates mastery of the sensorimotor stage responsive interactions with the environment with the exception of "responds to changes in the environment." Initiative interactions with the environment indicate weaknesses in the following areas: engages in self-stimulation and inappropriate use of objects (e.g., bangs them on his head). Elimination of these inappropriate behaviors are the focus of Cognitive Objective A. The next interaction with the environment skill (Table 61) is to show curiosity and explore the environment, which is the focus of Cognitive Objective B. The next skill to be acquired is indicating the need to toilet (Table 61). This objective is beyond Bud's current functioning level as self-help objectives focus on teaching him to sign "toilet." When Bud has a means to communicate this need, the objective can become an educational target. Therefore, no additional IEP objectives are needed at this time to assist in developing more interactions with the environment.

Self-Awareness

Self-awareness, a prerequisite skill to self-concept development, includes body awareness, recognition of attention, body image, and a beginning understanding of personal capabilities (Table 62). Body awareness and body image are very important skill prerequisites to the development of the following abilities: gross motor skills of locomotion and orientation in space, visual-motor skills requiring fine motor abilities, expressive language through body language and signing, and the cognitive concepts accompanying those abilities, as well as social and emotional and play skills. Body awareness and body image tasks are built into the skills hierarchies of these areas and are developed concomitantly with them.

Planning program objectives in the area of self-awareness involves analyzing the results of a systematic observation (Table 62) or locating the self-awareness factors on other evaluations and grouping for analysis.

Case Study: Sally

Sally was not administered a separate self-awareness evaluation. Her functioning, derived from other evaluation instruments, indicates the emergence following body awareness factors (Table 62): responds to sensory stimulation and awareness of own body (e.g., sucks her fingers). Her current objectives in vision, hearing, secondary sensation aim to increase responses to sensory stimulation and increase body awareness. An emerging skill for Sally is recognizing that adults are paying attention to her (Table 62). This skill, too, is built into current IEP objectives of sensory awareness, cognition, and language. The remaining Self-Awareness Skills of Body Image and Concepts of One's Abilities (Table 62) are predicated upon body awareness; thus no competencies exist in these areas. Additional IEP objectives are not necessary at this time because of the overlapping of initial skills.

Case Study: Bud

Bud was not administered a separate self-awareness evaluation. His functioning abilities can be derived from subskills of other evaluations, including Social Development Skills: Sensorimotor Stage (Table 60). By comparing Bud's Social Development functioning to the Self-Awareness Characteristics Checklist (Table 62), his self-awareness can be determined. Bud possesses the following Body Awareness skills: responds to sensory stimulation, shows awareness of own body, and explores with hands and mouth. Due to the severity of his vision deficit, he cannot visually explore his body nor study himself in the mirror. Thus, he currently possesses all possible body awareness skills. Bud possesses the following Recognition of Attention skills (Table 62): recognizes tactilely when others are paying attention, responds to others (adults or brother), attempts to play, stops action momentarily when told "No" very loudly. Bud does not recognize his name spoken. Differentiating positive and negative attention is an emerging skill since he recognizes "No." As Bud develops more concept of self and develops greater abilities in interpreting tactile signs, he will need to be taught a sign that stands for "Bud." Bud is making progress in body image development (Table 62) as he learns to walk and move about the classroom. Body image skills he possesses include the following: holds objects placed in his hands, differentiates self from objects and others, emerging concept of size of self as he chooses/prefers to sit in small chairs than crawl into large ones, emerging sense of self in space as he uses fixed furniture to pull to stand and moves about the room without always banging into things, emerging directionality as he finds favorite items in the classroom. He does not yet have the concept of separate body parts on himself or a doll. The emerging body skills are built into Bud's gross motor IEP program objectives. The concept of body image related to body parts is one of his secondary sensation objectives (Objective B). Therefore, at this time, there is no need to write additional Self-Awareness objectives.

Play Skills

"Play is the most complete of all educational processes because it influences the intellect, the emotions, and the body of the child" (Fallen

& Umansky, 1985, 415). Play activities enable the child to simultaneously practice gross and fine motor skills, cognition, sensory skills, communication, and social skills. Thus play should be an integral part of the life of a preschool-aged child.

Severely handicapped children do not appear to learn spontaneously through play and need a more directed and structured play (Lerner et al., 1987). During free play periods, severely handicapped children frequently engage in repetitive, nonfunctional actions, and/or inappropriate actions with toys such as banging on the table or floor until it breaks or banging the toy on their head. Handicapped children need to be taught directly how to interact with a toy and whether it should be pushed, pulled, put together, taken apart, thrown. Since the attention span of severely multihandicapped sensorimotor stage children is so short, they will require numerous patient hand-over-hand training sessions in an atmosphere of acceptance and encouragement before they will get "the idea" of how the toy works.

Stevens (1973) indicates a hierarchy of structured play activities including the following: (1) looking activities—at moving objects, at stationary objects, appearing and disappearing toys, peep games with people and equipment; (2) touching, grasping, giving, dropping activities; (3) carrying, emptying, pouring, filling activities; (4) manipulation activities; (5) reconstructing life activities; (6) simple construction activities; and (7) sorting, arranging, associating, sequencing activities.

Play skills functioning can be determined by analyzing the results of the Play Skills Checklist (Table 66) from systematic observation. The child's IEP program can then be planned using the hierarchial skills.

Case Study: Sally

Sally's overall evaluation results indicate functioning at the Exploratory Play level (Table 66). She engages in minimal sensory explorations of her own body (e.g., sucks her fingers). Play skills at the exploratory level overlap considerably with sensory stimulation, cognitive, and motor skills; therefore, a separate IEP objective is not needed at this point.

Case Study: Bud

Bud's evaluation report (Table 67) indicates functioning at the 10-to-12-month level in play skills with splinter skills at the 19-to-24-month level.

Using the play skills hierarchy (Table 66), the next realistic objective for Bud involves putting small objects in and out of a container. This is

TABLE 67
PLAY SKILLS EVALUATION REPORT

Name: Bud

Bud was evaluated using the Systematic Observation Form: Play Skills. Bud appears to be functioning at the 10–12 month level with splinter skills at the 24-month level.

At the Exploratory Play level, Bud possesses the concept of object, anticipates events, and explores himself and his environment. He explores objects with his hands and mouth, manipulates objects, and reaches for bright or familiar sound-producing objects in front of him.

At the Action/Object Play level, Bud understands that actions affect objects. He shakes, swings, bangs, grasps, and finds hidden toys using tactile cues.

At the Learned Movements/New Situations level, Bud squeezes dolls, stacks rings on a peg, dumps objects from a container, and is gaining facility in scooping with a spoon. Due to severe vision deficits, Bud does not roll balls or scribble with a crayon because he cannot "see" the result of his action.

At the Experimentation/Ritualized Play level, Bud engages in solitary play. He can crawl around the room, seeking preferred toys. He takes blocks out of a container, pushes a wagon, takes pegs out of a pegboard, throws objects. He reaches with one hand from a crawling position to manipulate toys. Bud does not scribble with a crayon, carry a toy, or watch objects fall.

At the Familiar Actions/New Objects level, Bud rocks on a rocking horse and swings in a classroom-sized swing.

one of Bud's fine motor objectives (Objective A). The next skill in the hierarchy—pulling wheeled toys and/or carrying a doll—involves stable walking abilities. Bud is learning to walk, but needs much more practice and stability before he can pull toys and carry dolls/toys. Thus there is no need to write additional IEP objectives.

IEP monitoring in social and emotional, self-awareness, and play skill development areas is merely a continuation of frequent systematic observation. The systematic observation should be used at least weekly to indicate the student's functioning levels—acquired/present skills, emerging skills, and skills not present. Developmental levels may be assessed frequently using data collection grids for social and emotional, self-awareness, and play skills. Utilizing the Developmental Skills Checklists will provide an age-based functioning range while systematic observation provides specific strengths and weaknesses in the task-analyzed programming skills.

SUMMARY

A child is a total being in which physical, mental, social, and emotional development are interdependent behaviors. Although children are not born social or antisocial, they are born with temperament differences that greatly affect their social relationships. The three-month-old infant shows social and emotional characteristics or behaviors. By two years of age, the child possesses an almost complete repertoire of emotions, but social interaction with other children is difficult.

Prerequisite to adequate social and emotional development is bonding or attachment, a special affectionate reciprocal relationship which does not occur automatically, but develops gradually, encouraged by both parties. Vision is extremely important to the bonding process. Bonding provides the basis for the development of cognition and language as well as social and emotional development. Initial bonding with the primary caregiver provides a pattern for future bonding.

The development of the self-concept begins in infancy with body awareness, recognition that others are providing attention, and body image. A positive self-concept or self-awareness is the core of successful functioning and one's willingness and motivation to try.

Play skill development is extremely important as the child practices, explores, and discovers increasing his/her abilities in cognition, fine and gross motor, communication, sensory, and social/emotional areas. Symbolic play emerges toward the end of the sensorimotor stage as the child begins to pretend and play house.

Deaf-blind severely multihandicapped children do not learn spontaneously from their environment by hearing and observing, then imitating. The visual deficit reduces or eliminates the visual communication that assists with bonding, reduces the child's curiosity and motivation to explore the environment, and interrupts or delays play development. The hearing impairment reduces or eliminates the social cues gained from intonation and pragmatics and interferes with the expressive communication system as well as receptive. The mental retardation reduces the child's ability to interpret what sensory information s/he does receive, results in very slow learning, no motivation, and little spontaneous play. The physical impairments of deaf-blind severely multihandicapped children delay or reduce abilities in fine and gross motor skills, interfere with play skills and social development, reduce exploratory behavior due to inability to control muscles.

BIBLIOGRAPHY

Ainsworth, M. D.: Patterns of attachment behavior shown by the infant in interaction with his mother. *The Merrill-Palmer Quarterly of Behavior and Development, 10* (1964): 51–58.

Allen, H.: Testing of visual acuity in preschool children. *Pediatrics, 19* (1957): 1093.

Anwar, F.: Vision and kinesthesis in motor movement. In J. Hogg & P. Mittler (Eds.), *Advances in Mental Handicaps Research*, Vol. 2. Chichester, MA: Wiley, 1983.

Anwar, F.: Cognitive deficit and motor skill. In D. Ellis (Ed.). *Sensory Impairments in Mentally Handicapped People* (pp. 169–183). San Diego, CA: College-Hill Press, 1986.

Appell, M.: Hospital Stimulation Programs. *Proceedings: Workshop for Serving the Deaf-Blind and Multihandicapped Child: Identification, Assessment, and Training.* California State Dept. of Education, Sacaramento: Southwestern Region Deaf-Blind Center (ERIC Document Reproduction Service No. ED 179 039), 1979.

Aslin, R.: Motor aspects of visual development in infancy. In P. Solapatek and L. Cohen (Eds.), *Handbook of Infant Perception, From Sensation to Perception,* Vol. 1. Orlando, FL: Academic Press, 1987.

Atkinson, R. C. & Shiffrin, R. M.: Human memory: A proposed system and its control processes. In H. W. Spence & J. T. Spence (Eds.), *The Psychology of Learning and Motivation,* Vol. 2, New York: Academic Press, 1968.

Ayres, A. J.: *Southern California Postrotary Nystagmus Test.* Los Angeles: Western Psychological Services, 1975.

——————.: *Southern California Sensory Integration Tests Manual Revised.* Los Angeles: Western Psychological Services, 1980.

Bailey, D. & Wolery, M.: *Teaching Infants and Preschoolers with Handicaps.* Columbus, OH: Charles E. Merrill, 1984.

Banks, M., & Dannemiller, J.: Infant visual psychophysics. In P. Solapatek and L. Cohen (Eds.). *Handbook of Infant Perception, from Sensation to Perception.* Vol. 1. Orlando, FL: Academic Press, 1987.

Barens, C., & Zucherman, J.: *Diagnostic Examination of the Eye.* Philadelphia: Lippincott, 1946.

Barraga, N.: *Visual Handicaps and Learning.* Austin, TX: Educational Resources, 1983.

Bayley, N.: *Bayley Scales of Infant Development.* Cleveland, OH: The Psychological Corporation, 1969.

Beyer, B.: *Practical Strategies for the Teaching of Thinking.* Boston: Allyn & Bacon, 1987.

Biehler, R., & Hudson, L.: *Developmental Psychology: An Introduction,* 3rd ed. Boston: Houghton-Mifflin, 1986.

Blackman, J.: *Medical Aspects of Developmental Disabilities in Children, Birth to Three.* Rockville, MD: Aspen, 1984.

Blaskey, J.: Head trauma. In S. Campbell (Ed). *Pediatric Neurologic Physical Therapy* (pp. 245–275). New York: Churchill Livingstone, 1984.

Bobath, B. & Bobath, K.: *Motor Development in the Different Types of Cerebral Palsy.* London: Heinemann, 1976.

Bower, G. H.: Cognitive psychology: An introduction. In W. K. Estes (Ed.), *Handbook of Learning and Cognitive Processes: Introduction to Concepts and Issues,* Vol. 1, (pp. 25–80). Hillsdale, NJ: Erlbaum, 1975.

Bradford, L. J.: Responsive Audiometry. In L. J. Bradford (Ed.), *Psychological Measures of the Audio-Vestibular System.* New York: Academic Press, 1975.

Bricker, D., & Dennison, L.: Training prerequisites to verbal behavior. In M. E. Snell (Ed.), *Systematic Instruction of the Moderately and Severely Handicapped.* Columbus, OH: Charles E. Merrill, 1978.

Bridgford, J.: Myelodysplasia. In S. Campbell (Ed.). *Pediatric Neurologic Physical Therapy* (pp. 205–244). New York: Churchill Livingstone, 1984.

Brown, A. L.: The role of strategic behavior in retardate memory. In N. R. Ellis (Ed.), *International Review of Research in Mental Retardation,* Vol. 7. New York: Academic Press, 1974.

Brown, D., Simons, V., & Methvin, J.: *The Oregon Project for Visually Impaired and Blind Preschool Children.* Medford, OR: Jackson Co. Educ. Services District, 1979.

Bzoch, K., & League, R.: *Receptive Expressive Emergent Lanugage Scales (REEL).* Gainesville, FL: Tree of Life, 1972.

Campbell, P., Green, K., & Carlson, L.: Approximating the norm through environmental and child-centered prosthetics and adaptive equipment. In E. Sontag (Ed.). *Educational Programming for the Severely and Profoundly Handicapped.* Reston, VA: Council for Exceptional Children, 1977.

Campbell, S. *Pediatric Neurological Physical Therapy.* New York: Churchill Livingstone, 1984.

Caplan, F.: *The First Twelve Months of Life.* Princeton: The Princeton Center for Infancy and Early Childhood, 1971.

Caplan, F. *The First Twelve Months of Life.* New York: Grosset & Dunlap, 1973.

Cattell, P.: *Cattell Infant Intelligence Scale.* Atlanta, GA: Psychological Corp., 1947.

Coats, A.: Elecronystagmography. In L. J. Bradford (Ed.). *Physiological Measures of the Audio-Vestibular System.* New York: Academic Press, 1975.

Cohen, M., & Gross, P.: *The Developmental Resource: Behavioral Sequences for Assessment and Program Planning,* Vol. I. New York: Grune & Stratton, 1979.

Cohen, M. A., Gross, P. J., and Haring, N. G.: Development pinpoints. In N. G. Haring and L. Brown (Eds.), *Teaching the Severely Handicapped,* Vol. I. New York: Grune & Stratton, 1976.

Connolly, B.: Learning disabilities. In S. Campbell (Ed.). *Pediatric Neurologic Physical Therapy.* New York: Churchill Livingstone, 1984.

Copeland, M. E., Ford, L., & Solon, N.: *Occupational Therapy for Mentally Retarded Children.* Baltimore: University Park Press, 1976.

Corn, A.: Low vision and visual efficiency. In G. Scholl (Ed.). *Foundations of Educa-*

tion for Blind and Visually Handicapped Children and Youth: Theory and Practice. New York: American Foundation for the Blind, 1986.

Cox, P. & Lloyd, L. L.: Audiologic considerations. In L. L. Lloyd (Ed.), *Communciation Assessment and Intervention Strategies*. Baltimore, MD: University Park Press, 1975.

Crow, L., & Crow, A.: *Child Psychology*. New York: Barnes, & Noble, 1953.

Dantona, R.: Implications of demographic data for planning of services for deaf-blind children and adults. In David Ellis (Ed.) *Sensory Impairments in Mentally Handicapped People*, (pp. 69–82). San Diego, CA: College Hill Press, 1986.

Deaf/Blind Resource Manual for Program for Exceptional Children. Georgia Department of Education, 1980.

Denhoff, E.: Medical aspects. In W. M. Cruickshank (Ed.). *Cerebral Palsy: A Developmental Disability*, 3rd rev. ed. Syracuse, NY: Syracuse University Press, 1976.

Dunst, C.: *A Clinical and Educational Manual for Use with the Uzgeriz-Hunt Scales of Infant Psychological Development.* Baltimore, MD: University Park Press, 1980.

Efron, M., & Duboff, B.: *A Vision Guide for Teachers of Deaf-Blind Children.* Raleigh, NC: North Carolina Department of Public Instruction, 1979.

Ellis, D.: The epidemiology of visual impairment in people with a mental handicap. In D. Ellis (Ed.). *Sensory Impairments in Mentally Handicapped People*, (pp. 3–34). San Diego, CA: College-Hill Press, 1986.

Fallen, N. & Umansky, W.: *Young Children with Special Needs*, 2nd ed. Columbus, OH: Charles E. Merrill, 1985.

Federal Register: Washington, DC: U.S. Government Printing Office, 1975, 7415.

Feldman, A.: Acoustic impedance—Admittance measurements. In L. J. Bradford (Ed.), *Physiological Measures of the Audio-Vestibular System*. New York: Academic Press, 1975.

Finnie, N. R.: *Handling the Young Cerebral Palsied Child at Home.* New York: E. P. Dutton, 1979.

Frost, J. L.: *Developmental Checklists for 3-, 4-, and 5-Year Olds.* Austin, TX: University of Texas, 1972.

Gard, A., Gilman, L., & Gorman, J.: *Speech and Language Developmental Chart.* Salt Lake City, UT: Word Making Productions, 1980.

Gellis, S., & Kegan, B.: *Current Pediatric Therapy.* Philadelphia: Saunders, 1976.

Georgia State Department of Education: *Deaf/Blind Resource Manuals for Programs for Exceptional Children*, Vol. X. Atlanta, GA: Office Instructional Services (ERIC Document Reproduction Service No. ED 276-226), 1986.

Gottesman, M.: A comprehensive study of Piaget's developmental schema of sighted children with that of a group of blind children. *Child Development* (June 1971), 573–580.

Gresty, M., Halmagyi, G., & Taylor, D.: Head thrusting and nodding in children with disturbances of ocular motility. In K. Wybar & D. Taylor (Eds.), *Pediatric Ophthalmology: Current Aspects*, (pp. 331–340). New York: Marcel Dekker, 1983.

Hallahan, D. & Kauffman, J.: *Exceptional Children.* Englewood Cliffs, NJ: Prentice-Hall, 1978.

Harris, S.: Downs syndrome. In S. Campbell (Ed.). *Pediatric Neurologic Physical Therapy* (pp. 169–204). New York: Churchill Livingstone, 1984.

Haynes, U.: *Holistic Health Care for Children with Developmental Disabilities.* Baltimore, MD: University Park Press, 1983.

Healy, H. & Stainback, S.: *The Severely Motorically Impaired Student.* Springfield, IL: Charles C Thomas, 1980.

Helms, D., & Turner, J.: *Exploring Child Behavior.* Philadelphia: Saunders, 1982.

Hood, D.C.: Evoked cortical response audiometry. In L. J. Bradford (Ed.), *Physiological Measures of the Audio-Vestibular System.* New York: Academic Press, 1975.

Hoyt, C. S., Nickel, B. L., & Billison, F. A.: Ophthalmological examination of the infant: developmental aspect. *Surv Opthalmol,* (1982) *26,* 177.

Hunt, H. & Wills, D.: The family and the young visually handicapped child. In K. Wybar & D. Taylor (Eds.), *Pediatric Ophthalmology Current Aspects,* pp. 95–104. New York: Marcel Dekker, 1983.

Jacobson, H.: The information capacity of the human eye. *Science, 13* (1951a), 292–293.

Jacobson, H.: Information and the human ear. *Journal Accoust,* Soc. Am *23* (1951b), 463–471.

Jones, C. J.: Analysis of the self-concepts of handicapped students. *Remedial and Special Education, 6* (Sep/Oct 1985), 32–36.

Kaiser, A., Alpert, C., & Warren S.: Teaching functional language: Strategies for language intervention. In M. Snell (Ed.), *Systematic Instruction of Persons with Severe Handicaps,* 3rd ed., pp. 247–272. Columbus, OH: Charles E. Merrill, 1987.

Kieran, S., Connor, F., Von Hippel, C. & Jones, S.: *Children with Orthopedic Handicaps.* Washington, DC: U.S. Government Printing Office, 1980.

Kirk, S. A. *Range of Human Hearing. Instructor's Manual to Accompany Educating Exceptional Children.* Prepared by F. E. Lord, p. 93, Plate No. XII. Boston: Houghton Mifflin, 1972.

Kirk, S. & Gallagher, J.: *Educating Exceptional Children,* 3rd ed. Boston: Houghton-Mifflin, 1979.

——————: *Educating Exceptional Children,* 4th ed. Boston: Houghton-Mifflin, 1983.

Lee, D. & Aronson, E.: Visual proprioceptive control of standing in human subjects. *Perception and Psychophysics* (15), (1974), 529–532.

Lee, S. P. & Chasin, W.: Otologic assessments. In L. J. Bradford (Ed.), *Physiological Measures of the Audio-Vestibular System.* New York: Academic Press, 1975.

Leisman, G.: *Basic Visual Processes and Learning Disability.* Springfield, IL: Charles C Thomas, 1976.

Lerner, J.: *Learning Disabilities Theories, Diagnosis, and Teaching Strategies,* 4th Ed. Boston, MA: Houghton Mifflin, 1985.

Lerner, J., Mardell-Czudnowski, C. & Goldenberg, D.: *Special Education for the Early Childhood Years,* 2nd ed. Englewood Cliffs, NJ: Prentice-Hall, 1987.

Lerner, R. M., & Shea, J. A.: Social behavior in adolescence. In B. B. Wolman (Ed.), *Handbook of Developmental Psychology.* Englewood Cliffs, NJ: Prentice-Hall, 1982.

Llorens, L. A. & Burris, B. B.: Development of sensory integration in learning disabled children. In J. Gottlieb & S. Strichart (Eds.), *Developmental Theory and Research in Learning Disabilities,* (pp. 57–79). Baltimore: University Park Press, 1981.

Lowenfeld, B.: *The Visually Handicapped Child in School.* New York: John Day, 1973.

Ludel, J.: *Introduction to Sensory Processes.* San Francisco: Freeman, 1978.

Lunnen, K.: Severely and profoundly retarded children. In S. Campbell (Ed.). *Pediatric Neurologic Physical Therapy,* (pp. 277–316). New York: Churchill-Livingstone, 1984.

Mahoney, G.: Ethological approach to delayed language acquisition. *American Journal of Mental Deficiency, 80* (1975), 139–148.

Mann, L. & Sabatino, D.: *Foundations of Cognitive Process in Remedial and Special Education.* Rockville, MD: Aspen, 1985.

Marks, N. C.: *Cerebral Palsied and Learning Disabled Children.* Springfield, IL: Charles C Thomas, 1974.

Mayer, R. G.: *The Promise of Cognitive Psychology.* San Francisco: Freeman, 1981.

McCarthy, D.: *McCathy Scales of Children's Abilities.* Cleveland, OH: Psychological Corp., 1972.

McInnes, J. M. & Treffry, J. A.: *Deaf-Blind Infants and Children: A Developmental Guide.* Toronto: University of Toronto Press, 1982.

Meichenbaum, D.: Cognitive behavior modification with exceptional children: A promise yet unfulfilled. *Exceptional Educational Quarterly, 1* (1980), 83–88.

Mercer, C.: *Students with Learning Disabilities,* 3rd ed. Columbus, OH: Merrill, 1987.

Meyer, S.: A total approach for increasing the quality of life for the visually and auditorily impaired child. *Proceedings: Workshop for Serving the Deaf-Blind and Multihandicapped Child: Identification, Assessment, and Training.* Calif. State Dept. of Education, Sacramento: Southwestern Region Deaf-Blind Center (ERIC Document Reproduction Service No. ED 179039), 1979.

Morrison, D., Pothier, P. & Horr, K.: *Sensorimotor Dysfunction and Therapy in Infancy and Early Childhood.* Springfield, IL: Charles C Thomas, 1978.

Mountain Plains Regional Center for Services to Deaf-Blind Children: *Guidelines for Certifying a Student as Eligible for Deaf-Blind Services.* Denver: Mountain Plains Regional Center, 1985.

Mullen, E. M., Danella, E., & Myers, M.: *The Psychological Stimulus/Response Evaluation for Severely Multiply Handicapped Children (PSR).* East Providence, RI: Meeting Street School, 1977.

Myklebust, H.: *The Psychology of Deafness.* New York: Grune & Stratton, 1964.

Nelson, L. B.: *Pediatric Ophthalmology.* Philadelphia, PA: Saunders, 1984.

Northern, J. L., & Downs, M. P.: *Hearing in Children.* Baltimore, MD: Williams & Wilkins, 1984.

O'Connor, N. & Hermelin, B.: Sensory handicap and cognitive defect. In D. Ellis (Ed.), *Sensory Impairments in Mentally Handicapped People,* (pp. 184–197). San Diego, CA: College Hill Press, 1986.

Paine, K. & Oppé, T.: *Neurological Examination of Children.* Philadelphia: Lippincott, 1966.

Papalia, D., & Olds, S.: *A Child's World: Infancy Through Adolescence.* New York: McGraw-Hill, 1975.

Phillips, C. & Drain, T.: *A Guide to Sensory Stimulation for the Home.* Raleigh: North Carolina Dept. of Public Instr., Division of Exceptional Children, 1979.

Pope, S.: Home program activities suggestions (xeroxed packet). Fayetteville, NC: Developmental Evaluation Center, Undated.

Reisman, J.: Touch, motion, and proprioception. In R. Salapatek & L. Cohen (Eds.), *Handbook of Infant Perception: From Sensation to Perception,* Vol. I. Orlando, FL: Academic Press, 1987.

Restak, R.: *The Brain.* New York: Bantam Books, 1984.

Robbins, N.: *Educational Beginnings with Deaf-Blind Children.* Watertown, MA: Perkins School for the Blind, 1964.

Rudolph, J., Bjorling, B. & Collins, T.: *Manual for the Assessment of a Deaf-Blind Multiply Handicapped Child,* 3rd ed. Lansing, MI: Midwest Regional Center for Services to Deaf-Blind Children, Undated.

Ruff, H.: The development of object perception in infancy. In T. Field, A. Huston, H. Quay, L. Troll, & G. Fenley (Eds.), *Review of Human Development.* New York: Wiley, 1982.

Samilson, R. L.: Orthopedic surgery of the hips and spine in retarded cerebral palsy patients. *Orthop Clin North Am, 12* (1981), 83.

Schieffe, W. & Foulke, E.: *Tactual Perceptions: A Sourcebook.* New York: Cambridge University Press, 1982.

Schmidt, M. B.: *Sensory Stimulation Training and Assessment Program.* Preston, 1979.

Scholl, G.: *Foundations of Education for Blind and Visually Handicapped Children and Youth.* New York: American Foundation for the Blind, 1986.

Seelye, R.: The deaf-blind child as a visually functioning person. *Proceedings: Workshop for Serving the Deaf-Blind and Multihandicapped Child: Identification, Assessment, and Training.* Sacramento, CA: State Dept. of Education, Southwestern Region Deaf-Blind Center (ERIC Document Reproduction Service no. ED 179 039), 1979.

Shepherd, R.: Brachial plexus injury. In S. Campbell (Ed.). *Pediatric Neurologic Physical Therapy,* pp. 141–168. New York: Churchill Livingstone, 1984.

Simmons, F. B., & Glalthe, T. J.: Electrocochleography. In L.J Bradford (Ed.), *Physiological Measures of the Audio-Vestibular System.* New York: Academic Press, 1975.

Slingerland, B.: *Slingerland Screening Tests for Identifying Children with Specific Language Disability.* Cambridge, MS: Educators Publishing Service, 1970.

Smithdas, R. J.: Psychological aspects of deaf-blindness. In S. Walsh & R. Holzberg (Eds.), *Understanding and Educating the Deaf-Blind Severely and Profoundly Handicapped: An International Perspective.* Springfield, IL: Charles C Thomas, 1981.

Snell, M.: *Systematic Instruction of Persons with Severe Handicaps,* 3rd ed. Columbus, OH: Charles E. Merrill, 1978.

Solapatek, P., & Cohen, L. (Eds.): *Handbook of Infant Perception, from Sensation to Perception,* Vol. I. Orlando, FL: Academic Press, 1987.

Sonksen, P.: Vision and early development. In K. Wybar & D. Taylor (Eds.), *Pediatric Ophthalmology: Current Aspects,* (pp. 85–95). New York: Marcel Dekker, 1983.

Sontag, E., Burke, P., & York, R.: Considerations for serving the severely handicapped in the public schools. *Education and Training of the Mentally Retarded, 8* (1973), 20–36.

Stein, L. K., Ozdomar, O., & Schnabel, M.: Auditory brainstem responses (ABR) with suspected deaf-blind children. *Ear and Hearing, 2*(1), (1981), 30–40.

Stengel, T., Attermeier, S., Bly, L. & Heriza, C.: Evaluation of sensorimotor dysfunction. In S. Campbell (Ed.), *Pediatric Neurologic Physical Therapy,* pp. 13–88. New York: Churchill Livingstone, 1984.

Sternberg, M.: Communication with deaf-blind children. *Proceedings: Workshops for Serving the Deaf-Blind and Multihandicapped Child: Identification, Assessment, and Training.* Calif. State Dept. of Education, Sacramento: Southwestern Region Deaf-Blind Center (ERIC Document Reproduction Service No. ED 179039), 1979.

Stevens, M.: *The Educational and Social Needs of Children with Severe Handicap,* 2nd ed. London: Butler & Tanner Ltd., 1973.

Stillman, R.: *The Callier-Azusa Scale.* Dallas, TX: Callier Center for Communication Disorders, 1978.

Stillman, R., & Battle, C.: Developmental assessment of communicative abilities in the deaf-blind. In D. Ellis (Ed.), *Sensory Impairments in Mentally Handicapped People,* (pp. 319–338). San Diego, CA: College-Hill Press, 1986.

Stremel-Campbell, K.: Communication interventions for students with sensory impairments. Presentation at Missouri State Deaf/Blind Workshop, Lake of the Ozarks, MO, Feb 1985.

Sweitzer, R.: Auditory assessment of the multi-handicapped deaf-blind child. *Proceedings: Workshop for Serving the Deaf-Blind and Multihandicapped Child: Identification, Assessment, and Training.* California State Dept. of Educ., Sacramento: Southwestern Region Deaf-Blind Center (ERIC Document Reproduction Service NO. ED 179 039), 1979.

Taylor, E. A.: Ocular-motor processes and the act of reading. In G. Leisman, *Basic Visual Processes and Learning Disability.* Springfield, IL: Charles C Thomas, 1976.

Thomas, A., & Chess, S.: *Temperament and Development.* New York: Brunner/Mazel, 1977.

United Cerebral Palsy Assoc.: *Infant Massage for Developmentally Delayed Babies.* Denver: United Cerebral Palsy Assoc. of Denver, Undated.

Van Dijk, J.: An educational curriculum for deaf-blind multihandicapped persons. In D. Ellis (Ed.), *Sensory Impairments in Mentally Handicapped People,* (pp. 374–382). San Diego, CA: College-Hill Press, 1986.

Van Etten, G., Arkell, C., & Van Etten, C.: *The Severely and Profoundly Handicapped Programs, Methods, and Materials.* St. Louis: Mosby, 1980.

Wadsworth, B.: *Piaget's Theory of Cognitive and Affective Development,* 3rd ed. New York: Longman, 1984.

Warburg, M.: Medical and ophthalmological aspects of visual impairment in mentally handicapped people. In D. Ellis (Ed.), *Sensory Impairments in Mentally Handicapped People,* (pp. 93–114). San Diego, CA: College-Hill Press, 1986.

Ward, M.: An overview of motor development: Implications for educational programming. In S. R. Walsh & R. Hozberg (Eds.). *Understanding and Educating the Deaf-Blind Severely and Profoundly Handicapped.* Springfield, IL: Charles C Thomas, 1981.

Wilson, J.: Cerebral palsy. In S. Campbell (Ed.). *Pediatric Neurologic Physical Therapy.* (pp. 353–414). New York: Churchill Livingstone, 1984.

Wyne, M. & O'Connor, P.: *Exceptional Children: A Developmental View.* Lexington, MA: Heath, 1979.

Yamamoto, K.: *The Child and His Image.* Boston: Houghton-Mifflin, 1972.

INDEX